FAITH
DOYLE
THE ULTIMATE CHALLENGE

They shook hands and then Doyle spoke. "I can accept that in the public mind you've won, Harry. But this is between you and me."

"What are you talking about?" Houdini was annoyed by this pertinacity of Doyle's.

"The contest is not over yet. I will prove everything to you once and for all," he mustered, challenging Houdini to one final endeavor.

"Why are you so intent on this . . . I don't know what to call it—this mission of yours?"

"Because I know. I know!" And he shook Houdini by the sides. "I want you to know, as well."

"What do you have in mind?"

Doyle smiled confidently. "Lock me in one of your contraptions, lower me off a cliff or into the water—it doesn't matter which—and I will get out, with the help of my dead son . . ."

BELIEVE.

About the Authors

WILLIAM SHATNER is best known for the role of Captain James T. Kirk in *Star Trek*, but he is also one of the few actors active on stage, in television, in feature films, and as a director. Shatner and his wife, actress Marcy Lafferty, divide their time among their ranch in northern California, their American Saddlebred breeding interests in Kentucky, and their hilltop home in Los Angeles.

MICHAEL TOBIAS is the author of eleven previous works of fiction and nonfiction, as well as the writer, director and producer of over sixty films, including his award-winning ten hour TV miniseries, VOICE OF THE PLANET.

BELIEVE.

A NOVEL

WILLIAM SHATNER
AND
MICHAEL TOBIAS

B

BERKLEY BOOKS, NEW YORK

BELIEVE.

A Berkley Book / published by arrangement with
the authors

PRINTING HISTORY
Berkley edition / June 1992

ISBN: 0-425-13296-X

A BERKLEY BOOK ® TM 757,375
Berkley Books are published by The Berkley Publishing Group,
200 Madison Avenue, New York, New York 10016.
The name "BERKLEY" and the "B" logo
are trademarks belonging to Berkley Publishing Corporation.

PRINTED IN THE UNITED STATES OF AMERICA

10 9 8 7 6 5 4 3 2 1

Authors' note

This novel is strictly a work of fiction. Most details that might have harbored even a shred of truth have been freely altered, embellished, imagined or altogether invented. The two principal characters with whom the story deals, both long-deceased, were very real in their day, of course, but very legendary as well. Those legends have grown in magnitude and poetry, like the proverbial fish that gets larger and larger through each retelling. We have fictionally explored the legends, rather than the reality, in hopes of gaining some modest insight into the blithe and brilliant worlds of Harry Houdini and Sir Arthur Conan Doyle.

All respects are humbly conveyed, with gratitude, to the memory of these two great men, and to their many survivors, as well as to their admiring public throughout the world.

For Jane Morrison and Marcy Lafferty

CONTENTS

BELIEVE.

PART
ONE

1

The Killing Steel

Montreal, October of 1926; in which Harry Houdini confronts his worst agony, only to be plunged backwards in time to a yet more horrifying moment . . .

"Pain, excruciating pain, keeps you on your toes, keeps you equipped," Houdini stated to the students seated in the auditorium before him, with the self-assured, rising voice of a seasoned general or maestro.

At McGill that morning he'd preached the religion of pain. Young men and women, bright-eyed, clad in woolen jackets and sweaters inside the lecture hall, looked up with half-open mouths. Many of those students had relatives or family members who had suffered or died during the Great War to end all wars. But there was no evident pain in the room, save for some aura that hovered around the wiry Houdini. His hair was parted with grease, and his own eyes darted about the room, seeking confirmation from those who knew little about him. The audience was what really mattered to him now.

"That's right. There's dignity in it," he went on. "Anyone who's paid for his ticket can be persuaded by a good show of pain. But it doesn't come easily, no sir. Pain must be achieved. You've got to win it. And when you do, when you can spit up blood as if it were a joke, why then you know you're on to it. Pain, for me, has always been the mark of success. It shows me that I tried. That doesn't mean I give in to it. Never!" He paused, pacing restlessly, scanning the room for young, following eyes. "You give in to pain, rather than control it, and you're finished. You'll sink lower and lower. There're no words, no discipline, no fair maiden's touch that can save you then. It's like religion gone sour if you should ever give up in the middle of it. You must never give up."

Houdini had a method for committing to memory certain aphorisms, helpful hints. For forty years he'd memorized tricks, subtle techniques.

But now—beyond the comforts of the lecture hall earlier in the day—the memory fails him. All that samurai sobriety that he'd cultivated throughout his life, that Talmudic logic and Brooklyn street smarts, even that P. T. Barnum–like bravado cannot protect him from an unraveling chain of events. His hands are numb. They've been numb before. But this time his dick is also cold, damn near frozen. Even his eyes are reeling behind a haze of cold that's slowing them down. The eyelids are sticking to the eyeballs. Everything's going blank.

The pain escalates. And with the pain comes the inner voice of reason. A voice Houdini had known for years, a second, inner self, his real name and identity—Ehrich Weiss— now spoke to him, as it had so often in the past.

Fingers, oh fingers, move, you bastards! Harry, you got to, you just got to! It can't be Canada. Lord don't make it be a sullen October in Montreal! Miami on the beach, maybe. Or better yet Paris in the spring. Bessie nudging up in her see-through black leotards and a heavy slab of hot apple pie and a wet full kiss like the French do it, for the road. One good night's sleep, first. Oh let it be fast. But not like this . . .

Six heaving workers from the city jail had hoisted him up above the snow-covered maples of Montcalm with a hand-driven winch and two hundred feet of steel cable running through a pulley that dangled beneath a high fire tower. Houdini stared downward and saw, to his disappointment, that there were too few in attendance to make an original trick worthwhile. It was too late to retreat.

A convoluted agony squeezed against his insides as the blood rushed to his head. He knew he was pressing his luck. At fifty-two, he was beginning to feel like some kind of schmuck hanging upside down by his ankles this way, one hundred forty-five feet up in the air. Everything was too tight, done too hastily. His balls were sore. He was mana-cled, mummified, straightjacketed; shackled in four hundred pounds of Georgia chain-gang leg irons. His waist and wrists were bound by straps stapled to wet, frozen leather. It seemed as if there were enough nails, concrete, glass and steel enshrouding the magician to furnish a construction site. The steel was the killer. He was pressed between two heavy sheets of eight-inch Pittsburgh steel. The whole apparatus reeked like an aerial coffin. But that wasn't all.

Houdini had carefully prepared an additional treat for his audience, a second suspended cable, alongside and slightly below the first, from which hung a huge barrel filled with water and an iron top that the crane would slide into position once Houdini's coffin was lowered into the hanging pool.

His assistants' hands were clasped forward in the front pouches of their jackets. They had no reason to expose them yet. Breath frosted around their mouths as they waited for the master to begin his routine.

The manager stepped forward and addressed the skeptical hundred or so people who had braved the weather to see the

American escape artist, King of Vaudeville, once again defy every sane rule of human existence. Only a hundred. The take was a disaster. There had been times when fifty thousand showed up on a quay, or beneath a building. When sixty thousand roared and lionized him in the London Hippodrome. But not today.

Harry couldn't hear the manager hype his act. He was not yet in the water, but he had a big problem. The leather had frozen as a result of the moisture between the straightjacket and the steel sheets. He couldn't get the slack he needed to spring the shackles around his waist or wrists, maneuvers which he normally accomplished before the actual countdown. There had been no time to test all the elements—the latches, locks, safeties, spring releases. Not in such cold. Furthermore, he'd never been placed in a straightjacket, under chains, upside down, underwater, in a smooth steel sandwich, in sub-zero weather. No sir. Never did that one. His mouth had been sealed shut with masking tape.

Houdini had had a temperature of a hundred and two even before he and his team boarded the train from Albany. Add to that a three-day-old migraine. He'd vomited twice early in the morning, first thing out of bed. There was blood in his urine. It was his kidney acting up again. A fifteen-year-old minor complaint. He'd had no sleep for four days and looked emaciated.

Houdini was fighting the numbers, declining numbers of paying customers. It wasn't the money, per se, that unsettled him. It hadn't been a question of money for years. His confidence was on the line. Vaudeville was drying up. Other stunts, out of real life, were competing. A nineteen-year-old gal from New York had just swum the English Channel. Big news. Bigger than Houdini, at least for a day. But that day hurt like hell.

But the greater problem was right now. Both shoulders had been dislocated and he couldn't maneuver to get them back in place.

His kidneys start to throb. His hand fumbles without success. The arthritis is acting up. As a kid he'd gotten caught in a crossfire of bullets during a robbery at the circus. Lead fragments remained beneath two of his fingers. Doctors had never gotten them out. Now the old shrapnel impedes the motion of his hand. And the ribs, one, maybe two of them, are definitely cracked.

The first touch of water. It is too cold, freezing up. If it freezes . . .

Harry starts to fight now. Sucks in the last breath. His every muscle poised to fire like a bullet from the trigger of that eternal source that has served him since the age of nine, when he first hung upside down and gathered needles with his eyelids. Stupid stunt. Got him into the circus. The faint beginnings . . . *GO!*

And then it snaps. An ankle. The left one. As loud as the Coney Island roller coaster riding the insides of his nervous system. The whole leg is locked in the searing of it. *Goddammit I broke my fucking ankle!* he screams. Nobody can hear. Not in this blizzard, beneath the masking tape.

Harry, Harry, think what you're doing. Move, man, move! Forget about the pain. Just do it, goddammit!

He's holding his breath now. Two hundred seventy seconds in the best of times. But not with a straightjacket to start things with. Figure two hundred seconds. He's racing. Every muscle bursting like dynamite. Frantic hands, wringing for slack, space. The cold cascades atop cold. He started frozen. Now it's going to his head. Hypothermic. The brain is slowing. Harry knows the syndrome. He rights himself, curling like a pathetic scorpion to see things in their proper plane. The water's burning his eyes. Hands are free now. Push the tumblers outward. Twenty at a shot. Locks are breaking free in a fanfare of urgency. Up above, down below, on all sides, a mighty blur.

Now the steel. He digs through the surgeon's cement that encases a minute picklock under his left heel. *Jesus, the break is bad*, he reckons. Swollen like a cantaloupe. The whole leg is freezing up. He's picking furiously. He checked the vault in public. But now something's wrong, deadly wrong. Harry loses it, blows out air. Takes in frozen water. The blue becomes total.

In the slow second he grapples against the steel, forgetting elegance of technique, slobbering in the overthrow of danger, he grabs hold of a similar moment, through the jerking-to-the-bone beeline of consciousness, a moment many long years before, neurons of memory stampeding neurons in search of . . . or as far back as—

Moscow. When was it, 1902?

Yes . . . He remembers.

The snow was falling. Houdini and Bess were led through underground passages reserved for royalty, and torturers, dirt and rock caverns that connected the river to Red Square along the Neglinka tributary of the Moskva. All of the former swampy banks were now underground, leading past the Spasskiye Vorota, or Gate of Salvation. Dark, hot pools teeming with cockroaches and rats, covered in algal slimes, protruding logs, chunks of discarded garbage, floating gobs of cess, provided a warm alternative to the outside chill. The armed contingent led the Houdinis past an area of skeletons, where prisoners of an earlier era had been left for the plague-carrying carnivores.

"*Vwee ponymaetye?*" Chief Lebedin asked the fur-clad "Roman Catholic" couple with an odd twisted expression.

"No, I don't understand!" Houdini replied, angered by this too obvious snub-of-an-approach route to the Kremlin.

But Bess did. She'd seen the coming trouble. While certain noblemen and most of the *myzhiks* had celebrated his shows, from St. Petersburg to the Nizhni-Novgorod fair, the Czar's Cossack guard and secret police, as well as a certain contingent of court consultants and dukes, were skeptical. There seemed to be a growing impatience that Bess had interpreted as danger. She was worried. And her fears were augmented by the unconventional, indeed disgusting, manner of their escort.

"*Izvenitiya Capitan?*" she said, at first meekly. "Excuse me."

Her husband gave her a look.

"*Da?*" the Captain returned. The Captain, or Chief as his fellows called him, was a huge man, draped in fox and rabbit furs that covered his woolen oversized trousers and just touched the tops of his black leather riding boots. He carried a Winchester over one shoulder, ammo on his belt, and a large butcher knife crudely stuck beneath a pouch at his waist.

"*Pochemoo mwee eedyome zdyess? Pochemoo ne troika?*" Bess carried on, enunciating with a rapid-fire flourish, almost understandable.

The soldiers ignored her.

"My wife asked you a question!" Houdini repeated angrily. "Why have we come this way? Why is there no troika to take us? This is ridiculous! Do you know who I am? We're meeting the Czar, after all!"

"You will meet the Czar," the Chief assured him in English. He could not be intimidated.

For four months the Houdinis had kept up the facade of a good Roman Catholic couple. Jews were not allowed into the country. The Houdinis spoke a poor Russian to their secret police escorts, a Russian that could not mask a *Yiddishkite* disposition, which Harry had inherited from his father's lingua Judaica, his Rabbinical lineage from Budapest. The police took it to be Polish. But others—spies, nobles, informants—had seen through it. There were those who were concerned about the British-born Czarina's gullibility.

A troika was indeed waiting to take the Houdinis up the final cobblestones into the acropolis, as nobles preferred to call the Kremlin. The horses were outfitted with linen muzzles to keep them from breathing in frozen air and harming their lungs. Four feet of snow engulfed the palace. They were escorted into the vestibule, handed their coats and bags and scarfs to liveried servants, and then made their way from one room of pink and yellow and Fragonard-blue splendor to another, finally attaining the Grand Salon, with its Louis XVI sofas woven in pure gold, ceilings bejeweled, and in the center of the enormous room, a royal troika, of solid gold, wheels and all!

The Houdinis were seated beneath the largest chandelier Bess had ever seen, before a French tapestry that covered a gigantic wall at the far end of a sitting room crowded with row after row of antique books, many having bindings fitted with precious gemstones.

It was here that the Houdinis were introduced by turn to one royal figure after another, some of them related to the late Queen Victoria. Houdini was never so off his guard. English, German, French, and Russian were spoken as a single language, while the Chief stood glowering at Houdini from the far end of the room, where they had entered.

Suddenly everyone stood up and bowed. Houdini did the same. Bess gawked at the beautiful thirty-year-old Princess Alix of Hesse, otherwise known as the Empress Alexandra Feodorovna, one of Queen Victoria's granddaughters. For eight years she'd been Czarina. The four daughters came out after her, and Houdini proceeded to entertain them all with such tricks as three-card monte and the old shell game. He pulled colored silk out of their ears, poured gold coins into their laps. Eventually Duke Sergius and the Czarina's sister arrived with their own party, and then Czar Nicholas II himself joined his wife and children.

Over dinner Houdini was animated and spoke frankly about everything that came to his mind. "Great diamonds!" he said. "I could make them disappear right before your eyes."

"Thank you, no," the Czar said with the same stiff humorlessness as the Chief.

Houdini focused on the dinner, which the chef formally announced, dish by dish. The food was set out smorgasbord style. They began with Red Mullet Algeroise, a roast leg of mutton Richelieu, Gigot de Chevreuil, stuffed filets that the chef called Edler Lungenbraten. Houdini was perplexed by all the French and German dishes, wondering aloud where a guy could get Russian dressing, or Russian beet soup, or even Russian easter breads. No one answered him. The Czar yawned repeatedly, and ate very little, but Alexandra stuffed herself with almond paste and Kirschkuchen, a Viennese cherry cake that Houdini himself succumbed to in large mouthfuls. "*Prekrastne koushen!*" the Duke said, gently touching his pearl-studded napkin to his lips. It was still early when the Czar excused himself.

The Empress, though, was impressed with Houdini's reputation, and she asked the Houdinis to stay after the others were dismissed. Duke Sergius and his wife remained while two German-speaking nannies swept the children away toward their pearl-laced canopy beds in some part of the Kremlin.

The Empress was direct. "Perhaps you could help me," she began.

She paused, looking at Bess. Then she returned her regal gaze to Houdini. "You are a miracle worker, are you not? That's what the people are saying. You are in touch with spirits."

"Well, no, I wouldn't say that." Houdini looked at Bess. They had masqueraded as mediums back in the States, but only for a year or two, at a time when they were unable to get work any other way. They both felt bad about the experience.

Bess noticed that the Duke looked discomforted by this turn in the conversation. He did not take well to his sister-in-law discussing such delicate state matters, but he was not at liberty to impede the Empress.

"How would you describe yourself, Mr. Houdini?"

"Well, I have certain powers, but they're definitely powers of the body. I mean to say, tricks, like Yoga. I work out. I practice. I perform. That's all."

"But what about . . .," and she proceeded to recount the many stories she had heard, feats that seemed too incredible to be explained by mere chicanery and practice. She didn't believe him.

He remembered launching into a rhapsody that emerged from depths he rarely tapped. "The pain is crucial!" he'd said. "Pain connects the living with the dead."

"Is there no happiness in your world, Mr. Houdini?" the Czarina asked.

"There is happiness in plenty, Your Highness. My feats are the byproduct of a supreme joy, the joy of seeing through the limitations of the body, escaping death even for a moment, and feeling the profound immanence of life, before and after. I have touched the dead and they have spoken through me."

That was what Alexandra Feodorovna wanted to hear. The Czarina passed a look at her in-laws. The Duke was frustrated.

"Could you communicate with the unborn?" the Czarina pressed. "Can you tell me if I might hope for a son?"

"In a séance, perhaps," the magician said boldly.

"Excuse me. May I speak with you a moment?" Bess said to her husband.

"Not now, Bess," Houdini muttered with a becalming smile.

"Harry, now!" she fired, in firm matriarchal tones the Czarina could not help but appreciate.

Harry and Bess stepped back to one side while the Duke took the opportunity to whisper something to his wife, who in turn whispered to her sister, the Czarina.

"Your Highness, my wife is feeling the fatigue of so much excitement," Houdini concluded. "It's better that I take her back to the hotel. Perhaps we could have a séance tomorrow at this time?"

The Czarina agreed. She was desperate.

Houdini and his wife left the Kremlin in their waiting troika and took it all the way back to the hotel this time. No midnight trudges through the sewers. Bess kept Houdini out in the hall for an hour. She was fuming over her husband's bout of arrogance. *Communicating with the dead!* Talk of *unborns*. It was too much nonsense. Finally, the penitent husband threw his earmuffs into the room and waited. Five minutes later, Bess had not yet thrown them back out into the hall. That was a sign of reconciliation, their way of resolving a family squabble.

In the morning an all-out blizzard had engulfed Moscow. The wind tore through alleyways, ripped at flags, kept people off the street. The temperature must have been minus forty. Icicles ten feet high hung like glistening guillotines before the Houdinis' window two floors up. The ancient city lay frozen and still beneath the morning pall of storm.

There was a knock at the door. They were expecting tea. Instead, Chief Lebedin and half-a-dozen Cossack guards were there to take Houdini to the downtown prison. The men's beards were frozen from moments before outside.

"Good morning to you, Mr. Houdini," Lebedin said with a snort. The Chief nodded to his assistant, who stepped up to Houdini and slapped handcuffs on his wrists.

"Heh!" Houdini was perplexed.

"You will prove your magic, Mr. Houdini."

Houdini turned toward the window and five seconds later turned around and handed the cuffs back to the Cossack, expecting applause.

Lebedin frowned. "Get dressed. We will see what you can do."

Houdini had boasted of his ability to escape any form of incarceration within Russia.

Now Chief Lebedin had arrived to meet Houdini's boast. Houdini knew where they were going: Establishment Yard. It was the notorious prison of Moscow where special people were tortured. The jail was considered to be the worst in the world. No prisoner who entered Establishment Yard ever left, not even in a coffin. Those tortured to death were thrown in ovens, their ashes tossed into a great yawning hole in the outhouse or fed to the inmates. The wardens never failed to remind the men which lucky compatriot of theirs had become food for thought.

"They call it a *carette*, sweetheart," Houdini explained to Bess with a wink, referring to the cell in which he'd be tested. "I'll be back for lunch."

The Cossacks led Houdini to the prison. They descended iron steps into a certifiable dungeon. Houdini studied the surroundings. He knew at once how he'd extricate himself.

"Your clothes," Lebedin said. "Off!"

They stripped Houdini bare. It got cold very fast. They laid him on a metal surgical bed. Houdini noticed years' worth of blood stains. They spread his legs, and six men began an intensive search of his entire body, beginning with the balls of his feet. They stuck a horse prod up his rectum, shone a flashlight down his throat and up his nostrils; they used the point of a scissor to probe inside his ears.

The primary investigator took Lebedin aside and whispered something to him. Lebedin came back to Houdini's side.

"Now take a shit," the Chief ordered.

"Why?" Houdini asked, annoyed.

"Just checking," Lebedin said.

Houdini forced some business in the adjoining latrine, where the stench would have felled a lesser man.

The chief investigator poked at the excrement.

"*Nechevo*," he then said to Lebedin with a quick and singular shake of his head.

"Fine. We can proceed. Mr. Houdini, after you. Please." The Chief gestured gentlemanly with his hand. He bore a knowing grin.

The Cossacks led Houdini out of the dungeon into the open courtyard. The snow was well above Houdini's knees. He was still naked. The others were of course heavily outfitted in many layers of wool and sable. Still they were cold. It had to be one of the coldest days of the year in Moscow. The snow swirled in bitter cross-gales over the depressing exterior, plastering the red outside walls of the prison with *verglass*.

Houdini looked around. "But, I thought—"

Suddenly Houdini saw three horses entering the court-yard, a soldier riding the lead horse. The animals pulled behind them a large sleigh on which rested a strange gleaming vault. It resembled a safe Houdini had cracked in Berlin.

"This is your *carette*?" Houdini asked Lebedin.

"Naturally," the Chief replied.

The horses stopped. They were fighting the wind. The snow flurries were blinding them. "After you," Lebedin proffered, once again with the generosity of a sweeping arm.

Houdini quickly sized up the sadistic little box. It was made entirely of smooth steel. He shook Lebedin's hand and in the process—though no one but Houdini was aware of the dexterous sleight—managed to retrieve a small picklock he'd earlier affixed to Lebedin's coat, just prior to the search in the dungeon.

There was a small hole in the *carette*, the width of a thumb. The lock was thirty-six inches below, on the outside. Houdini crawled inside. The sinister vault had just enough room inside for him to sit hunched up like a chimpanzee. The steel was as cold as dry ice. Houdini immediately felt a profound stinging sensation on his bare feet and buttocks and shoulders. He had to work fast.

Lebedin withdrew a key chain from his pants pocket, locked one of two outside bolts and returned the key to his pocket.

"I should inform you, Houdini, that this key does not re-open the *carette*. Only one key in the world can do that, and it is in the hands of a warden in Siberia, twenty-two days by horseback from here. Have a good trip!" He laughed with a loud bite, nodded to the soldier atop the lead horse, and slapped the rear of the closest of the beasts. Lebedin meant to kill the magician.

Houdini knew the Duke and other nobles had put the Chief up to it. He worked frantically. They'd totally missed a narrow integument-like strand of wire along his scalp. They'd also failed to detect a needle fitted beneath the skin of his left palm and a minute metal hook that had been inserted beneath a large scar on his waist. The skin there formed a subtle flap, providing Houdini with a place to insert one or another tool, however tiny. In addition, he had the picklock and a length of string taken from his hair.

As the horses left the prison, moving out through the deserted streets of Moscow, Houdini drew in his breath, shrunk down in size by several inches all around, and exerted prodigious puissance in order to get the varied elements into one working implement. He had to get the tool out the hole and down toward the lock. The hook would have to be leveraged with the wire into the tumbler device. It was an agonizingly difficult maneuver. Houdini had never had so little room to work. His whole body was quickly going numb. The pain from the steel was something new. It stung with the ferocity of a swarm of angry hornets.

Tears started to form, and freeze, on Houdini's cheeks. By his calculations, he'd be dead in less than an hour. Even if he were to cry out foul play, to insist on being released, he knew that Lebedin had told the truth about the key. They'd have to blow up the *carette* to open it anytime during the next twenty-two days. And if they blew it up, Houdini would be a dead man.

The horses were now trotting. The movement made his efforts with the dangling tool in his hands even more difficult. His skin stuck fast to the frozen steel, burning, blurring the world within that hellish black vault. Every jolt atop the sleigh smashed one of his limbs, a knee, or a joint against the unrelenting insides of the box. Unless the metal hook caught on the tumblers, he knew that he was finished.

A half hour must have passed. Houdini was dying. Every part of his anatomy seemed to be on fire, compressed to the point of breaking. The stinging had passed through the skin. He felt streaks of ulceration, slippery blood, fingers clawing dumbly. His nerves, tissues, corpuscles were flattened against the killing steel. Every move required him to rip his skin from the metal to which it was now bonded. The skin literally peeled away with each effort.

Compelled by the horrors of Russia, galvanized by a pain from long ago, into action now, here . . .

And then suddenly . . . suddenly . . . Light! Montreal!

Houdini hears screaming. His eyes burst open. He is in steel, frozen in water. The horses have vanished, but the wind and the snow continue to howl. With one mighty exertion, Houdini explodes upward, breaking the shackles that still hold him in. His free hands feel nothing now but know instinctively how to disengage the broad iron plate that holds down the hanging apparatus. The sleeve in which he's been sealed is removable. Houdini's out of air. One last chance. Now he thrusts upward with all his benumbed weight against that sleeve. He cracks through the leaden mass of water that has already formed a half-inch surface of ice. As it shatters, the water splashes over the top, the iron piece, weighing a good two hundred pounds, slides free, the chain-gang irons drop, along with the strands of asphyxiating leather.

Go, go go! the voice calls to him. Houdini lunges out, gasping, throwing himself over the top in one last desperate motion. His throat is screaming for air, fighting off the death that was all around him, in him. He's been there before . . .

The exorcism is over. His arms hang limp. Lock hard and frozen. The blizzard engulfs him.

I'm alive, he thinks.

Somewhere down below, the impresario shouts through a megaphone—"He's done it again!" The winch operator immediately begins to lower the cables. The crowd below can barely make out the spectacle through the thickness of the squall. Many have already left, having found even six minutes of such weather too much to bear for a mere light entertainment.

2

The Hit

Following the stunt atop Mount Montcalm, while Houdini tries to get some rest, and practice a new trick, he has some unexpected visitors who will change his life . . .

By the time Houdini came down from the fire tower, the crowd had thinned out to a mere smattering of admirers. He was in bad shape, spooked by the Russian memory that had seemed to be an eternity of anguish. And he was riddled with myriad pains shooting throughout his body. His ankle felt like cold jelly.

One of Houdini's traveling assistants, Dexter Baxwell, a callow, thirty-two-year-old secretary-cum-magician's-assistant, was there to help his white-faced boss into a waiting vehicle. He then drove Houdini back to the hotel suite in the complimentary Packard twin six, along the unpleasant snow-laden road down the Montcalm Mountain, past McGill

University, where Houdini had lectured that very morning. It was a forlorn Thursday. Montreal shivered beneath a mantle of snowdrifts. Driving was hazardous.

Houdini slumped across the backseat, his eyes closed, forehead sweating, his shattered left ankle atop a bunched-up raccoon coat.

Bess had arrived earlier in the day by railroad from Providence. She was deathly ill with food poisoning. The couple's private Pinkerton, Frank Lattimer, picked her up at the station and rushed her to Houdini's suite. As was customary, Houdini had taken a half-dozen rooms on the top floor. He needed the space not only for an entourage of seven loyal assistants, but for the nearly four tons of equipment that accompanied his traveling retinue.

Frank had his own problems, which he had sworn to keep secret from Bess. There had been widespread voodoo attacks on Houdini in Boston. Dozens of spiritualists had fashioned wax dolls of Houdini and stabbed them with blood-coated pins. There were threats brought against him from anonymous ministers, men of learning, irate citizens appearing in newspapers across America and Europe. Angry letters poured through his mailbox at the house. And dozens of hungry lawsuits abounded in the courts. Houdini loved to testify on his own behalf in court, testing the limits of his adversaries. He thrived on this new hobby of séance busting, goading ghosts, making fools of those who trusted in the beyond. Houdini displayed a crusader's zeal in his bouts of vigilantism. He was protecting America, in his mind—the freedom to think clearly, openly, as opposed to the narrow fundamentalism that was gripping Americans from all walks of life. To Houdini, that narrowness was the result of the insane spiritualist calling whose most visible and outspoken champion was none other than the famed Englishman Sir Arthur Conan Doyle.

Both Bess and Frank were deeply concerned by Houdini's ongoing fixation with Doyle. The initial friendship between the two men had been mired in public controversy. Now, three years later, it remained cloaked in ambivalence and lack of resolve. Houdini suffered by it. Bess wondered what had really happened that fateful last day. Houdini had spoken of a miracle, then called it nonsense. No one knew the truth.

Despite the vehemence of his position, and the clever public displays of his malevolence, most of the consternation Houdini inspired among spiritualists had posed little risk to him personally. But then the magician wrote a letter to the editor of the *New York Mercury* questioning the legality of murdering any materialized spirit that should happen to cross his path. "I don't see that I should be breaking any law were I to fire a pistol at a ghost," Houdini had written. In New York one night, bullets riddled one of the cars of a motorcade, initially marked for Houdini. By a miracle no one was hurt.

Bullets and kisses. Frank noticed that Houdini inspired one or the other from the public. In spite of his own expert knowledge of gadgetry, Frank was baffled by Houdini's uncanny abilities—pranks perfused with a Zen master's solemnity; mischief that had the look of mysticism; vaudeville charm laced with transubstantiation. Houdini transformed chicanery into an Olympics. Doyle had been convinced it was no chicanery. Frank was unsure, but he had no time to probe such heady uncertainties. He was more worried about the bottom line, namely, Houdini's safety.

There was one medium in particular who had given Frank Lattimer cause to be on the alert for several years. A woman who weighed two hundred and eighty pounds, more mass than the first washing machines, with eyes that blazed bloodshot and cruel, the "Princess," or "Madame," as she was variously known, had been with Houdini and Doyle that night in Denver. Then she had vanished. Now, Frank's sources suggested she might have crossed into Canada.

By four that afternoon Dexter Baxwell brought Houdini into the front lobby of the hotel. Houdini's "Olympics" looked as if they'd backfired. He leaned against his assistant for support, collapsed onto a sofa and had Dexter call Frank and the others to help him up the stairs. There was no elevator in the hotel. It was already dark out and still snowing.

Frank was the first to come into the lobby. "Jesus, you look like shit. Dexter, get the house doctor. Layton, watch the car."

"No medicos!" Houdini blurted. "Just get me to bed. Did Bess arrive yet?"

"She's asleep," Frank replied. "She's still got the bug. Where's your left shoe?"

"I bruised the ankle," Houdini said, downplaying the injury. "Nothing a good cold bath won't mend."

Frank and Dexter, along with Royale and Joe, helped Houdini up the stairs. These latter two assistants were mechanics, both in their twenties, both from New York. They rigged the gear, kept spring-activated locks well-greased, did the packing, and unloading, and maintained a constant vigil over the needs of Houdini's machinery. They were Houdini's official engineers.

Layton was Frank's number two. He had replaced a Pinkerton by the name of Byron some three years before, after the murder attempt business.

Bess was awake in bed, warming her hands on her belly as her husband hobbled into the room.

"How you feeling?" Houdini murmured, snuggling up to her.

She stared at him. Then, "What happened?"

"Nothing happened."

"Harry, you look horrible."

"Thank you."

"I mean it!"

"You sound like your mother." He meant that to be no compliment.

Houdini examined the menu.

"You want anything?" he asked Bess.

She just grimaced.

Houdini skipped his order, shuffled out of the bedroom,

started a bath, climbed in and then examined his injuries. Later he crawled back into bed, careful not to wake Bess.

In the morning a knock at the door signaled the arrival of breakfast and the morning paper. Houdini sipped mineral water, flipping through the news, looking for notices of himself. Bess buttered a roll and swigged strong black coffee.

"What do they say?" she asked.

" 'Visibility made it all but impossible for anyone present to see, or appreciate, Mr. Houdini's stunt.' " He threw down the paper. "Pisses me off!"

"Serves you right!"

Houdini was too tired to argue the point.

The Houdinis had one more day scheduled in Montreal before heading to Detroit on a midnight train for the last stop on their fall tour. A performance was scheduled for the following evening, Saturday. Frank, Layton, and Dexter were to go in advance and prepare things. Joe and Royale always stayed with the gear. Houdini still needed some hours with the equipment. He'd worked out a variation on an old gag but needed practice before Detroit.

Houdini spoke to a small crowd of students and fellow magicians at noon. Despite an outside temperature in the low teens, he was burning up. He forced his left leg to move normally, without admitting to a limp. He figured he could get the ankle checked out properly back in New York the following week. In the meantime, there was one more audience to please. Detroit was important to him. The season had to close with a bang, not a whimper.

Bess was greatly improved by the afternoon and sat reading in their bedroom while Houdini was in an adjoining suite, working through the particulars of the new variation on his guillotine trick. The sprawling suite was cluttered with the great illusionist's array of iron traps, hanging contraptions, cocoons of ropes; there were special suits of steel, a straightjacket, a water tank and a dozen suitcases along one wall. In the middle of the room sat a bizarre jungle gym device. Houdini was testing its trip locks.

A large turnscrew activated a hoist that raised six gleaming guillotine blades. Houdini lay on his back atop hundreds of nails that covered the solid base of the contraption. Normally his arms would be shackled and he would have all of a second to spring the releases by bulging his muscles in just the right way. In that second Houdini—and the audience with him—stared at certain death. He instantly had to get his various appendages out of the steel constraints and slip cautiously away, foot by foot, before one deadly blade after another sliced down through his legs, arms and neck. One false move would prematurely trigger the blades.

In his act, he planned initially to demonstrate the unpredictability of the guillotines. They were precariously set, like the springs of a rat trap. Houdini had to squirm free of the shackles without causing the slightest tremble in the apparatus. Of course he had secret methods—friction devices that prevented the blades from coming down until he had depressed several minute lever arms orchestrated throughout the bench on which he lay.

From the audience's point of view, it seemed that even a contortionist's cool was unlikely to prevent the inevitable. Those blades were as finicky as a time bomb. Houdini would make sure that the audience appreciated that fact.

Down in the lobby a group of young men had just entered the hotel and went directly to the concierge. The youngest, a lad no more than eighteen, wearing an argyle sweater and baggy breeches, and carrying in his arm a large leather satchel, asked for the room number of Harry Houdini.

"He expecting you?" the concierge said curtly.

"Yes," the young man responded.

"What's in the bag?"

The young man withdrew two pen-and-ink drawings he'd made of Houdini performing. Imaginary portraits. "Mr. Houdini lectured at the school."

"I know," the concierge said, not bending an inch.

"He's already got one of my drawings. He asked me to come by today with the others."

The concierge studied the group carefully. One of the boys was Japanese. Frank, when he'd left for the train station with Layton, had flashed his private detective's badge and cautioned the veteran hotelman to keep an eye out for any nuts trying to get to Houdini.

"And who are *they*?" the concierge asked the young artist, looking at his pals.

"Just friends of mine from school," the boy reassured him.

"What's with the Japanese?" the hotel guardian said.

"What do you mean? He's Japanese, that's all. An exchange student."

Ordinarily the concierge would have called up to the room. But the students seemed OK.

"All right, then," he said. "Room 311. But if I hear you boys made a nuisance of yourselves . . ." he threatened with a warning finger.

The young men raced up to the third floor. There were four of them, the Japanese fellow older than the rest, perhaps in his mid-twenties, unshaven. He was a family friend of one of the others, and an alleged autograph hound.

Houdini was in the middle of his trick. He expanded his right bicep, popped the leather straps holding down the arm, which he deftly moved three inches to the left, and depressed the hidden button on the bench with his right elbow. Instantly, a twenty-pound metal blade plunged downward, smashing neatly into the steel plank. A raised and fitted groove received the guillotine blade without damaging its razor-sharp quality.

Houdini bulged his left bicep with the same resulting effect. Now came the tough part—neck, ankles, then waist.

Down the hall, the boys knocked on room 311.

"Who is it?" Bess called out.

"My name's Richard Bizankin, ma'am. Mr. Houdini asked us to drop by. We have a present for him," the shy painter reported.

"What kind of present?" Bess asked suspiciously, starting

toward the door from her bed, where she had lain propped up on pillows.

"Drawings, ma'am."

Bess let them in. The Bizankin youth showed her the two pen-and-inks and explained how Mr. Houdini had liked an earlier drawing several days before and recommended that the students drop by the hotel on Friday. Bess led them down the hall.

The Japanese wiped sweat from his brow.

Standing outside the closed door, Bess shouted, "Harry, you've got visitors."

There was an anguished "Huh?"

Still in the hallway, Bess and the boys heard a crash, an agitated scrambling, the sound of steel against wood, then the word "Shit!"

Houdini's concentration had been obliterated at the worst possible moment. His neck had been turned, and then, while he was caught in the distraction, in all of a spellbinding flash the blade roared downward. He inflated the veins, muscle and flesh of his throat, yanked his head violently to the side and just missed having himself killed. The violence, at the same time, triggered the left fore blade. It too, after a slight hesitation, crashed down. He pulsed his ankle, broke loose of the cuff and swung it free just in time. The spasmodic jolt to an already injured ankle plastered his entire body with pain.

Now the right blade crashed. And then the center one. He wriggled, half a second, motion imploding all around him. With a pickpocket's agility and one agonizing howl, Houdini rolled off the bench onto the floor, screaming, as the three remaining blades smashed, one after the other into the steel.

"Harry, get off the floor, you've got visitors!" Bess scolded him, having just let the gaggle of devoted boys in. They were seconds too late to see the guillotine blades come down.

"Jesus, Bess, knock first!" Harry gasped furiously, dragging himself off the floor onto a couch, where he slumped down, totally spent.

No one but Houdini could appreciate the extreme physical exertion required to burst shackles with a single expansion of the musculature. He lay sucking in air, holding onto his gut for dear life. It felt as if his insides were falling out. His forehead, kidney, ankle, ribs and now his neck were all on fire.

The students introduced themselves while Bess returned to her bedroom.

"I brought you the other two drawings," Richard Bizankin said, reaching into his satchel.

"Sure I remember. Have a seat, boys. Nice of you to drop by," Houdini said, breathing hard. He glanced up at the foursome. The older one caught his eye for an extra second.

Two of the students walked over to the jungle gym and lightly touched the steel. The artist pulled up a chair and sat next to the master, nervously awaiting confirmation that Houdini liked the new drawings. Houdini studied them intently.

Outside in the hall, Houdini could hear Joe and Royale moving a large crate down toward the stairs. They'd be getting everything to the train station in advance so that he and Bess didn't have to deal with it. The older boy, standing behind the artist, mentioned something about certain claims of endurance. Houdini wasn't listening. He simply nodded, and said, "Uh-huh."

Suddenly, the older boy stepped up between the artist and the reclining magician and, with tightly clenched fists, exploded, tearing into Houdini with one maniacal punch after another. The blows were expertly delivered to Houdini's stomach, heart and lungs.

"Hey!" the others shouted hysterically. "What the hell are you doing!"

Houdini fell to the floor without a sound. His throat was locked.

"He said it was OK!" the Japanese boy explained coolly. "You all heard him."

"Are you out of your mind!" his family friend shouted.

Bizankin was scared. He realized he didn't really know a thing about the Japanese guy, who was obviously a madman. And now they'd all be implicated. He started to mutter something, then paused, trying to help Houdini off the floor.

"Jesus, I'm sorry. He's crazy; I don't really know him. Let me help you."

Houdini wasn't hearing anymore.

"Better get his wife," Bizankin said, his chair having fallen behind him as he stood up to escape the fray. He couldn't believe that this had happened.

The Japanese youth stood his ground, studying Houdini on the floor. He thought to leave, but then checked the impulse, deciding to remain with the group.

Again he repeated, "You all heard him. Big tough guy, bragging about taking punches to the stomach. Hell, he felt like cheese to me!"

3

Death Train

Concealing a serious medical condition from Bess, Houdini meets a wraith on board the train to Detroit. Later, while performing before a crowd of several thousand screaming fans at the Garrett Theater, he senses the provocative presence of Sir Arthur Conan Doyle . . .

By moonlight, the Quebec Consolidated quietly made its way toward Detroit, past one snow-blanketed town after another, stopping only in Ottawa and Toronto. Houdini stared out at the stars, lying in the lower bunk of the compartment he shared with his wife, a pen of solid eighteen-karat gold resting in his hand, his diary open. Bess slept above him, composed like an angel.

Montreal had ended disastrously for the magician. Houdini now felt an unrelenting pressure in his abdominal region. In the hotel bathroom he'd looked down at droplets of blood diluting in his unsteady urination. His temples continued to burn. His entire left leg, beginning at the toes, pronounced at the ankle, was numb with a cold fire. The sensation in his kidneys, and rib cage, was acutely uncomfortable. And he'd only managed to realign the dislocations in both shoulders several hours after they were separated with the shredding and crunching of cartilage.

Houdini wiped his forehead, left the berth and hobbled down to the bathroom. In the rattling open passageway where the two lurching compartments were held at bay, he encountered another night owl, a young freckled towhead, with mischievous gray eyes, dressed for tobogganing, who stood mesmerized by the cold blur of rhythmic black track and glistening snow underneath. The boy was wearing the same tam-o'-shanter and loose-fitting corduroy jacket Houdini had donned as a kid of twelve, having run away from home for a life on the road, and for Texas.

"Hey, mister," the boy asked, as awake as chewing gum. "What do you think would happen if someone jumped off going this fast?"

Houdini grunted impatiently. A snow crystal zapped his eye from the open window. He paused to rub it out. When he opened his eyes, the passageway was empty.

He shot glances up and down the adjacent compartments and rushed to the side, examining the fast-receding trail below. It was as if the boy had never been.

Houdini felt too sick to deal with the possibilities. A daredevil stunt? A freak suicide? A hallucination? He decided to forget it and shuffled on toward the bathroom, with the intention of applying an emollient to soothe his muscles. He locked the door behind him, sprinkled warm water on his face and stared into the mirror by a dim twenty-watt light bulb.

He saw a frightened stranger there, a tired-looking man contemplating himself in middle age.

A shock wave assaulted his groin, overwhelming him now like an opium overdose, injuries crying out from every muscle. He threw himself down on the toilet and sat groaning minute after minute.

Seeking solace, his mind drifted back to his initial engagement—at a police station, when he walked into the Mount Holyoke city jail in 1895 and stated matter-of-factly to the officers that no set of handcuffs in the world could hold him. It was an impulse, amidst the belligerent outburst of guffaws, a way to get some kind of write-up in the local papers. His escape came as a total surprise—not only to the cops, but to Houdini as well. No gyves, no darbies, would ever hold him for long.

Later, he tried his hand at jail cells. In Chicago, naked, shackled, desperate, the press thronging to all sides, he finally proved his point: Houdini was more than a magician. He was something inexplicable, a new honest-to-god phenomenon in an era accustomed to mere two-bit showmen.

From prisons to straightjackets, to every species of shackle and constraint. He remembered breaking out of Scotland Yard, blast furnaces and bank vaults, dungeons and mummifications. The one-hundred-fifty-eight pound magician would simply swell his muscles during any internment, then deflate them in order to get the needed slack.

Houdini always left knots in the same tied condition as when he began. He resealed bags, crates and tanks, and accomplished that covering of tracks within a very few seconds. His trail was incalculable. No one ever figured it out. He'd had all his employees sworn to secrecy before official notaries. And even his employees were ignorant of many of Houdini's machinations.

Houdini no longer challenged others. Now he accepted challenges, wagers of all kinds. It was open season for sadists, malicious inventors, vengeful locksmiths. All approached him, gleefully pitting the boastful magician against their lethal machine entrapments. Needle-spitting labyrinths. Oxygenless cul-de-sacs. Certain death. People turned out in droves to see him commit suicide.

When most families were living on eighteen dollars a week, Houdini and Bess were taking in nearly two thousand. And yet, Houdini was never satisfied. How could he be, when a Jack Dempsey earned a quarter of a million dollars in three and a half minutes in the ring, to live radio! When mediums were raking in millions by a psychic scam surely no more appealing or efficacious than Houdini's own powers?

The taste for risk, and its acquired strategies, had built a career, but left their permanent scars on his body. He had aged prematurely. He was broken, scoured, swollen and punctured.

Suddenly, he thought of Conan Doyle's knowing smile and animated hands gesturing toward some heaven. How that burly, one-man janitorial service for the Great Gate infuriated him; mustachioed, tanned, Teddy Roosevelt–like, an insane summons full of first principles and ultimate assurances. There was more to Doyle than met the eye. That thought came to Houdini just now. He had taken the large Englishman to be an old senile Victorian.

He began to tremble. "Ehrich?" his acrid lips whispered to his inner self, between the stench of sulphur on his breath. "Is that you?"

He put his fingers to his mouth. He was shaking all over. His eyes gazed painfully into blank space. Moonlight stippled the bathroom with a cold aura of cobalt blue. Outside, the clacking of steady tracks dissipated in near darkness, across snowy fields and the occasional smokestack of a warm hearth.

Houdini returned to his cabin. Bess had not moved a jot. He took up his diary, thought for a few minutes about the freckled kid he'd passed earlier, fiddled with his pen, then put it aside and got into bed. He retied the ace bandage on his ankle, flattened out the sheet beneath his back so that not a single wrinkle disturbed the fragile balance against his kidney, propped a second pillow lengthwise under his neck to aid in fortifying his wounded shoulders, and gingerly applied more of a demulcent to his rib cage.

He lay there feeling a horrible sensation in his stomach where he'd been hit. One more performance. That's all he had to worry about. He'd spend the day sleeping in the hotel.

Head to the theater and make it brief, then get himself home. A whole winter of rest. Write a few books. Figure out what he was going to do. At fifty-two, he had a whole lifetime ahead of him.

The Houdinis stepped off the train at 7:05. The "Team," namely Dexter, Joe and Royale, commandeered a dozen sluggish porters to help ferry the several tons of equipment into a waiting truck, while reporters surged around the Houdinis.

Frank kept them away. "Back off, guys. Come around tonight at the Garrett Theater. 8 P.M. That's where the action is."

"Is that a limp?" a pressman shouted at Houdini.

"I said shove off!" Frank threatened, all seventy-five inches and two hundred ten pounds of him.

Houdini didn't speak. Bess had seen him leave their berth on the train an hour before, only to return as colorless and waxen as a ghost. She was attuned to the smell of his illness, having just had the stomach gripes herself. She heard the laboring in his breath.

"Harry, I want you to cancel tonight," she had insisted.

To which he only shook his head, with a brief, exhausted negation she knew to be inflexible. Houdini would not let down fans, ever.

Now she kept her arm around him as much for physical support as comfort.

Layton deployed additional porters to handle the Houdinis' personal belongings, which included over one hundred books. Houdini always carried magic books, which he read carefully, despite nagging claims by some that he was illiterate.

Detroit was in bitter fog. Out in front of the station, Frank and the Houdinis crawled into the back of a leased charcoal-gray Pierce Arrow with a velvet interior. Layton drove, heading down a deserted Woodward, then Washington Boulevard to the hotel. The Houdinis had planned to tour the parklands of Belle Isle in the middle of the river. There were said to be a lot of geese. Now no one mentioned the outing. Houdini's evident discomfort had cast an admonitory silence over them all.

Layton rubbed out a Lucky Strike cigarette and turned up the Magnavox. He loved radio, having invested most of his savings in RCA stock. "Free money," he'd say. Though he didn't have to convince anyone. They'd all poured bucks into the market. RCA was the hottest. You'd have to be a fool or a Commie not to have bought some, Layton would say.

Frank read from the morning *Star*. Thomas Edison had avowed the innocence of a condemned medium whom the courts of New York had judged a money-grubbing fraud. "It says here that Edison was hoodwinked but that his pride prevented him from owning up to it," Frank said, paraphrasing the details. Houdini hardly listened.

They arrived at the Academy Hotel. Houdini was allowed to keep his vehicle directly in front of the drab brick exterior, within visual range of the glass revolving door, making Layton's task of keeping an eye out easier. He'd be able to remain indoors, rather than in the cold front seat.

Layton scoped out the lobby and chose a strategic warm couch. Four or five Cokes, a jar of pickles, potato chips, a couple of egg salad sandwiches wrapped in the classified section, a radio which he kept low, and secreted girlie magazines. That was his station, those were its particulars, until dinner, when he'd gobble down something in the hotel kitchen, then get the Houdinis off to the theater, where he'd continue his patrolling duties outside the back entranceway. That was his routine, and had been for nearly three years.

As she was exiting the foyer with the bellhops, Bess stopped a minute, took Frank aside and mentioned the incident that had occurred in the Montreal hotel room with the students.

Frank was addled. He asked her what their names were. She said she didn't know, though she had no problem describing the assailant. She thought it was all pretty innocent stuff.

Bess rejoined her husband.

Frank lodged himself in a hotel phone booth, rung up the concierge at the hotel in Montreal and obtained what information he could. He then called a local Canadian detective contact to help him track down the young Japanese. He had a hunch that the kid, or man, might have been an imposter, perhaps working with the Madame. Houdini was lucky to be alive.

Frank headed over to the Garrett, where the boys had arrived with a truck of gear and were setting up.

Houdini undressed as if he were disarming dynamite and crawled into bed, while Bess was in the other room pouring him a warm bath. When she announced that his water was ready, he couldn't get up.

"Later," he mumbled.

"Harry, let me see your ankle."

"Why?"

"Don't argue with me."

Houdini normally relished the tomboy in his wife, that girlish charm and rural moxie. But he had little patience for anything now. Bess never got past seeing the ace bandage and figured that was good enough. She lay down next to him and gently scratched his head.

"Don't." He winced. His forehead was dented in with fever.

"Is there anything you want?" Bess asked, feeling helpless.

He hesitated dreamily, then said, "Tits."

Bess undressed without a word and dutifully stroked his face with one breast so that its nipple rested against his desiccated lips. She watched him suck himself to sleep.

Bess then got up, took a bath and afterward called for room service. She hadn't eaten anything since the foul oysters a few days before. Now she had an urging for spaghetti with spoonfuls of grated Parmesan, and a hot fudge sundae.

Outside the theater, three sandwich men with billboards suspended over their backsides and chests advertised the evening showcase. Around two o'clock a line started forming. Dexter, who kept tabs, could see there would be a good take that night. Frank checked for bombs, looking under every seat in the hall. He examined Houdini's dressing room, and the rooms on either side. He checked the orchestra pit, the galleries overhead. He probed inside the lights, under the stage, in the curtains, and did a detailed search of all the backstage paraphernalia. Frank was thorough. His own life was involved.

Joe and Royale set up Houdini's special performance cabinet, with its numerous hiding places, slip walls, trapdoors, fake curtains. He and Bess would do their old trunk trick tonight. Houdini wanted no Chinese torture. Nothing upside down that would involve the ankles. The local papers had been advised to convey one of Houdini's open challenges to the public. Blacksmiths all over Detroit—as well as binderers, metalworkers, crate and barrel manufacturers, locksmiths from police departments, engineers and inventors, even former convicts—were invited to try out their best escape-proof contraption on Houdini. Such contests always escalated the hype associated with a performance.

At seven o'clock sharp two bifocaled sisters, self-important secretaries specializing in shorthand, from an agency, showed up at the theater with legal pads of lined yellow paper and a box of pencils. It was their job to record anything Houdini, or members of the audience, might say during or after the performance. Houdini's lawyer Kirchner had recommended the practice as a result of all the libel cases that had been brought against the magician. There were spiritualists suing him for upward of $100,000. Since you could never be too sure who was against you, the shorthanders were always placed at opposite ends of the auditorium, their notes plucked up before they might have time to confer.

By 7:20, nearly five thousand people had entered the large

theater hall, each paying fifty cents. The atmosphere was electric with anticipation. A survey had shown that Houdini's name was known by more people than Woodrow Wilson's, Babe Ruth's or Einstein's. Joe and Royale had finished their preparatory work on stage. The wide blue curtains were down. Where was the master?

In the hotel, Layton knocked four times in short succession on their door. Bess awoke in a start, looked through the dark blinds toward the slivers of twinkling light out on the street, then silently lay back down, hoping not to rouse Houdini. But it was no good. Layton knocked again. Houdini's eyes flew open. Bess heard him groan.

Houdini grabbed his gut, took a deep breath and willed himself in the direction of the bathroom.

Bess turned on the light beside the bed.

"Harry, my God!" she cried, lurching up. She saw the blood stains on Houdini's sheets. "You're bleeding."

He closed the door, turned on the water and didn't answer.

She threw off the sheets, exposing the whole bed. "I'm going to be sick!" she muttered, seeing the dark, acrid pool of blood. It penetrated deep into the mattress.

"Never mind that," he said, hearing her panic.

"Never mind?" she screamed. She tried to open the bathroom door. He'd locked it.

"Harry, open the door."

There was silence.

She kicked it. "Open the goddamned door!"

"I'll be out in a minute," he whimpered.

"Harry, I'm calling the doctor. You're not going out."

"After the performance."

Fifteen years before, a doctor in St. Louis had diagnosed his bad kidneys, with their broken blood vessels, and had had the audacity to advise the Great Houdini to give up his profession. Since then, Houdini had taken great relish in periodically pestering that doctor with good-natured postcards of scorn. "Jumped off a bridge today," or "Broke out of Sing Sing . . . still goin' strong, Doc! Never heard from my kidneys. If I'd listened to you why I'd be sick and poor and no-body!"

Bess was desperate. As Houdini got dressed, she put her hand in the puddles of blood on the bed, then smeared it all over her face and confronted him. She looked like a squaw on the warpath.

Houdini shivered and turned away from her. Then he said, "Go on. Wash yourself off. That's bad luck."

"You were always a stubborn superstitious fool!" she de-creed with useless insight.

There was another rap on the door. "Harry? Bess? You all awake? It's time, just letting you know."

Houdini grinned at his wife. He loved her solicitous fury. "You've never once been on time since the dawning of his-tory." He looked at his watch. "Come on, Bessie. Put your getup on before Layton bangs down the door."

Bess acquiesced. "I love you," she moaned. "And I can't stand to see you do this to yourself."

"It's the last time, I promise," he replied weakly.

Layton drove them to the theater. There was ice on the road and they were late. Houdini and Bess could hear a com-motion a block away from the theater. The audience's impa-tience had reached audible proportions. The whole assemblage was pounding its feet against the wooden floor and rhythmically clapping in unison for the show to begin.

Houdini entered the building through the rear stage door, where Layton would remain. Frank was on the inside.

"They've been going this way for ten minutes, Boss," Frank said.

Royale and Joe were on hand.

"We got a challenger?" Houdini asked them above the din.

"Oh yes," Royale said. "Looks harmless enough. Some older fellow with a bunch of cuffs and some iron. Looks like no sweat."

Bess had shed her overcoat and now stood in black ballet tights and a sequined blouse with frills that showed off her boyish figure. She replaced her pumps with gymnastic slippers.

Houdini had become a magnet of concentration. Having retightened the ace bandages, he'd now exorcised the demon from his ankle, renounced any sign of a limp and shut off his stomach, bowels and chest from his head, the source of his powers. He'd stuffed Kleenex up his anus to hold back the blood.

Bess and Houdini looked at one another. Houdini winked and they entered the stage. The crowd went wild. It had been over a decade since the Great Houdini had performed in Detroit.

"Good evening," Houdini began, squelching further applause. He was in a hurry.

The theater impresario stepped forward on the stage and introduced the challenger, a Mr. Hodgekiss and his assistant, representing the Society of Psychics, down from Windsor. As stipulated in the printed conditions set forth by Houdini of all challenges, the magician had a few minutes to examine the shackles put forward. He did so, then took the microphone to convey his dissatisfaction.

"These locks have been heated and bent and broken inside," Houdini proclaimed. "They are not regulation cuffs, which are the rules. This is no legitimate challenge, therefore." He started to withdraw from the contest. But there was some booing in the audience.

Hodgekiss took the microphone. "The rules stated that the challenger should bring his own irons. Nothing more!"

The effect was a dramatic one. The audience expected nothing less than that the challenge should be met.

To Bess's grief, something in Houdini could not let down the crowd. He was losing strength rapidly just standing there.

"Sure, why not," he conceded heroically, throwing Joe and Royale a look of desolation.

Bess closed her eyes. She wanted to cry.

Frank was nervous. He had no undercover contact in

Windsor, so he called the police on behalf of an anonymous client. He preferred to keep Houdini's name out of these matters, as invariably it showed up in the papers. Frank wanted a rundown on Hodgekiss.

Meanwhile, the show had begun.

First the assistant trussed Houdini's arms firmly at his side with hoops of steel locked behind his back. Then he padlocked Houdini's wrists, arms, thighs, knees and ankles with separate devices. As if this weren't enough, he then entwined chains from various irons in and out of other chains, wrapping Houdini up the way the mob made short business of those destined for the East River.

Houdini was seated and helpless beside his closet. He was holding back vomiting. Padlocks were sealed atop padlocks, his arms pulled back so tightly that he was forced to protest out loud, "It is not part of the challenge that my arms should be broken!"

Hodgekiss apologized but did nothing to relieve Houdini. Bess whispered to Joe, who, with Royale, stepped forward to curtail the challenger, who was still ardently yanking and pulling. Houdini was in agony, losing circulation all over his body. His stomach felt as if it had been cut open with a butcher's knife. For all of his yogic training, he could not control his breath—he was hyperventilating. His heart was pounding out of control, and his chest caving in under the avalanche of pain. He could feel that blood had overwhelmed the stuffed Kleenex that he'd fitted up his rectum. Any minute the blood would percolate onto the stage floor.

"I'm finished," Hodgekiss announced, throwing up his hands with shrewd apologies for all the inconvenience.

"Me, too," Houdini uttered to himself, in a near faint. The only human ever capable of threading the eye of a needle with his toes now felt powerless inside the labyrinth of steel and iron manacles.

Hodgekiss dragged the heavy chain leading from Houdini's mess of leg irons across the stage until it was taut, then wrapped it around a freestanding steel ballast and locked the knot.

Now the crowd watched and waited.

"Don't leave me," Houdini quietly implored Bess. Never before had she heard him sound so pitiful.

Joe and Royale dropped the curtain over Houdini. This was a normal part of the stage presentation. It was 8:40 P.M. Joe provided Bess a chair. She sat uncomfortably a few feet away from the closet, looking composed, before the thousands of hushed paying customers. Hodgekiss, his assistant, the theater impresario, other technical hands, and Joe and Royale stood to the sides watching from backstage.

The whole theater was dramatically darkened, save for a bald spotlight aimed from high in the ceiling at the closet in which Houdini worked. Bess was caught peripherally in the glare.

Down below, a small twenty-piece band launched into a section of Gershwin's "Rhapsody In Blue." This was followed by a rendition of "Can't Help Lovin' That Man," as sung by Helen Morgan. Bess got all teary a second time.

Inside the closet, Houdini had vomited all over himself, just before passing out.

After a few minutes, Bess smelled it.

She controlled her panic. "How you doin', Boss?" she whispered.

There was no answer. Nor did she hear any sound. She got up, walked the few feet over to the closet and called through the curtain to Harry.

Her voice magically stirred the unconscious in him. Houdini awoke in a flashing combustion. The pain was unbearable. He fought back in a sudden paroxysm of motion, breathing yogically at the top of his lungs.

The audience buzzed with private commentaries all over the hall. Bess stood back, perplexed, looking from the closet to Joe and Royale, then back toward the closet.

She sat down.

Hodgekiss bit lightly down on his bottom lip, looked at

his assistant and nodded his head with favorable anticipation.

Ten minutes transpired. There was not a yawn among five thousand people. Every person in that hall was tensed, sitting forward fitfully.

The band did Gus Kahn's "It Had to Be You." Still Houdini did not emerge. They played jazz renditions by Jelly Roll Morton, in just the style of his Red Hot Peppers.

Finally, triumphantly, Houdini thrust his face from under the curtain into the blinding white light.

Immediately the crowd stood up, some hats were tossed into the air, and the roar of approbation shook the whole hall. But the fanfare was premature.

"I need you to unlock the steel bands on my back," he said. "Just for a minute or two. I've got no blood flow."

Bess stood up and shouted for a doctor in the house. A well-groomed gentleman left his wife, rushed up onto the stage, took one close look at Houdini's face and neck and started to speak.

No words formed. He didn't know where to begin. Houdini was blue.

"What?" Bess harried him.

The doctor shook his head. "Loosen the locks at once!" he insisted, totally befuddled.

Hodgekiss came forward with a key in his hand. "This is a contest, no love match!" he reminded Houdini.

"Fucking son of a bitch!" Houdini mumbled. "All right then!" He looked at Bess. She was horrified by what she saw.

"No . . . ," she cried, begging him, begging Joe and Royale. Beseeching the doctor.

But Houdini disappeared again under the curtain. He would not give up. He uttered a Hebrew prayer to himself. Then he set about resignedly to use the half inch of slack he'd thus far achieved. He knew that that half inch, by itself, was worthy of an Olympic gold medal. But it was only the beginning. He consoled himself with the knowledge that there had been hundreds of other times in his life when death hovered all around him, even as the crowds watched and cheered just a few feet away.

But there was a stronger sensation than mere physical agony. There was a specter in the air, again. Houdini felt the presence of Sir Arthur Conan Doyle. Had he seen him actually seated there in the audience? It had been more than three years since they last had anything to do with one another. And yet, during that time, Houdini had not stopped thinking about Sir Arthur and their final "combat." The strange and sensational outcome had haunted him, refilled him with a grueling and damnable self-doubt. But that fateful day had also endowed Houdini with a freedom too rarified and exquisite to even begin to analyze.

Houdini had suffered torments of the damned, on account of Sir Arthur. His hopes had been raised, dashed, then left dangling. He never knew for sure whether Doyle had in fact touched the beyond, as he said he would do.

And in the aftermath, Houdini sank deeper and deeper in the mire of mixed convictions, guilt, hope.

Now, he was certain that Doyle was out there, in some form or another. If it were so, then Houdini must not fail. He struggled even harder. For Doyle's sake; for the sake of those ghosts, madding spirits, and final judgments, that would not sleep.

He managed to get onto his knees, facing forward, an excruciating way to forge more slack and begin untangling himself. Pinioned in the position of knighthood, or of execution.

There was little time left.

Meanwhile the audience, which had already sat patiently for more than an hour, was going wild with excitement. This had to be one of the greatest entertainments all year in Detroit, certainly worth half a dollar.

PART TWO

4

The Contest

Three years prior to Houdini's agonizing moments in Detroit. It is New York, the Spring of 1923. In which the publisher of the well-known magazine Scientifica Americana *comes up with a bold and inspired plan to save his faltering empire . . .*

Police had cordoned off the crowd. Reporters flashed their cameras. Everyone craned their heads upward ready to catch the romantic instant the young couple leapt to their death from the twentieth story of the brick building above.

"Sorry, mister, ma'am. . .," the cop said, pushing back two determined individuals.

"Do you know who I am? Ralph Harrington, that's who!"

The cop wasn't listening. He had other crowd control problems to contend with.

"But my office is in there and I'm expected at an important meeting!" the dapper, middle-aged Harrington went on.

"Careful!" the twenty-three-year-old Miss Amy Beckwell

warned. She saw that her boss was about to step in fresh horse manure.

"Well this is just the damnedest nuisance, if I say so!" Harrington snapped, squirming out of the mob. He and Beckwell crossed the street, avoiding the manure trench where others had blundered in their eagerness to get a better view—the gutters still ran freely with fertilizer after the night's thunder shower—and entered one of twenty breakfast speakeasies in the neighborhood, where they could sit until the nonsense played itself out.

"Hello, sucker!" a bawdy barmaid said, slapping her friend Harrington on the same shoulder she slapped every fella.

"Good morning, Darla."

"Little early for my big butter and egg man, isn't it?"

"Two coffees and toast if you don't mind."

"No problem. You catch the action?" she said, peering out the windows to the street.

He grunted.

"A tragic thing," Amy added softly. She adjusted her bottom on the stool, crossing her svelte legs as the sun caught a minute glow of fine platinum hairs leading innocently to her exposed knees. Harrington couldn't help but notice. He figured she'd never shaved. The idea excited him.

He took out his morning paper. From her briefcase Amy withdrew a file that contained the day's agenda.

For five years, Harrington had been the publisher-in-chief of the nation's leading scientific magazine, *Scientifica Americana*. Throughout that time it had been a struggle to keep up circulation, requiring more and more advertisements. Now, when the magazine should have been in the black, it was failing. This day demanded a decision from him which he'd been avoiding: secure another lien without telling his wife, cut staff drastically, shorten the number of pages by half, eliminate the color cover, go with cheaper paper or come up with some miracle. He'd already pressed his luck with "Daddy," his condescending hosiery-manufacturing father-in-law, who'd bailed him out twice before.

Harrington restlessly scanned the *Times* with a dark knot in his chest. He noticed that Sarah Bernhardt had died suddenly in Paris. She'd evidently been preparing for it all along, sleeping at night in a coffin lined with rose petals and faded letters. A Mr. Shuh-shee-ahsh of Montana, the only survivor of the battle at Wounded Knee, was pronounced dead from cancer. Mohandas Gandhi was failing to stir the masses in India, and in London, the Prince of Wales had dismissed another marriage rumor. The country was reported to be "benighted with angst over his protracted bachelorhood."

Harrington looked out at the street; then his eyes darted to Amy, irresistibly drawn to her cleavage, the rouge on her lips, the dab of self-conscious powder on her high cheekbones. He liked the new look of her bobbed hair and cloche hat. He imagined that she was wearing silk underwear. He'd heard about a special room upstairs above the bar and contemplated his next move.

Amy averted his intermittent gaze. The magazine was desperate. Forgoing a trip in a topless Model T to see Lillian Gish in *The White Sister*, Amy had spent the previous evening diligently compiling new sources of advertising. She wanted her own magazine some day. A periodical devoted to maternity dresses, wedding gifts, how to plan for the big day, dishes and floral arrangements and, of course, bringing up babies.

"The way I figure it, Ralph," she began, "the magazine's been carrying machine ads, radio ads, battery ads, for five years. And the rates haven't gone up, they've gone down. Why? 'Cause nobody's flocking to read ads about batteries. Everybody's got a personal problem, see. You've got a problem. I must have a problem. So we go after advertisers who are offering solutions to personal problems that are scientific."

"Such as?"

"The All-Bran people," she declared. "And the makers of

yeast cake to fight pimples. I went to the store around the corner from my aunt's place and found all these products that fight some of the biggest problems. Toothpastes to prevent pyorrhea, pills to combat B.O. and halitosis. Of course, cod-liver oil for darn near everything else."

"That's good, Amy." He put his hand on her hand. "That's *very* good."

The barmaid brought them their order. Harrington smeared preserves on his toast.

There was suddenly a loud crescendo of alarm from across the street.

"Oh gosh!" Amy blurted. She stepped out onto the street. Harrington and others inside the speakeasy followed her.

They could make out horrible goings-on atop the building. The couple had resisted efforts by two rescuers. Now they had moved to what looked like the very edge of certain death.

Harrington's senior editor on the magazine, Bertram Fennell, was one of the rescuers. He usually came in to the office early. *Scientifica Americana* operated out of a large penthouse suite on the twentieth floor. Fennell had heard a strange lovers' quarrel from above. From what he could make out, the young man had not found employment since returning from the War. The couple had engaged a Justice of the Peace the night before. Thinking for the both of them, the groom had now resolved that they should join their souls in the eternal bliss and full-time employment of the Hereafter. She was unsure about it.

Fennell made out all of the loud soul searching coming from above. Then he heard sirens. He ran up the stairs and climbed onto the roof. He was not unfamiliar with the causes and consequences of this so-called epidemic. Just three days before, the *Times* had commented on a woman in Trenton who'd killed her baby, then done herself in by swallowing Lysol, in the apparent belief that her recently deceased husband was calling to them from "Summerland." And according to a Swiss daily, thousands of otherwise conservative locals had been driven to suicide, or insane asylums, as the result of a spiritualistic mania that was sweeping Europe.

Now Fennell found himself in the thick of that ague, trying to talk the couple down.

"Just get away. We know what we're doing!" the groom shouted. They inched forward on their butts to the very brink of the concrete ledge.

A cop had arrived and was seated beside Fennell. He motioned that Fennell should keep talking to them. Other hidden cops were secretly moving into positions with a net one floor below.

"Look, I'm a scientist," Fennell started.

"Just don't listen to him," the groom told his bride.

She was shaking. Eye makeup streaked her puffy cheeks. She didn't like all the hundreds of people staring at her.

"Before that, I was a writer, in Paris," Fennell continued, speaking calmly.

The bride got interested and turned. "Did you ever meet Zelda?" she asked anxiously.

"All the time," Fennell replied.

Suddenly, the impatient policeman, annoyed by his task, lunged for the bride. "Save it for the confessional, you jerks!"

"No!" Fennell screamed.

The groom panicked and deflected the cop's arms. Fennell also lunged, just as the woman fainted and fell headfirst off the building. But Fennell had her by an ankle. Now the cop seized part of her rayon wedding dress. She hung facedown into the abyss, a matrimonial missile distinguished by its plainly visible undergarments. Petticoats and bloomers dangled over her head. Her colorful wedding bouquet dropped from her hand and floated down toward the street, where the crowd cried out, arms rising to catch it.

Amy, whose small, pale hand clutched the side of Harrington's woolen tweed jacket, let go and ran through the maze of stopped traffic. By some extraordinary tingle of destiny, which Amy would never forget, the bouquet happened to fall into horse shit right before her.

She reached down and claimed it. White lilacs and lilies of the valley.

Other envious young women flocked beside her. Above, the groom was not going anywhere without his wife. He struggled with his two rescuers.

A sort of trampoline was awkwardly extended from the windows of Harrington's world headquarters on the twentieth floor. Harrington was furious.

Both Fennell and the cop were lying flat on their stomachs, extended way out. The bride had hit her head and now awoke as from some surreal dream. She started to bawl and kick. The groom collapsed, leaning back against the building.

Together, Fennell and the cop tried to drag the girl back up. It wasn't easy. Her silk stockings slipped. She wore no corset. Her panties had come off. Fennell didn't dare turn away. The groom was jolted to his senses.

"Hey!" he hollered, wrapping his arms around his wife's immodestly exposed thighs. He joined in and yanked. Other cops appeared on the scene. All were now anxious to ensure the bride's well-being.

It was over.

"Fool kids!" the first officer carped.

Harrington was immersed in thought, walking through the jubilant chaos of sympathizers. He had sized up the near-tragedy. He had an idea. Maybe a great idea.

Entering the offices of *Scientifica Americana*, Ralph Harrington and Amy Beckwell met chaos. Harrington was besieged by copy editors, linotype operators, print stewards and waiting telephone calls. Today was press day. He would have relished the excitement and the veneer of power had he not been lugging around the horrible foreknowledge that the magazine was going broke. As publisher, it was his job to prevent that.

He threw down his things in his office, took off his shoes,

propped his legs up on his mahogany desk and surveyed the "blue line" final galley of the magazine. It was his last chance to make any changes. Within three days, it would be on the newsstands.

The one-hundred-fifty-page magazine contained a better-than-average-looking spread of new and exhilarating inventions—a paring knife, a mail chute, hair curlers requiring no heat, a gauze cage used with a cigar to corral its smoke, a filling station for fountain pens, a stand-alone douche, something called a snowplow, a shoe tree and an alarm bell that would catch burglars. This was a big month for ingenuity.

He glanced at articles detailing new findings in the galaxy. The universe appeared to be expanding, starting just behind the parking lot of Mount Wilson Observatory above Pasadena. Meanwhile in China, big things had been going on. A revival of ancestor worship following the purchase of some teeth in a Peking drugstore. One tooth led to another. Molars, then a complete skull dated at half-a-million years, were recovered. A few days later, another fellow happened upon million-year-old dinosaur eggs.

Harrington yawned.

He noted stories about underwater painting, germ-plasm and telegony theory. The nuggets of gold discovered inside the skeletal private parts of the once beautiful Queen Aashait, whose sarcophagus had been dug up the previous year in Egypt. Meanwhile, hornets had been seen swarming to King Tut's mausoleum, following confirmation that the coffin was to be opened and subjected to X rays. A little better, Harrington thought.

He leafed through other essays, interviews, letters from the reader. He tapped his finger on an article entitled "Genetics of the Future," which chronicled one Mr. Burbank's new plums and prunes and thornless blackberries.

An in-depth account of the revolution in endocrinology suggested whole new possibilities for longevity. Harrington read it more carefully. He learned of new hormones coming onto the market that could easily be obtained from plants and animals, even little girls. There was centronervin, a brain hormone, which, when served to frogs, somehow expedited their ability to catch flies.

Harrington noticed a preponderance of advertisements for radios. Kennedy, France, Doubleday-Hill, General, RCA. The ads were paltry and token, each one looking alike—inexpensive.

He read a letter to the publisher from British physicist Sir Ernest Rutherford, who wished to dispel the ludicrous notion that useful energy could ever be derived from an atom, adding that the process of radioactive disintegration was as slow as glaciers.

A U.S. Naval astronomer denounced Einstein as a plagiarist, offering radical new interpretations of the bending of light, as measured by two expeditions to the tropics.

Now something caught the publisher's eye: the majority of other letters to the magazine had been prompted by what Harrington generally termed "oddities." An anonymous airman from Port Clinton claimed to have flown 37,000 feet, thus beating Sadi Lecointe's and Lieutenant Macready's respective altitude records. The respondent said that he had witnessed "ghosts" up there, traveling in a V, like swallows, but not south, and many of them wearing U.S. Army fatigues, as well as old Reichswehr uniforms.

Yet another writer commented upon the recent disclosure that Arthur Rubinstein allegedly played the piano in "telepathic rapport with members of the audience." This fellow had had the same "outer body" experience on a Sousaphone.

Harrington examined three particularly striking letters, each responding to an anthropological assessment he'd published two months before, in which a certain medium from Bolivia, Silverio Viracocha, had come to New York, dazzled observers and made the news. Using wooden sticks called *hantis*, he was reported to have healed several ailing widows. One of them was dying from a nervous addiction to sugar, another from an undisclosed social disease.

Silverio, wearing a ceremonial poncho, a Panamanian straw hat, an embroidered white scarf, and carrying a leather *chuspa* or coca bag, tossed kernels of corn into the gathering, had everyone chew a pleasant juicy concoction of coca, quinoa and amaranth, then sang in some Quechuan dialect that nobody understood. He explained later that he was addressing Andean spirits that also happened to be visiting New York. Then he clicked the wooden sticks repeatedly until all those present had gotten sleepy and "taken the step" over some bridge "to the other side." Everyone present agreed that they had taken a long ride atop llamas, looking out at all the sights.

One man, a wealthy superior court judge, was consoled when Silverio enabled him to speak with his dead wife, who'd been run over a few months before by a red Buick roadster. Somehow in the interim she'd turned into the Goddess of Potato Peeling for the whole Inca Empire.

Silverio was taken to see Fannie Brice in the *Follies*, where he laughed boisterously, and then disappeared from New York several thousand dollars the richer. Readers were crazy to hear more.

Harrington slapped down the galleys. *That's it*! his brain rattled. "Amy!" he shouted.

She came running into his office. "Yes, Ralph?" She knew how to manipulate his temper by her familiarities.

"Assemble the staff," he said, with a finality that gave her the chills.

Amy gathered the entire group near the coffeepots outside Harrington's book-lined den. Four editors, a dozen technical people, two bookkeepers and Fennell. The editors knew their boss had just scanned the issue. They stood anxiously.

"I have something to announce," Harrington declared. He saved up his breath, beaming. "A contest!"

"A . . . contest?" Fennell said inquisitively.

"That's exactly right. Now listen . . ." And he proceeded to remind them how the magazine had grown up, made a

name for itself and promoted all the fruits of science and reason. But how, of late, it had strayed from its mission.

"Mission, Mr. Harrington?" Fennell's associate editor,
Barkwaithe, stammered.

"Mission!" Harrington sliced back at him. "By that, I
mean interest! Novelty! Flair! We have to compete to stay
alive. We've ignored something up here in this dry scholas-
tic aerie that really *matters* to people."

Amy was radiant. She could tell that Ralph was about to
disclose some brilliant variant of her solution. Some contest
involving All-Bran, or anti-pimple sponsors, something really big.

"People are searching for something and science isn't
providing them the answer," Harrington continued. "We're
not being read, and advertisers aren't paying attention to us
either, because we're stuck on Einstein. Radios. Expanding
universes and prehistoric teeth."

"But isn't science the reason this magazine exists?"
Fennell contested, losing patience.

"Of course it is, and we'll continue to be the best. But not
if we're broke. We need a cash infusion. And I mean to get
it."

Harrington's senior bookkeeper raised his hand.

"What is it, Jeffrey?" Harrington reared impatiently.

"If it's a loan, forget it. I had lunch recently with the
banker from—"

Harrington cut him off. "I'm not talking about any loan.
As I've unfortunately learned, that only delays an inevitable
flaw in the structure around here. I mean a contest. A battle!
Lances and fire and ghosts. Something that's half-real, half-
imagined."

Amy waited for her big moment, solemn and serene.

"It'll get Americans thinking, reading, arguing, and best
of all, subscribing."

"Ralph, what will?" Fennell said, trying to see beneath his
boss's characteristic bluster.

"I propose to publicly offer five thousand dollars to anyone who can prove beyond a doubt that there is life after death."

Harrington looked around the room, his hands still raised. "Well?" He was waiting, buoyed by his own momentum.

But so far the impact was still settling. There was an awkward moment. Amy's expression turned to one of disgust. She felt pity for her boss, and personally humiliated. It was a horrible idea, she thought.

"*Scientifica Americana* will select half-a-dozen umpires—men who will judge the veracity of evidence presented by contestants from—well, hell—from all over the world!"

"Evidence?" Fennell inquired.

"Where you gonna get five thousand—" Jeffrey started.

"Don't even think about it," Harrington said breezily. He was a torch, driven, inspired. "No one's going to win that money." He gathered his employees closer and whispered conspiratorially, "Because we know—don't we—that when you die, you're dead!"

Amy was confused. She *didn't* know. She stepped back.

"It's good," Fennell finally avowed. "Eh, Barkwaithe? Heller? Bistro, what do you say? Madigan?" All the editors, with the exception of Barkwaithe, started to grin in accordance with Fennell's reaction.

"It's *very* good!" they all agreed.

"Brilliant!" Fennell continued. "You've done it, Ralph!"

There was general applause for the publisher. He wiped sweat from his brow. "Amy, dear, some coffee."

She got him a cup without answering.

Barkwaithe was troubled and not a little indignant. He'd had his own inner experiences, which some had said made him a "sensitive," and he didn't take kindly to Harrington's whole tone. "How do you expect to attract candidates?" he said.

Harrington was ready. This was his master stroke. "That's the question, isn't it?" He stepped forward, pinched some sugar in his brew and stated with a faraway look, "Two giants in the public eye. Men upon whose words and deeds millions of readers will hang. Exclusive coverage by this magazine. Two advocates. One for, the other against."

No one ventured a guess. Lips bristled, eyes grew liquid with forethought. Harrington delayed their suspense, then said the names.

"I'm referring of course to Harry Houdini and Sir Arthur Conan Doyle!"

5

The Enormous Madame

*The next day, following the inception of the contest,
Frank Lattimer exposes evil and Houdini receives a
tailor-made invitation . . .*

It was still dark, drizzling and fog-bound when Frank
Lattimer headed out of Brooklyn along Jamaica Bay in his
silver-gray Stutz. When he reached the Cypress Hills cemetery, he turned off the engine, blackened his headlights and
coasted silently down a dirt road to the undertakers' compound. Frank saw two vehicles parked before one of the
buildings. He removed his semi-automatic short-recoil
Webbley from his waist harness and double-checked its
loading indicator. The cartridges were in place and fresh. He
slipped out of his car, bolted across the grass and ducked to
the side, gun raised. Light was coming through the grill in an
underground window. Frank kneeled low, inched his sleep-

less eyeball forward and peered directly down into the morgue.

He saw a badly pockmarked meat-packer of a man reaching into an old beat-up leather case on the floor, from which he retrieved a small sack of plaster of paris. He then approached the naked, middle-aged stiff that lay on a pathologist's table. Death had left the man's hefty private member erect, swollen with rigormortis.

Body parts immersed in formaldehyde jars cluttered the shelves. Frank saw an open casket on the wet concrete floor. There were mud stains where it had been dragged from an open rear door. By its gold satin lining he could confirm what he had already suspected: billowing gold interiors were a trademark of the Bravo Coffin Company. That and the eight-inch screws.

Two other men stood by. Frank recognized the short one, bunched up under a woolen trench coat. He was the capper all right, the creep who'd scoped out easy spots at the private séance the night before. Frank, in his own disguise as a librarian with the New Rochelle College of Pastors, had watched the man fraternizing with the sitters in the early minutes of the evening, expertly seducing personal information from two bereaved widows—one of them gorgeous, probably early thirties—details that were exploited later that evening by the veritable giant who posed as a medium. There were strange happenings that night, which Frank intended to take up with Houdini as soon as possible.

A second cretin, taller, twitching, obviously with Bravo, an insider, kept hurrying the proceedings. Dawn would soon be upon them.

"I don't like it," the pockmarked ghoul complained.

"There's money enough in this one," the shorter rogue stated matter-of-factly, scratching his jaw and hunkering down.

The scapegrace continued by taking a mold of the dead man's face, careful to work the plaster into every facial nook and cranny.

The plaster dried within minutes. The mold taker pulled out a vial of liquid rubber from his bag and filled in the cast with it. Soon enough, Frank could see that a perfect facial replica had been created.

"What do you say?" the mold taker asked, anxious to get the hell out while the going was good.

"I don't have to tell you, Charlie. Natty gets what Natty wants. She promised that dame a biblical experience."

"Please, gentlemen. If you wouldn't mind completing your business—" the Bravo man whined.

"Ah shut the fuck up!" the capper ordered. "Come on, Charlie, I'm startin' to feel like breakfast."

Charlie growled. He stared at the dead man, then turned to the capper. "You do it then." Natty had ordered them to cut off the dead man's penis, keeping it erect with the plaster. She had her own perverse designs. But neither man had the stomach for grabbing hold of that yellowing scrotum and severing the member.

"Let's get outa here," the capper said, paying the insider cash and gathering their things. The two toughs headed for the door.

Frank ran for it, got into his Stutz and peeled off up the dirt road. As he crested the hill, he caught a flash of light in his rearview mirror. They had seen him speeding away. It had warmed up and the cemetery was cloaked in rain. Reaching the main entrance, Frank skidded into the thoroughfare, turning down Woodhaven. The sun had risen to the surface of Queens. Frank passed a streetcar crowded with immigrant types on their way to work in the city. There were plenty of horses drawing ice, loads of hay and other necessities out to the island. The ghouls were following him.

Frank speeded up, turning on to Cross Bay.

"Who is he?" Charlie said, weaving in and out of congestion.

"Don't know," the capper said, heated. "But we're gonna fucking find out. Move it!" He pulled out a military Mauser from his trench coat, specially outfitted with extra muzzle velocity.

Frank thought he'd lost them at the Bay. He was wrong. Around a hairpin curve, they suddenly appeared directly on his tail, roaring down in a black Budd.

"Jesus!" Frank pulsed, swerving toward the dunes on the far right. There was no way his Stutz could outdrive a thirty-thousand-dollar Budd.

They started to pass him in the oncoming lane, careened back to avoid an open poultry truck, then pulled out again.

Frank smashed out his driver's window as the ghouls started to pass him on the Bayside. He raised his gun, just out of sight. The vehicles were running parallel now.

The capper looked Frank over.

"What do you think?" Charlie said, at the wheel and keeping apace with the Stutz. "Should I cut him off?"

"What and dent Natty's Budd? You outta your mind? Fall back."

The capper recognized Frank, but he didn't know from where.

Frank breathed again, gained distance and finally lost them.

"I know that face . . ." the capper puzzled.

Within half an hour, Frank was at the County Clerk's office. He had a contact there he frequently used to gain access to all court records and police file backups in the city.

Madame Natty Sublime would be performing this night at the Harlem Theater on 125th Street. There were billboards all over town advertising "the most famous medium in African history." Whatever the real story, there was no record of that name.

Frank got two other gumshoes down there from the agency to help him, men frequently used by Houdini. They called the principal Budd dealer in New York, only to learn that nearly fourteen hundred had been sold, countless others leased in the last month alone.

Frank conferred with his in-house man, who ran a cross-reference search through the hallway of three-by-fives. The County Clerk had adopted for its police records a comprehensive system, first instituted a few years before by Attorney General Palmer's twenty-four-year-old paranoid exemplar, J. Edgar Hoover, during the Red Scare. All the Pinkerton files had been hand-copied and incorporated here.

After several hours, the in-house man had come up with over two hundred female mediums who'd been busted in New York state during the past twenty years. There were descriptions, dossiers, but no photographs.

"I'm looking for the ugliest pig you've ever seen," Frank was quick to point out. "Talks with an accent, possibly South African, maybe British Jamaican. Hard to say exactly. And she's a giant of a woman. I mean like Hannibal."

"That narrows it some," the in-house man quipped.

"Look, Jonesy," Frank confided in his friend, "this woman's a slime. She's hooked this super-rich dame whose husband died last week, see . . ."

"I got the picture." Jonesy sobered. "But unless you catch the medium taking money from the deceived, there's no case, Frank."

"You don't have to explain the law to me. Whoever Natty Sublime is, she's smart. Too smart to take money outright. That's why I've got to find any other dope on this broad."

"What's your interest in her anyway?" Jonesy finally asked.

"My boss plans to blow her show wide open tonight. You know what he thinks of mediums. I've got to protect him."

"There'll be thousands of people there."

"Yeah. Some of them with guns. She's got solid backup, Jonesy. Real grease monkeys. I already had a scrape with them. This woman's tied to the mob. I'm sure of it." Frank cocked his head, looking for the angle. "If I had the goods, it might make all the difference."

"You're gonna alert the police?"

"Can't do it," Frank said. "Not without the goods. Houdini's been burned too many times. He can't handle that kind of publicity. If I don't think there's probable cause, I keep the police out of it."

It was two o'clock. That gave Frank and his cohorts a little over five hours before Houdini would leave for the theater.

Jonesy, Frank and the two other gumshoes pored over the records pertaining to the many female mediums who'd been in either Sing Sing or the Tombs during the last two decades, beginning with the most recent. By dinner, they'd eliminated every medium going back as far as 1904. That left one more year, and twelve final cases.

The wall clock now read ten after seven. Frank rubbed his eyes. He flipped down yet another index card in his hand. His mind was blurred. He'd gotten up at 3 A.M. Suddenly, something clicked.

"Wait a minute."

He picked back up the previous card to see what he'd just overlooked. The original booking file had been neatly taped to it. The name on it was Vita Adama. Weight, two hundred sixty-four pounds. There was a policeman's hand-written bit of marginalia that read, "Or more!"

"Bingo!" Frank said.

Vita Adama, alias Eunice Holstein, alias Princess Anne, alias Ada Porimisimo, alias Countess Atilia Corregio De Borgia, alias Madame Evi Lucas De Lair, etc. etc. Her crimes were numerous, her dossier a thick one. Frank's eye was first caught by the name Bruhod Merriweather of Manhattan, at one time a very rich attorney. At least until he fell in with Adama. In 1903 Merriweather, for some reason that baffled his friends, had turned over to Adama his Central Park manse for the sum of one dollar. Merriweather's brother, who worked in the same firm, hired detectives to look into his sanity, and the woman who had apparently swindled him. What those detectives found was one of the most sinister Svengalis in recent times.

Frank scanned the file. Adama claimed in court to be the offspring of King Louis I of Bavaria and the magnificent *femme fatale* Lola Montez. The prosecution brought in an el-

derly witness claiming to be Adama's sibling and former
partner. She stated that Adama's real name was Eunice Holstein, of Baltimore, born in 1877 to a black prostitute and her
Hungarian pimp. That would make her forty-six. Eunice had
gone bad, according to the sister, because she'd been raped
so many times by their father starting from the age of four.

Eunice got ninety days. A detective's notes accompanying
the police blotter indicated that Eunice's sister was full of
shit, angling for mercy from the court, which is what she
achieved. It was suspected that the two of them had worked
together in Prague, in Rio, in Venice, cities where they'd
been accused and frequently convicted of charges ranging
from murder to public exhibitionism. In every case, they'd
managed to elicit pity and greatly reduced sentences. In
some instances, Eunice had engineered spectacular escapes,
invariably leaving her sister behind (Frank detected a bit of
the Houdini-turned-criminal here), or manifested magic of
such an order as to mystify judges, wardens, and jailers into
simply releasing the both of them.

In the meantime, according to the notes, Eunice—or
whatever her name was—had accumulated a fortune. Her
sister, however, became a bride of Christ and retired to a
convent outside of Elko, Nevada.

Eunice went on to get arrested for poisoning the entire
water supply of Morecambe and Heysham, her motive completely unknown. After spending forty-eight hours in Aylesbury Prison, she escaped, it is believed to Paris, where she
managed to baffle authorities at the Louvre, making off with
the *Mona Lisa* long enough to have several credible copies
churned out. One of them showed up in Kyoto, another in
Montenegro.

She was next heard of at the Bloomingdale Asylum, then
in Joliet Penitentiary, where she strangled a guard but was
released on a self-defense technicality. Sometime later,
under the name Princess Anne of Bohemia, Eunice turned up
at the Onset Bay Spiritualist Community in Massachusetts,
then in Cape Town in 1900, where she led a spiritualist revo-

lution, or something like that. Several people died in the up-
shot, and Princess Anne, claiming diplomatic immunity,
slipped out of the country with millions of dollars' worth of
diamonds stolen from the Smutts Banking Cooperative.

By 1901, she had returned to London under the name of
Countess Atilia Corregio De Borgia. It was known for certain that she possessed two stolen works—bathers by
Fragonard, and a reclining nude of Dosso Dossi's from an
estate in Ferrara. At that time she had apparently gained the
confidence of a well-heeled widower from Sussex—a
cricket companion of Sir Arthur Conan Doyle, no less.

Frank paused and looked up. *Doyle?* His head began to
reel. With Doyle's friend's financing, the Countess had
started her own Theocratic Church of London. Detectives
from Scotland Yard, upon hearing of her claims to Victoria's
lineage, investigated. Two pretty young infiltrators were
found slain, their vaginal regions excised. Fifty of the Yard's
best men surrounded the church one Saturday night. Upon
breaking in, they discovered dozens of female sex slaves,
many of them in their teens, chained in the basement. They'd
been repeatedly raped and sodomized over a period of
months by the Countess and her associates.

But the Countess had vanished.

That was 1902. In 1903, she arrived in New York, heavily
disguised, in steerage and set out to conquer Bruhod. There
was the sensational trial, the exposure of the sex abuse, the
short sentence, during which time it was claimed Eunice had
been a "model prisoner."

Then, on August 28, 1906, the *Times* reported that
"Countess Eunice of Aylesbury, recently famed here for
having produced certain inexplicable manifestations, left
for Sante Fe to found a religious order of painters."

The file on Eunice Holstein of Baltimore went blank for
nine years. But then, as if by terrible providence, Frank read
that a Princess Eunice was reported to have spent three days
in Sarajevo in 1914. Three years later, a mysterious Baroness Adama Rosenthyme was spotted in the company of

Lenin, in Zurich, hours before the activist's return to Russia. The witness, a South African gemologist, confirmed that the Baroness "was as enormous as she was unattractive, resembling that Princess Anne who'd started a revolution in Cape Town many years before and made off with priceless jewels."

That was it.

This is big, Frank reckoned.

"Jonesy," he said. "Quick. What's the score on extradition of British criminals?"

"Forget it," Jonesy replied. "Palmer abolished such things. Parta the new isolationism, League a Nations backlash and what all."

Sex slaves twenty years ago on a Saturday night in London. No proof of her involvement. Frank knew he'd lost. His only hope now was to give elephant woman Holstein, or whatever the hell her name was, enough rope to strangle herself. If anyone could lead her down the path, it was Houdini.

Frank made haste for Houdini's house. Upon arriving, he reached through his broken car window and rang the buzzer in four short bursts outside the electrified port cochere. He could hear Houdini's fox terrier, Shalom, yapping from inside the cloistered garden.

The gate opened. Frank drove inside. It was dark.

"Evening, MacIntosh," Frank said, greeting Houdini's archivist-cum-butler.

MacIntosh, in his late seventies, hailed from Cambridge, Mass., where he'd spent thirty years organizing two of Harvard's specialty libraries—Divinity and Crime—before coming to work for Houdini. The magician's own enormous collection of alchemical books and memorabilia was renowned.

"He's still in the laboratory," MacIntosh informed Frank, shaking his head with a look that Frank knew to mean "You're not going to believe what he's been up to all day!" By the "laboratory" MacIntosh was referring to Houdini's testing grounds downstairs, part gymnasium, part machine shop, part torture chamber; a proving site cluttered with contraptions, pipes and pumps, a small portable pool, hanks of rope and wire, tinted mirrors and physicist's lights, surgical equipment, engine parts, ladders, trick mechanisms, vaults, and locks dating back five centuries.

Frank doffed his hat, then passed his assistant, Byron, as he continued to the lab. Byron had also started with the Pinkertons, was a great gun handler, seemed to know his way around the underworld well enough, was single, addicted to the job and kept relatively to himself. Furthermore, he had come highly recommended, not just by Frank, to Houdini's staff. He was on his way to pull the car out of the garage. He frequently shared driving duties with Dexter, especially if a lookout was called for.

Frank knocked first, calling from outside the door. "Harry, you got a minute?"

There was silence from within. Frank waited, then called to him again. "Harry? It's Frank."

The door slowly opened. Houdini was sitting quietly some thirty feet away.

"How did you manage that?" Frank asked, to which his boss grinned punkishly.

"Magnetism," Houdini replied evasively. "Now, what is it? You look frazzled. Where you been? We're leaving in five minutes."

Frank quickly filled Houdini in on the day's major points, and continued to describe the remarkable dossier as the attentive Byron drove them to the Harlem Theater uptown.

The white-gloved, heavily Slikumed Byron, his weapon in his chest harness, stayed with the car, as he usually did, reading comic books, or girlie magazines, and sipping spirits wrapped in a newspaper. Houdini rarely interacted with this anti-social solitaire, the butt of occasional jokes. Even Frank knew little about him other than that he'd scored high on the Pinkerton tests and had proven to be loyal and hardworking.

It was ten minutes to show time. Houdini was certain he could get the goods on this Madame, based upon everything

Frank had told him. Houdini commandeered a street cop marking his beat. The policeman asked for his autograph. Houdini signed a matchbook and explained the situation.

Frank, Houdini and the cop joined in with the cascade of tens of hundreds who were entering the theater all eager to see a ghost, as the advertisements had promised.

"We got a problem," the cop admitted, once inside. Houdini was not unaware of it. There had been no charge for admission. Whatever deceptions Eunice Holstein had in store, she'd not charged the public for it and was therefore breaking no law. Two enterprising merchants, no doubt attached to the medium's circle, were set up at tables doing considerable business selling Lydia Pinkham's Compound and Radom's Microbe Killer. The cop confronted them. But they too were in the clear, flashing bona fide business registration papers.

The policeman was ready to leave. He had his beat to walk and no legitimate cause to hang around the theater all night. While he appreciated Houdini's vigilantism—most cops who weren't on the take did—he also knew Houdini's reputation for going overboard and missing the mark.

The theater was filling up. Houdini and Frank stood to the inside of one of the entrances. Suddenly, Frank caught sight of the knifeman.

"Hey!" he whispered to the departing cop, keeping low. "That face mean anything to you? The stocky one with bad acne, over there?"

The cop squinted. "Well I'll be damned," he said, reaching quietly for his gun. "That's Charlie Moranis. One a Legsie's goons."

"Wrong," Frank proffered. "That's no goon. He's a ghoul. I watched him cut off the balls of a dead man this morning. And he's working for her."

"Stick around," Houdini advised.

Frank and the cop inched their way toward the front rows. Frank was on the lookout for the widows he'd seen the night before at the séance. Especially the beautiful one.

Houdini meanwhile positioned himself in the rear corner of the theater, out of sight.

The lights dimmed as half-naked black African drummers sounded the commencement of the performance. Houdini watched the curtains rise to reveal a spectacle less monstrous than pathetic. There was the self-styled Madame Natty Sublime, standing center stage, her head bowed, her hands in a gesture of prayer. Appearing almost as wide as she was tall, the Madame was deep in meditation, dressed to kill, she no doubt imagined, in a diaphanous getup, like one of Degas's ballerinas. The effect could not have been more ticklish had a hippo been clad in diapers, but the audience was prevented from a good laugh by her solemnity. Her breasts, polka-dotted with glowing little stars, were all too visible, and of a size hard to calculate. She was barefooted. Her calves were the size of her breasts and hung down with a similar gravitational bulk. The Madame's face was painted with lampblack in keeping with the color of her confederates. She stood before a large circular structure draped in opaque fabrics.

Houdini noticed an ardent-looking fellow, bespectacled, coming after him just behind the rear rows. Something didn't set right. Houdini changed locations. The fellow kept on. Frank, separated from his boss by a hundred feet of crowds, hadn't seen him yet. Houdini carried no weapon, other than a penknife.

"Before we get started I would like to introduce Mrs. Ginger Riddles, recently widowed as a result of the tragic and untimely death of her beloved husband, the illustrious brain surgeon, Irwin Mayakovsky Riddles. He succumbed only six days ago while ice skating at Central Park. A good man, Irwin. He and his wife were still newlyweds, so much in love. Come up here, my dear . . ."

Mrs. Riddles, who was seated in the first row center, walked onto the stage. She was the beautiful one, dressed for mourning in a sinuous, loose-fitting caftan, like an Arabic princess. In the concentrated lighting of the stage, her face shone white. Frank was smitten.

"With Mrs. Riddles's help, by the force and purity of her grief, as well as by the powers invested in me from Africa, the holy place of my upbringing, I shall attempt to bring back her husband. Ginger," she said with sturdy commiseration, taking Mrs. Riddles's hand and placing it to her bosom, "you will know this miracle to be so by the ecstasy of reunion it will induce."

Ginger sniffled, as did many of the women in the audience. She lifted a corner of her caftan to wipe away tears and heartily thanked Madame Natty Sublime.

"Now I must insist that everyone remain in his seat," the Madame announced. "As is the custom at these events— where any hooting skeptic could likely ruin the atmosphere of piety—my assistants have been placed strategically at the front of the audience to protect against any possible collusion on my part with hidden members in the audience. That should satisfy any unbelievers among you. For what you are about to witness is truly of supernatural origin and it would be a cruelty to the grieving widow were any critics or newspapermen to vocalize their doubts."

Several figures moved into position. Frank and the cop quickly took up their own spots on either side of the blackened orchestra pit, where they were fully inconspicuous. Frank spied a wooden latch that should provide access to the center of the stage, from below.

Houdini, judging the source of light on stage, made his way upstairs. He was still being followed.

Natty Sublime ushered Ginger Riddles into the chamber on the proscenium. The house went black.

Suddenly, a thin, gassy light wove a pattern in the air, there was a lightning blast—the audience screamed—and then the voice, unearthly, forbidding, called from a far-off land.

Sublime's rasping, coming from the chamber, sawed through the tense air of the theater, calling on divine powers, and accompanied by weird howls from her drummers. Children in the audience clutched their mothers. From where Frank and the cop stood, the goings-on sounded like a Zulu uprising.

Houdini moved to the upper balcony, searching for what he knew to be the "holy source" of the Madame's powers. As he approached a sealed stairwell, he heard the audience groan. Turning, he saw a remarkable effect: a man's face, no doubt Irwin's, hovered high in the air over the auditorium.

"Ginger . . . ," a man's voice spoke yearningly. "I need you . . . I want you . . . I am here for you . . ."

Frank heard hundreds of sneezes. Houdini looked down at the patchwork of hankies. *Gullible shut-eyes*, he thought. An entire audience of believers.

The spectral manifestation descended toward the chamber. No one could see what Ginger or the nympholeptic Madame were doing in preparation for this visitor from the other side.

Another bolt of lightning shot out of the ceiling. Houdini climbed up the hidden stairs. He stopped midway, listening. Ten seconds later he could hear steps quietly approaching after him.

Houdini took out the penknife he carried in his back pocket and moved quickly. He came to the steel rafters that formed a corner of the ceiling and the lighting grid for the theater. Leaving his jacket behind, he pulled himself up into a crawl space, shimmied along the metal beamwork and arrived finally at an ingeniously concealed compartment that was locked.

Houdini could hear a projectionist inside operating the various chimeras. The hoax infuriated him. Within seconds he'd silently opened the lock, tiptoed along the transverse edge of a steel girder, his fingertips clinging to the cross brace, and prepared to pull himself up. His fear of heights was unsettling to his stomach. He concentrated, then made his move, gymnastically slithering out over the aerie into the compartment.

"Hey!" the spry youth running the projection apparatus shouted.

Houdini ripped off his tie and jammed it into the machine. The celluloid melted, the cinescope ground to a halt. A fire quickly started inside the mechanism and the lad smothered it with his jacket. Houdini grabbed one of the spotlights and turned it toward the audience just as the moaning and groaning reached its zenith.

"Ohhhh!" Mrs. Riddles howled from behind the curtain, bleating like a woman in the midst of sexual transport.

The hall went dark, save for the spotlight Houdini controlled. Noxious smoke was billowing from the compartment where the nitrate had ignited and been suppressed.

A loud, startled "Huh?" went up from all quarters.

Faces turned from below. Houdini leaned out where the audience could see him, holding on to the steel brace with one hand, and addressed what must have been some twenty-five hundred people.

"She's a crook, ladies and gentlemen!"

"It's Harry Houdini," someone's voice called out.

"If she truly wishes to hoodwink the public, perhaps Eunice Holstein—the Madame's *real* name—had best find a better hiding place for her accomplices!"

The projectionist panicked, pushing the apparatus, with its electrical discharge machine and the hanging mask of Mr. Riddles, away in an effort to get out. In so doing, he slid the heavy machine from its edge. Houdini grabbed on. Its weight pulled his feet from under him. Still he held on, keeping the smoking contraption from crashing into the spectators below.

"Get her, Frank!" Houdini screamed.

A bullet rang out, then two more, bouncing off the steel not three feet from where Houdini hung in a dizzying frenzy to right himself. He swung away.

The cop fired back. It was Moranis, running for cover. His other accomplices were firing at the orchestra pit and at

Houdini. Sparks flew. A machine gun sprayed the rafters. People stampeded toward the exit.

The theater lights went on all over the house. Frank forced open the latch behind the orchestra pit and lunged upward, emerging in the middle of the Madame's chamber.

"Nobody move!" he hollered, pointing his gun in one hand and his badge in the other. The cop joined him, holding Madame at bay. Before Frank stood the ravishing widow, naked as a dream, groping after her caftan which lay on the floor. Something beyond his immediate ken had evidently taken place on the stage. Beside the widow, still growling like an interrupted monster, was the Madame, ripping off the rubber molding of Irwin's own face, which she wore. Frank remembered it from the pathologist's table.

"Okay, lady. Move it," he ordered the Madame.

Up above, Houdini struggled to regain his stance. His fingers were coming unglued. Just then, a fleshy palm, backed by little muscle, offered itself to the vertigo-frayed magician. Slipping, Houdini lunged for the helping hand and pulled himself to safety, while the machine crashed below into now empty seats.

The ungainly looking galoot who'd been trailing him all along took off his hat and energetically shook his hand. It was the zealous Jeffrey, certified accountant.

"Mr. Houdini, sir, a great pleasure to meet you. I'm with the magazine *Scientifica Americana*, and I've been authorized to inform you of an important contest. My boss, the publisher Ralph Harrington, wants to make you a significant offer!"

"Contest? What are you talking about?" Houdini was befuddled amidst all the goings-on.

"That's right. A contest pitting science against religion. Mediums like that fat lady from all over the world. And expert observers from universities. You'll have one adversary, a judge on the opposing side." Jeffrey paused, thrilled by what he had thus far conveyed.

"What judge?" Houdini demanded with glowering ambivalence.

"Sir Arthur Conan Doyle, all the way from England."

Houdini stepped to safety, and a faint thrill of providence flushed the tight flesh of his face.

6

The Voice of Pheneas

While Houdini is savoring his victory over Eunice Holstein, Sir Arthur Conan Doyle awaits the momentous return of someone dear to him—from the grave . . .

Across the entire southeastern coast of England, from Dover to Weymouth Bay, the freakish snowstorm had plastered everything. Freakish because earlier that day, the temperature had reached sixty degrees in the direct sunlight.

But the night brought on cold winds from France, winds that howled across deserted battlefields where the blood of young men felled in the war still soaked the roots of thistles and brambleberry.

The snow bombarded the ruins and castles of Sussex, slamming against Pevensey and Hastings, sounding the bells at the cathedral of Chichester, freezing the moat of the stone fortress at Bodiam. The snow and ice swept over the farms on the Weald, the ancient stands of beech, continuing across the slopes of the Downs where once, twelve hundred years before, Aethelwald had been murdered by the savage prince Ceadwalla, and Aldbryht forced into melancholy exile.

Sir Arthur Conan Doyle had dipped his quill into this regional realm of spine-tingling, pre-Norman romance. He felt the allure of the land, with its ghosts and its winds. And he also knew, this day, by the unceasing tinnitus, or ringing in his ear—*les oreiles fiflent*, as the strange psychic foreboding was called across the Channel—that something far more momentous than a mere blizzard out of season had come hither, to his sprawling estate in Crowborough, Kingdom of Sussex.

Twenty million had died in the Great War, followed immediately by another twenty million who perished from influenza during a single month in 1918. The Doyle clan was devastated. First Malcolm Leckie, Doyle's brother-in-law, was killed, then Doyle's own younger brother Innes, followed by two nephews, innumerable friends, more distant relatives, his mother and finally his beloved son Kingsley. All perished in quick succession. For poor Kingsley, death came slowly. For endless days, following his wounds suffered at the Somme, he slipped deeper and deeper into the mucousy, implacable pall of double pneumonia. His maker arrived just before Armistice Day in London, 1919.

Those who were closest to the Doyles could see how such concentrated carnage had deeply affected Sir Arthur and Lady Doyle. At least forty million dead souls were floating between Earth and Heaven. The Doyles were in touch with at least some of them.

"Those we love *must* continue to live," Sir Arthur had insisted on numerous occasions. "The souls of millions flourish and are speaking to us."

Lady Doyle tended to agree and found her deepest satisfaction by way of comforting her husband. She had suffered her own losses, like everyone else, and found in her heart the capacity to give without question or degree. Lady Doyle was well educated and proud, but never too proud to withhold that affection upon which Sir Arthur depended for his writing, his lecturing and his apparent sanity.

They were a loving couple who lived a good, adventurous life. But what surely accented their relationship was the evolution of an ideal that they both shared—a profound belief in life after death.

By morning, the spring sun had warmed things up. Sheep were back out digging for grass through the thin cover of snow.

Betcham, the Doyles' impeccably dressed and dignified handyman, butler, social secretary and occasional nursemaid, had run the Doyles' three children (Bottles, Doodles and Inches, as they were so-called) off to school for the day, leaving the front door wide open so as to channel the welcome sunrise and heat up the night's chill indoors.

At first light, four special guests had also come through that door. Doyle's wife, Jean, was conducting a séance. The storm, in both her and Sir Arthur's minds, was a miraculous sign, a fitting prelude to the urge that had been swelling in them for weeks. This was not the first time such "swells" had occurred.

The house was huge, containing a central oak-wood corridor angling past fourteen rooms in all, snaking around a hodgepodge of memorabilia on the walls; a standing suit of medieval armor, Battle of Monmouth period, its hatchet poised above plastron and hauberk; a movie poster from the previous year's *Sherlock Holmes* by Goldwyn, starring John Barrymore and Roland Young and based upon the William Gillette play; a library case specializing in the British campaigns throughout France and Flanders; spirit photographs; magazine covers from *Punch* that Doyle's uncle had drawn; first editions of Doyle's nearly fifty volumes to date and framed samples of Lady Doyle's recent "automata," those literary effusions conveyed through her own hand at the behest of departed spirits.

And at the end of the long passageway was a special

room, the door ajar, in which sat several yearning, mesmerized believers, close friends of the Doyles, all en rapport,
hand in hand, singing "Nearer, My God, to Thee."

Lady Glenco, an Australian Jew, had removed to Sussex
three years before, following her spiritualist conversion in
Melbourne, where Sir Arthur had lectured on his so-called
"New Revelation." She and Lady Doyle had immediately
sparked to one another, shared a pen pal in the beyond and
posted unaddressed letters sealed with kisses of smeared
cochineal, honey and gum arabic. They also played rousing
games of mah-jongg together.

Sir Henry Dabacourt was a well-known "sport". In his
customary plus fours, he and Sir Arthur had taken a ride in a
hydrogen-supported dirigible, followed Red Grange's every
ball carry in America and could grab numerous wickets in a
single inning on the bowling field. Dabacourt was rich, with
loads of beachfront property in the newly emerging city of
Miami and vast numbers of shares in US Steel and AT&T.
And he was generous to boot, often competing with Doyle to
set high standards of philanthropy. Weeks before, he'd given
two thousand pounds to an orphanage so that the children
could enjoy Prince Albert and Lady Elizabeth Bowes-
Lyon's wedding day in style. But he had a long way to go to
catch up with Sir Arthur, who'd given away—by his own
estimates—nearly 250,000 pounds to spiritualist causes.

Sir Henry was as eager to become immortal as the next
man, and when Sir Arthur guaranteed his friend on that
point, it cost the gamesome sixty-seven-year-old nothing to
have go at a séance or two.

Lionel Vercombe was an avid proponent of the new Coue-
ism, an "auto-suggestive self-mastery" rage based upon the
teachings of the French guru-pharmacist Emile Coue. He
was himself a physician of the old school who had treated
Sir Arthur's late alcoholic father, Charles, the painter of fairies, after he'd been committed to a home. Lionel believed in
Greek homeopathy and could not bring himself to accept the
new mercenary style of profitting through unnecessary

drugs. He knew of one doctor in London who'd become a millionaire prescribing eighteen pounds of morphine to his clients in one year—830,000 doses.

Lionel preferred herbs, and still wandered the heath in search of nature's own wonder drugs. It was during one of his gathering expeditions that he saw his darling granddaughter fall from her pony, hit her head on a rock and die. Now, his only wish in life was to regain contact with the child.

And finally, there was Sidney Mosbacher, a man of many "suppressed desires," as he put it scientifically, who had only three days before seen Doyle in one of his greatest moments of triumph, hitting a century in a cricket match at Lord's. The two friends went way back, had hunted for whales in the Arctic together in their early twenties and decades later seen action side by side as medics in the Boer War, where the two of them helped bury as many as sixty men a day in the red ant-ridden soil of the Veldt.

Sidney's marriage had disintegrated when he started taking Freud to heart. Though there were recent signs of contrition on Sidney's part, it had put a strain on his relationship with Sir Arthur as well. Doyle, after all, was a prude, or that's how Sidney thought of him; he had never once contemplated an affair and had even tried to have removed from Hyde Park a nude bas relief by the "anarchist" Epstock. There was not an ounce of English swank in the grand, late-middle-aged creator of Holmes. During the period when Doyle's first wife was dying of tuberculosis, he had fallen in love with Jean Leckie. The disease lingered. Doyle remained faithful in the old-fashioned, Victorian manner, keeping his acquaintance with Jean strictly platonic for many years. When his wife finally died of the consumption in 1906, he buried her quietly, then married Jean, fourteen years his junior, kissing her for the first time.

Doyle had been called "a good giant." Unlike his friend Sidney, who had abandoned his wife without remorse and taken up with a forty-three-year old blond bombshell banker in London, Doyle's whole person was about honor. Though he'd once renounced religion in favor of theosophy, the mature Doyle was a Roman Catholic to the core. In Doyle's universe, to doubt was to sin. Doyle was firm on the business of monogamous love, was a vehement anti-suffragette, a patriot who loved to fight, had enlisted in the Great War at the age of fifty-five, and revered Napoleon. He had written of the bloody Boer uprising, "Wonderful is the atmosphere of war," and come back from Pretoria rejuvenated.

Sidney, who was in the process of shifting the center of his ripe years from sleepy Sussex to erotic London, now had little patience for his old friend Sir Arthur, "that Edwardian mire of contradictions," as Sidney would tell mutual friends, a shot of brandy in his hand.

How could this bold fighter, master sleuth, scientist in his own right, speak so confidently of life after death, not to mention—yes—fairies? Sidney found such faith absurd, though he was not above playing along, just in case there was something to it.

Just a year before, in 1922, Doyle had written a book entitled *The Coming of the Fairies*, in which he presented two revolutionary photographs—"Alice and the Fairies" and "Iris and the Dancing Gnome." There was sufficient technology at hand to support the miraculous images. To doubt is to sin, Doyle had repeated to critics.

"You can't expect us to take these pictures seriously?" one reporter had scoffed.

"God is here and now," Sir Arthur made clear. "I am a man of science, which is why I am able to accept certain phenomena without misgiving. Why be surprised if the phenomena should happen to be messages from God?"

These messages were more palatable in Scotland. But to the largely Episcopalian reading public of England and Wales, faith was for Sundays, and sin was fashionable. Moreover, publishers demanded it. And the messages *they* were getting were from their paying subscribers. The editors of the *Beeton's Christmas Annual*, who had first brought out

A Study in Scarlet, in 1887, were not interested in a Roman Catholic, upright Holmes. They had paid (albeit modestly) for deception, murder, cunning, as well as an addictive, seven percent solution.

Doyle, however, was tired of Holmes. His life was still populated with dead people, but this time they were not merely the product of ingeniously wrought detective yarns, but rather the real, delicious glimmerings of life after death, as captured on rare photographic plates, in the floating objects of a séance or the myriad notebooks and slates of living mediums.

It was only in the last four years that Lady Doyle had come fully around to her husband's adamant new way of thinking. Throughout the war, she'd stayed clear of such matters, even ridiculing, when pressed, the whole notion of spiritualism, which she'd termed "uncanny and dangerous." She was more concerned with the family income and Sir Arthur's general happiness. Her husband was not a good businessman. She still recalled how one day Sir Arthur had descended one thousand feet into a coal mine he'd recently acquired, only to learn—too late—that the veins were junk, incombustible. Moreover, with the exception of the Holmes tales, which Sir Arthur now actively detested, his other books were doing very little for their bank account.

For Doyle, who had fanatically pursued psychic experiences for thirty years, her unfriendliness in public to the spiritualist arena had given him minor heartburn. By 1916, his missionary zeal had gone international. He was lecturing widely on spirits and had become as famous for his work with mediums, healers and sensitives—many proven to be frauds—as for his prodigious output of fiction and nonfiction.

Something then occurred that was extraordinary, and dramatically changed Lady Doyle's mind on the subject so dear to her husband.

An obscure man calling himself Pheneas, a prophet whispering in Aramaic, began communicating to Lady Doyle, first in her dreams and then through uncontrollable calligraphic impulses. Sir Arthur, initially jealous that Pheneas had exclusively chosen her with whom to chatter (after all, wasn't Doyle more deserving?) came to greet these preternatural visitations as the "Miracle of Sussex."

Pheneas had foretold a chance meeting at dawn between three influential men—Hoover, Keynes and Jan Smuts—on a street corner in Paris. He'd gone on to describe the tragic failure of Wilson, even at the moment of his glory in Europe. All of this astonished the Doyles, who kept up a constant vigil on world affairs. But that was only a test, as it turned out, of Lady Doyle's receptivity to the spirit world (or that's how her husband would describe it). For what came afterward was far more compelling than mere prediction.

Pheneas—a self-described bedouin caliph who'd ridden across desert sands with the best of them, prior to his later life as court astronomer to Charles V, Holy Roman Emperor—started speaking through Lady Doyle at lunchtime, then at breakfast. Finally, the garrulous Pheneas wouldn't shut up, even during quiet, romantic dinners. For reasons of his own—and he did keep his counsel where such motives were concerned—he intended, with the help of Lady Doyle, to serve as a clearinghouse for certain souls still wandering in confusion since the war. Sir Arthur had witnessed such wonderworks among dozens of other mediums.

The magpie Pheneas began with Lady Doyle's very own dead brother, Malcolm. Malcolm, in turn, spoke in an avalanche of greetings from the other world.

Then came forth Hugh Lawsons, an editor friend of the Doyles', recently deceased, of *The Times*, who stated unreservedly that "a pleasant home is being all fixed up for you."

Then her mother-in-law (the "Ma'am") came through in her traditional clishmaclaver accent.

"Aye now, such a good boy," she'd told her son. "But it's time you be growing up, don't you think?"

The voice had spoken quickly in her ear, while Lady Doyle wrote furiously to keep up, page after page.

"What do you mean, Mother?" Sir Arthur pressed.

Lady Doyle listened for the answer, then wrote, "Holmes. That's what I mean. Enough is enough, child . . . And that double-crossing scoundrel of yours, Moriarty . . . Why don't you just finish off the bastard?"

"Just one more book, to pay the bills, you understand. But tell me, what's it like up there?"

There was a long pause and then Lady Doyle, suppressing her amusement, taking down the inner dictation of Pheneas, who in turn was conveying Doyle's mother's words, wrote, "I never saw any home on earth to compare with our home here."

Sir Arthur lifted up the slate on which these words were written, turned to his wife and trembled with everlasting joy.

"Can she be more specific?" Lady Doyle asked Pheneas.

There was an inner commotion. And then Pheneas added, "They've apparently got cricket, brandy, smoking jackets and Church. 'We're all taken care of here,' she relays."

"Materialism is dead!" Doyle stated jubilantly.

Lady Doyle ceased to be troubled by these moments, though she never offered to discuss their reason for being. In her darkest corners of doubt she wondered whether she hadn't somehow conjured the visitations, the voices, to please the man she wanted more than anything to please; to bring back the source of his youthful confidence; to restore the assurance to their household that so many deaths had shattered.

She was responsible. She was the medium, and whatever ambivalence she may have harbored, there was no denying the rich vein that had been opened in her, giving Lady Doyle a new sense of power, and thus of freedom in an otherwise male-dominated universe.

And there was no question that these revelations—jealousy aside—imparted a surefootedness to Doyle himself.

The children had their own concerns. Their parents were not exactly *normal*. They weren't even *paranormal*. These bouts were more intense than that. But there was no turning

back. They were too much in the public eye. There were demands upon their time and their social calendar. Nearly every utterance, each pronouncement, carried the weight of
Great Britain's interest or the country's sentiment and invariably reached the press.

Then, on a certain afternoon, Lady Doyle's inner connection to Pheneas, her reams of silent transliteration, were
greatly augmented by a genuine chorus of voices that anyone who happened to be in a room with her could hear.
Voices from Pheneas's earlier incarnations; groans, directives, ruminations and, added to these, Lady Doyle's own involuntary vocalizations. She began speaking in Aramaic,
supplementing the trance dash of written prose with a volley
of unrecognizable vocables. Sir Arthur, who'd dabbled in
lexicography, thought he recognized Chaldean, then Gaul-
ish, or Old German, and Anglo-Saxon. Chaldean proving
unwieldy, Pheneas adopted proper English and before long
was speaking through Lady Doyle, as one of the family.

"Freud has a term for this," Sidney Mosbacher had informed Sir Arthur. "Have you taken her to see a specialist?"
He was thinking of a place he knew in Switzerland.

The Doyles went to Switzerland, but only for a skiing hol-
iday. For Sir Arthur himself was the specialist, and he knew
without the slightest doubt that what ailed his wife, if you
will, was inspiration.

One night, over dinner, Sir Arthur noticed that Lady
Doyle was looking paler than usual. Suddenly, without
warning, a profusion of their broccoli soufflé and leek soup
came pouring from her mouth, followed by a bizarre off-
white substance, like cream or oil paint. Lady Doyle gagged
and fell onto the floor, clutching at her throat. The stuff
drooled from her nose and dripped from her ears. This had
never happened before to the Doyle clan. A triumph, thought
Sir Arthur.

But Lady Doyle was scared to death. Things were getting
out of hand. She'd taken it too far, but didn't know whether
it was she, or Pheneas. She had lost track of truth, margins,

delineations. Her psyche reeled between dualisms; her innermost controls faltered before this altogether unexpected emergence.

Betcham whisked the children away while Sir Arthur ran for his camera, leaving his wife retching and begging for her life. By the time he'd run back from the study, the substance—which Sir Arthur knew at once to be first-phase white ectoplasm—had dissipated. Lady Doyle was exhausted, in tears. She'd become Pheneas's slave.

"Darling, you've done it! By God you've really reached the other side!"

"I've made a mess I'm afraid," she cried apologetically.

"Do you realize what this means?" Sir Arthur crooned, helping her off the floor where she'd fallen.

"It's going too far," she whimpered.

"You have no reason to fear. Your brother, our son, all of them now will have an open channel of communication. You are like a precious radio, my darling. Open to the dead souls. Open to the cosmos."

"I don't want to be a radio." Nor did she want to vomit ectoplasm. She wanted to be sexy.

Sir Arthur took her into the bedroom. In the adjoining bathroom, she cleaned up and there discovered that the ooze had come forth from between her legs as well. Lady Doyle suppressed a scream. Now she was shaking. The ooze, she thought, was like what one might expect from a ghost's ovulation, a kind of milky discharge that could serve no purpose other than to remind her that she'd become a freak.

Calm yourself, her brain hastened.

But there was little calm to be found. The world had changed for her, and she'd never be sure what had actually triggered it—her love for Sir Arthur, a strong urging to please, to be all things to all members of the family, or a brutal, selective destiny that had singled her out.

Lady Doyle rejoined her husband, who waited in bed like a proud king, prepared to do his duty by his mate. He sensed her self-consciousness, stroked her wise face, then straddled her backside, not for purposes of carnal union—though that too was on his mind—but rather, in the most loving fashion, to soothe her churned-up nerves. He rubbed her shoulders, fiddled with the muscles in her fanny and made her remember that she was a woman, beautiful, strong, brilliant—all of those assets for which a woman was rarely complimented out in the rural sticks of Sussex.

In the days that followed, Sir Arthur was ecstatic. His greatest hope, the one fundamental in whose service he'd crusaded and sacrificed since the age of twenty-one, had materialized at his very dinner table. This was the same species of ectoplasm that had converted four of the greatest scientific minds alive, men who were his own examples: Sir William Crookes, discoverer of the element thallium and a courageous pioneer in the field of X-ray tubes and electric lighting; Sir Oliver Lodge, bereaved physicist and true believer, knighted side by side with Doyle years before; Alfred Russel Wallace, coauthor of the theory of natural selection with Darwin; and Camille Flammarion, astronomer extraordinaire, a man obsessed with the notion of life on Mars. Doyle himself believed in Martians, having had first-hand experience of them through the soul of a dead Australian teenager he'd encountered at a séance while writing his second batch of Sherlock Holmes stories.

And now he had another example from which to derive evidence and courage—his very own wife!

Science and religion had merged in the wake of broccoli soufflé. In time, Lady Doyle learned to control, even exploit, her spirit guide Pheneas. She came to rely totally on Sir Arthur's encouragement. She had no reason to be embarrassed any longer. And soon, she stopped questioning the voices and the oozes. If they were her inner self, then that self had powers beyond the behavior of every day. There was a reason for it. She was not crazy. Her friends at tea confirmed that. The way the children related to her also reaffirmed it. And while her husband had his own eccentric biases, he was, nevertheless, a man of science, reason, acute observation.

And he was certain that she had broken through. Life was wonderful.

Within a short time, the ectoplasm ceased to flow significantly. It had not been necessary. Pheneas, Lady Doyle came to understand, had been showing off; he had wanted her to know who was boss. But with Sir Arthur's loving complicity, Lady Doyle soon cultivated the strength to put Pheneas in his place. Sir Arthur enjoyed that. It meant asserting her own awkward desires in the face of overwhelming male might, with the result that Lady Doyle became someone worthy of fearing, endowed with unquestionable powers that had stood up on the battleground of psyche. Their friend Sidney Mosbacher, like most of their close friends, was not unaware of these inner struggles within the Doyle household. Sidney ascribed such turmoil to the normal psychological fallout from menopause. He offered Freudian explanations as well.

Whatever it was, Lady Doyle and her spirit were the best of friends. Sir Arthur took her to Egypt. They snapped pictures of each other riding camels before the Pyramids. This enormously pleased Pheneas, who was no longer the braggert or prankster of his early days in Sussex. He restricted himself to simple predictions—like a devastating earthquake in Chile—and homilies devoted to peace on earth, as well as the messenger service that the Doyle household had become so grateful for and dependent upon.

The snowstorm had unleashed a strong premonition in Lady Doyle: none other than Kingsley! From across the ghost-strewn battlefields, from the Somme itself, Kingsley was coming home. Every ice crystal declared his name; in the halo of light suffusing the morning, glancing off each rivulet, streaking the air with untold freshness, Sir Arthur's son was on his way.

She was certain of it.

To meet the twenty-six-year old, who'd been gone now four years, the Doyles had invited their inner circle of intimates.

The singing was over. The guests, seated at the séance table since before dawn, were ready. Lady Doyle prepared to call on Pheneas for assistance.

Doyle detected the odor of ozone, peculiar to ectoplasm.

"He's coming!" Pheneas murmured.

"*He's coming!*" Lady Doyle hearkened.

Sir Arthur's walrus mustache was glistening with sweat. He wiped off his brow.

"Do I hear something?" Lady Glenco ventured diffidently.

"Yes! I do as well!" Dr. Vercombe attested.

Sidney and Sir Henry Dabacourt looked at each other, then to Lady Doyle, who started to push her chair away from the séance table. Her body was beginning to tremble. Doyle thought he saw a light growing in intensity through the partially opened door.

Now they all heard it, clear as a bell. Sounding once, then twice. Followed by more rapping.

The room was dark, the blinds pulled down. The only light source was that door.

Lady Doyle's trembling increased. "Pheneas. . .," she began.

"*F-f-forggggii . . . Forgive!*" the voice called out, straining, stuttering.

Doyle was startled. "My son!" he said. His son had always stuttered.

Now all eyes were turned to the father, whose instincts had been right.

"Are you happy, son?" Sir Arthur asked, feeling a hand across his forehead.

There was no reply, but a gentle kiss on Sir Arthur's lips. He shed tears in rapid succession, wincing with intimacy.

"Footsteps!" Lady Glenco said.

"Coming!" Pheneas cried through Lady Doyle.

"Yes, I can hear them!" Sir Arthur hastened, making ready for a second-phase materialization.

Now Lady Doyle was groaning. The door started to creak.

"Now!" she blazoned, flinging her arms. A glass crystal slid off the table and exploded on the floor.

All were drawn into a collective wail that called out to the spirit gathering force outside the door.

"*F-ff-ffffaaather!*" Pheneas pledged in a resounding show of affection.

Sir Arthur stood up, mesmerized, walking toward the door, which now opened full.

The light burst in upon them. They shielded their eyes, having been in the near dark for forty-five minutes.

"Kingsley!" Sir Arthur yowled, extending his arms, with an adrenaline rush of sweet memory, toward his gurgling offspring.

The ectoplasm, standing the same height as his dead son, came through the door, dressed in a uniform.

Flabbergasted, Doyle stopped short, in the limbo of unknowing.

"Excuse me, folks . . . Sir Arthur? . . . . I've brought ye a telegram. Now the door was open so I reckoned . . . Anyway, ye more than likely heard the ringin' of me bicycle. Mornin', missus . . . Just sign right here . . ."

Doyle sat down. Everyone blinked.

Sidney started to laugh. Then Sir Henry succumbed to his own show of relieved humor.

Nervous release consumed Lady Doyle as well. Seeing the flush of near apoplexy in her friend Lady Glenco's face, she declared self-consciously, "These things happen, I suppose. . . ."

Sir Arthur scanned the telegram. He saw by its envelope that it was from America.

DEAR DOYLE: THE MAGAZINE *SCIENTIFICA AMERICANA* HAS JUST INITIATED A CONTEST, TO BE MADE PUBLIC, WHICH SHALL DETERMINE ONCE AND FOR ALL THE SCIENTIFIC FEASIBILITY OF LIFE AFTER DEATH STOP YOU AND MR. HARRY HOUDINI HAVE BEEN SELECTED TO

STAND AS PRINCIPAL ADVOCATES, FOR AND AG-
AINST STOP NEED YOU IN NEW YORK SOONEST
STOP ALL EXPENSES PAID STOP PLEASE WIRE
ACCEPTANCE ASAP STOP RESPECTFULLY,
RALPH HARRINGTON, PUBLISHER STOP

7

The Lazarus of Pittsburgh

One day in the life of Harry Houdini, and Sir Arthur's reaction to it all . . .

Sir Arthur and his wife *knew* from whom the telegram had *really* come. While Pheneas had laid the psychic ground-work, and the postman had delivered it, and Harrington had dispatched it, the *source* was obviously the Doyles' son Kingsley. This was a revelatory moment, "*the* turning point in my life," Doyle exclaimed.

He called Harrington, first to agree, then to set terms and conditions. "We're on our way, and God Bless You!" Sir Arthur had stated with conviction.

"Harry Houdini, imagine that!" Lady Doyle said with a look of puzzlement the Doyles had shared about Houdini ever since first meeting him backstage at the London Hippodrome. At that time, Houdini's peculiar fame in Europe was unequalled. There were those who thought him to be a god, the greatest athlete in the history of mankind, a magician so uncanny as to transcend the profession entirely. Lady Doyle found him odd but unaffecting. Athletic to be sure, but middleweight, smallish, short. His reputation had no cause that she could see. Toward what end did he slink and crawl and extricate himself? He was unmasculine, in the British or warring or political sense. Almost like a gigolo. He certainly dressed like one, she thought. But her own husband had a far more considered and affirmative response.

Sir Arthur had carefully watched Houdini's needle and trunk tricks. He believed that he had seen something of a privileged nature and that Houdini was himself a medium, clearly in touch with spirits that enabled him to pull off such feats. He waited for his wife to recognize the signs. They talked about the little man.

"But he's so obviously uncouth, don't you think?" said Lady Doyle.

"There is no accounting for his magic," Sir Arthur insisted. "I don't care if he speaks like an American. He must have a Pheneas of his own who enables him to do such things with his body."

This disturbed Lady Doyle. "Can such a man be trusted?" She was wondering aloud, considering the various possibilities about which the British press had already speculated. If Houdini turned to crime, there would be no stopping him. He could cause physical injury to others through his own psychic agency, reinvent voodoo, rob banks.

"It's not trust that's called upon. It's contact," Sir Arthur said.

"He scares me." She was looking out for her own Pheneas, trying to apprehend in her mind the coming collision that this contest had unleashed.

"He's just a misguided bullet. Stubborn. From the same lands as your Pheneas. A semite. And like Pheneas, he will come around."

"I really don't like this idea of a contest," she protested. "It cheapens everything."

"I quite agree, dear. But it is necessary. The Americans have little guidance in these matters. Houdini himself is floundering."

"They have their Wall Street, their gang killings, their Wild West. You won't convert them to the Laws of Pheneas so easily, Arthur."

"No, perhaps not. But you will!"

She put down her tea. They were seated in their den, taking lunch. "Me?"

"Yes," he affirmed. "You will win." And he went on to assure her that she was the greatest ace-up-a-sleeve in all of Britain.

Lady Doyle felt like something of a spiritual wench just then, but kept back the rush of nausea and apprehension.

Doyle had already weighed his strategy and felt confident that his wife would ultimately prove a devastating weapon. He had read Houdini's book, *Miracle Mongers and Their Methods*, a mean-spirited exposé of alleged con artists posing as mediums. Houdini likened them to two-bit circus freaks and rural showmen. Doyle had meditated on Houdini's obvious anger. There was rage in him, as well as a pathological insistence on public self-denial. Here was a man, Doyle would explain to his wife, who could have acquired a worldwide religious following, or, conversely, become the greatest criminal in history. Only capital punishment would have sufficed to stop him had he turned his talents toward evildoing. Houdini himself had bragged that he could have become the most important fellow in Russia.

And yet, in Doyle's opinion, Houdini preferred to remain a slightly embittered trickster.

After some months of familiarity with the showman— who had toured repeatedly across England—Doyle finally figured it out. Houdini was a mama's boy. Doyle recognized the signs. And there was more.

Houdini *had* to deny his spiritualist powers, just as the

earlier famed Davenport brothers had denied their own mediumship in the late nineteenth century, so as to uphold the appearance of innocence, as well as the entertainment value of a performance. Otherwise, as had happened to the Davenports, he might have triggered ambivalent responses, been booed off stage floors as a dangerous cult figure, run out of town, ridiculed, even murdered. By insisting that everything he did was mere chicanery, he stayed on the right side of most existing laws. What was spiritual to Doyle, Houdini was quick to write off as an everyday commonplace. Doyle came to view Houdini's renunciations as the highest state of asceticism. He was a tragic figure, trapped in the narrow confines of vaudeville, confined to the psychological limits of his audience. Houdini's whole approach insured a certain type of audience that expected greater and greater thrills, new tricks, stunts promising disaster.

"This man reminds me of a St. John," Doyle admitted to his wife.

"More like a carnival huckster," she said. "Or door-to-door salesman."

Lady Doyle could not stop contrasting the unlettered Houdini with her own husband, who was so good, so wise, so . . . Renaissance! In her mind, this Houdini was all noise, perhaps to compensate for being ill-spoken, negligible in appearance, badly dressed. She might not live by her first impressions, but no one was going to prevent her from enjoying them. One thing was for sure: there was certainly nothing saintly about Houdini in her view. She rather pitied Houdini's wife, whom she'd met only briefly. How could any woman live with that? she wondered.

"You're so stuck up, dear," Doyle had said on the matter, grinning appreciatively.

"Thank you, Arthur," she replied.

But for himself, Sir Arthur was undeterred.

"His stage-floor contraptions, rope tricks and underwater hells are his wilderness, which he frequently embraces in the nude, or nearly so," Doyle went on. "Don't you get it? His needles are his nettles of remorse."

"Your comparisons are appalling."

"I'm sure they are, dear . . ." But he couldn't help wondering. Why had this Wisconsin farmboy come out so vehemently against spiritualists? There was, Doyle believed, something of a Judas in Houdini. He told his wife so.

"That's utterly absurd," she said. "You are building this brussels sprout of a man into a Pharaoh. You'll demolish him. He'll be eating out of your palm. Food for finches, trust me." But she really wasn't engaging in this business anymore, involved rather in the composition of her traveling cosmetics bag. It was unfair to have to gather it together so hastily. She suffered for not having the time to make well-deliberated choices.

The disturbing, indeed inexplicable, irony, Doyle went on thinking, and saying, lay in the fact that this Judas of Brooklyn was having *himself* crucified, of sorts, four nights a week according to his current sellout schedule of appearances.

"Who's he betraying?" his wife asked, glancing up from her priorities.

Doyle was not rushing through this train of thought. He was captured by the evanescent appeal of his comparisons.

"I believe, to use the parlance, that he may be schizophrenic. He betrays that side of himself which constantly yearns for, no . . . which is fully in touch with the beyond! He turns himself in, cowers before his own strength, the way Moses resisted the burning bush."

He stopped himself, looked upward, then put down his sandwich. "That's it! That's the proper analogy. Moses refused God. Houdini refuses his powers. Don't you see? He *must* succumb. He will lose, not only this contest, but his own fears. He will surrender, Jean. Mark my word."

"Really, Arthur. You haven't properly met this man and you've already got him on a couch," she said. "Off to America to judge a contest with a mentally unstable Judas, or Moses, or whatever he is. At least the shopping in Manhattan's as fine as in Paris."

Doyle wondered what Houdini was likely to make of Pheneas. And this thought led to more fearful speculations. Though Doyle had boxed in college, the idea of entering the psychic ring to fight this heavyweight vigilante, Houdini, left him more and more agitated, as he finished gathering all his necessary belongings for what was expected to be a three-month expedition to America, including a journey as far west as the Rockies. It might prove to be a disaster, or the biggest international boon for mediums—for humanity— since the Fox sisters first heard unexplainable rapping sounds in the basement of their Hydesville, New York, farm-house in 1848. Those noises turned out to be the restless soul of a corpse buried years before, beneath the house. The cele-brated incident had engendered the modern spiritualist movement, with all its fervent and consoled followers, as well as its share of raucous skeptics. Now it was up to Sir Ar-thur and Lady Doyle to keep the faith alive.

Lady Doyle was won over, with reticence. Though it was not the Doyles' plan, exactly, to introduce her as evidence, or as a contestant. Not in the beginning. She had her modesty to maintain. As a couple, the Doyles did not wish to appear self-serving. Doyle had scientific credentials to safeguard (his having been an eye doctor), a detective's perspicacity to uphold. Lady Doyle had no wish to be seen as liberated. She knew how to stay in charge, to quietly run things, to manipu-late her husband's state of mind without so much as raising a finger. All she had to do was produce ectoplasm once in a while and that kept Sir Arthur spellbound.

But the bottom line, of course, was their genuine love for each other. It transcended any histrionics, or need for fame. Lady Doyle had her tacit game plan and it was matriarchal, not feminist. All who came into contact with Jean and Ar-thur were invariably struck by the old-fashioned puppy love they exuded. He opened doors for her. She constantly touched his hands with a wispy tenderness. It was first love that reeked of infatuation. Heaven was always close by.

The contest could not have come at a better time for the Doyles: the children would be off to camp for the summer in another month, and Betcham and his wife, Harriet, could look after them just fine until then. The Doyles had long been planning a major lecture tour of the United States. Sir Arthur's North American manager, Captain Pushcart, was on top of it, and now they'd simply move everything up.

Sir Arthur's agent at Thomas Cook's in Hastings informed him that, as luck would have it, the *Baltic* was already in port at Southampton and would be departing within twenty-four hours for New York, to arrive at the end of April. This being prior to the summer season, a first-class cabin was available.

Betcham took them to the station. The Doyles kissed their children and patted them all on the behinds, telling them to be good, to avoid sugar, and the rear ends of horses, and not to bully poor old Betcham beyond what was fair and square.

The train came and the Doyles boarded with a cumbersome load of things and headed off towards Southampton. Sir Arthur stared out at the country coming into bloom.

They reached port, got on the ship and slipped quietly away from England. Doyle found the ocean voyage uneventful and noisy. It gave him plenty of time to think about the upcoming battle.

He was dizzy with the possibilities. He sensed the wild continent before him, this melancholy America, a country that was struggling to find happiness and was thus ripe for conversion. The war had depleted the younger generation. Women were still mourning.

In addition, America had other problems. He'd read that there'd been twenty-five hundred floggings of Blacks in one month just in Oklahoma. And, as Lady Doyle had informed him, the Chicago suburb of Cicero, through which they were scheduled to pass sometime after their engagements in New York, was totally owned by the gangster Al Capone. Some five thousand people were killed each year in America as a result of mob-related violence.

People were hurting and Doyle was ready to rise to the occasion. Some years before, he had written the odd medical pseudo-autobiography, *Stark Munro Letters* and acquainted himself with America's morbidity and epidemiology. He knew that millions of Americans were drinking dangerous substances in order to circumvent prohibition—mothballs dissolved in gasoline; tri-ortho-cresyl phosphate; and adulterated Jamaican ginger. Tens of thousands were suffering from what was called "jake paralysis." They were going blind. Nearly one hundred billion cigarettes had been nervously consumed, along with one hundred fifteen pounds of sugar per person per year. Cancer, heart attacks and diabetes mellitus could now be said with certainty to be wiping out the American multitudes, along with heroin and influenza.

The year 1923 was a period of medical revelations. By Doyle's way of thinking, it would be the year of spiritual cures. The doctor in him felt the summons to make house calls on a massive scale—not in order to dispense medicine, but new thinking, a religious breakthrough that could well rejuvenate nations. If only the audience could be properly prepared for such an epiphany.

In that department, Doyle was not ignorant of politics and public relations. He had become a great speaker and carried the weight of enormous authority in several disciplines. With tens of millions of readers, and a persuasive and generous joviality, he knew how to campaign to get what he wanted.

He'd once written a three-hundred-page brochure defending the British concentration camps in South Africa, in the interests of his upcoming election. He'd joined the Conservative Unionists, though he failed, barely, to get the necessary number of votes he was seeking. He did manage to reform military garb throughout England in anticipation of chemical warfare, as well as sensitize the War Ministry to the threat of German submarines.

Doyle had taken up training at a London turnverein with the most famous strongman of the times, Eugene Sandow. Action precedes Faith, his own family doctor had told him, when he was growing up. Doyle embraced difficulty, contact sports, crime sleuthing, science, war, manly duty. And now as never before in his life, he was ready to dive headlong into the spiritualist fray.

As their ship's prow turned at last toward the receiving harbor, passing the first signal boat at Fire Island, Doyle stared in wonderment at the great skyline of New York. There was Raymond Hood's American Radiator building, black and gold and touching the clouds. And all the other high palaces of polished aluminum and jet-black marble. Bauhaus Himalayas. High in the center was the Woolworth Building, fifty-seven stories. Incredible! Contemplating all that was before him from the rear hurricane deck, Doyle took a deep, regal breath and prepared to conquer not only a nation, but one man. His American Moses.

Captain Pushcart was there at the quay to greet them, as were a number of obstreperous newspapermen. The vigorous war veteran, Pushcart, in his rakish beret, harangued various negro porters, waving a cigarette in one hand and a leather portmanteau, filled with messages for Doyle, in the other.

The press was eager for comments. After all, between his Holmes and his spiritualism, Doyle rated as one of the most famous foreign names known to Americans. Added to former celebrity was the current film production of his book *The Lost World*, a science-fiction epic of Amazonian proportions that had been surrounded by great secrecy and clever public relations. Pushcart had had little trouble setting up an ambitious tour for the Doyles. He'd worked out a schedule with Harrington that coincided with Houdini's own calendar and booked Doyle on seven speaking engagements in the coming fortnight, commencing with a "debut" at Carnegie Hall.

"You all know about the contest for which I've come," he declared.

They nodded and pressed with the normal queries.

"Let me just say for now that the world is about to change. What has languished in darkness is coming into the light of day."

They busily took down his words.

"Must you dramatize everything so!" his wife chastised him moments later, as she and her husband stepped into the waiting white Cadillac. She hated his heavy-handed prognostications but had long ago given up trying to curb such dramaturgy.

"It makes them think," he replied softly. "Now, Captain Pushcart!"

"That's me, sir."

"The stranger I've been writing to for three months finally materializes. Good. Now take us first to the Woolworth Building," Sir Arthur said, jubilantly. He'd surmised that there might be intriguing atmospheric, perhaps religious, inspiration to be gotten up there.

"But there are pressmen waiting at your hotel," the Captain replied.

"I always start at the top and then work my way down," Doyle insisted.

Lady Doyle closed her eyes and stretched out so that her head rested on Sir Arthur's lap as they drove into downtown. Her stomach had been queasy on and off for the full nine days at sea.

Within an hour, they stood in the clouds, felt the cold spring wind on their faces, saw bursts of minutiae down below and heard the far-off horns and bustle of a new world. Descending to the first floor of the building, Doyle then managed to part with one hundred twenty dollars on shirtwaists and souvenirs, saw a hungry Polish woman arrested at gunpoint for making off with a chicken, picked up a paper and read about himself with reference to the contest. Page two of the *Tribune*.

By late that afternoon, they'd checked into a suite at the Ambassador Hotel on Park Avenue and Fifty-first. There were twenty-four long-stemmed black roses and a box of chocolates on their bed, with regards from Ralph Harrington.

"How kind of him," remarked Lady Doyle.

The next morning, Harrington joined them for breakfast. He was at once surprised by Doyle's height and arrested by his wife's beauty.

"And when will we see Mr. Houdini?" Sir Arthur asked.

"Today, he's in Washington—you won't like this—he's testifying before Congress to put an end to all mediums in the nation's capitol."

"That's just like him." Doyle smiled.

"Tomorrow, weather permitting, he's in Pittsburgh doing one of his suicide tricks. Back here in New York day after tomorrow for two performances. The morning after that, we begin the auditions. We've already got dozens of submissions from mediums all over the eastern seaboard— even the world—who will be presenting their various acts"—Harrington caught Doyle's judgmental eye—"their psyches, if you will . . ."

In chilly Washington, Houdini had arisen at dawn, leaving Bess asleep in the hotel room, jogged to a nearby cemetery where many of the stones were still under snow, then headed to the Federal Prison for an engagement that morning. Byron and Frank positioned themselves in a waiting vehicle behind the prison. The afternoon would see Houdini and Bess on the Hill.

Houdini relished his prison stunts and never failed to irritate the wardens, who always looked inept in the newspaper aftermaths. Houdini had hung out at various times with yeggs and Gay Cats, men right out of Runyon's later *Guys and Dolls*. He'd seen how the "oil man" held hot water bags filled with nitro while an inside man sealed up cracks in a safe door using soft soap. With a fuse wedged in, a single shot of so-called soup would do it. They would snuff the drum, or break it open with an acetylene torch, working to the watch, while an outsider kept tabs on the escape route.

Cells were harder to break because of the many invariable squirrels who'd bring down the authorities for some esoteric favor like a cigarette, but similar principles were applied. Short fuses. Forks and knives from the kitchen.

Houdini, of course, cultivated a different world of subtlety in his escapes. He had studied the techniques of one of the great criminals, the late Max Shinburn, whose diagrams on the art of safecracking and jail breaking were inspirational. Houdini had devised special electric dials, as well as calibrated, razor-thin origami paper, glued to his skin, for discovering lock combinations. With his great strength, endurance and arsenal of minute tools, hidden usually with surgeon's cement on his person, as well as an intuitive grasp that defied either scrutiny or analysis, Houdini could make a sport of any penitentiary.

This one held particular interest for him, not only because it would serve to prove his point before congressmen later in the day, but because this prison had held Charles Guiteau, President Garfield's assassin.

The press were there, including Walter Simpson, the young *Manhattan Tribune* reporter assigned nearly full-time to Houdini.

The jailers stripped him naked and proceeded with the customary search. The head warden stood by without the slightest concern. No one was getting out of his pen. No one ever had; no one ever would.

Photographs flashed. "Hope you guys have got plenty of fig leaves when you go to print," Houdini sparred amiably. The reporters all laughed. The jailors laughed.

They immured his legs in three-foot chains, impounded his arms, constrained his shoulders. The shackles—standard in this prison—weighed twenty pounds. Houdini was led into the maximum security region. He noticed large cells with numbers of men chained together. He'd only seen that once before, in the outback of Georgia.

"What happens when someone needs to pee in the middle of the night?" Houdini asked.

"You get beat up," the jailer said.

There was one cold water spigot for the entire section, one hundred men. No soap. No towels. Food consisted of baked corn pone, aged pork bellies, lima beans, lots of sand and plenty of worms to go around. They passed one cell where a prisoner had just finished taking a beating. He'd evidently been flayed with leather straps. Blood still ran in puddles. The prisoner was mad and mournful.

"What did he do?" Houdini inquired.

"That's for doin' nothin,'" the jailer said.

Men stared from behind bars at Houdini. Some recognized him and called out his name.

"Stay calm, fellas. I'll be letting you out shortly." There were unamused chortles.

The jailers escorted Houdini down a flight of stone stairs. Here was Guiteau's cell, empty, sunk in a heavily barred cubby of brick masonry, dank and dismal. As they opened it, Houdini listened, watched, understood. Five tumblers.

They slammed the door and rebolted its exterior.

"Have fun, Harry!" the three escorts said, licking their chops.

Part of the conditions set forth by Houdini was his need to work without any wardens present. The jail was not emptied of observers, however. Houdini was surrounded by scores of hardcore inmates.

Within two minutes Houdini had removed every shackle and neatly pushed forward his cell door. He was free. He ran up the stairs and entered the main two-story jail house, putting his finger to his lips to encourage the prisoners not to say a word. They complied, as he emptied one cell after another, thinking nothing of the possible risks involved.

Within minutes, Houdini had opened every cell, and the hundred or so men clustered around him.

"If a fellow wanted to escape from this joint, where's the

nearest crawl space to the outside?" he whispered so that all could conspire with him.

There was silence. Finally, a giant of a man, bald and un-impeachable, with stitches all the way across his frontal lobes, nodded toward a recently done-over brick section in the rear. Houdini thanked him, raced to the wall and dug out the superficial mortar with his own picklock. The cement was still drying from an earlier escape effort. Houdini pushed the bricks forward and crawled rapidly down a space between two walls.

Twelve minutes had transpired by this time. The reporters and jailers were several hundred feet away, behind walls, standing around the warden's office.

Houdini soon reached the inner yard. He cut through a fence, dashed across the playing field, climbed another wall, snipped through barb wire and triggered the alarm.

"Shit!" he exclaimed, jumping down and running in the direction of his two waiting gumshoes.

Shots rang out from a tower; machine gun fire sprayed the courtyard across which Houdini now skipped. Bells and horns blazed throughout the penitentiary. Armed soldiers amassed. Men on squawkies called in auxiliary troops from the surrounding annexes. Hell had broken loose. But Houdini was gone.

By the time an embarrassed warden, the dean of persecution, had assessed the damage, the prisoners had been returned to their cells and a dozen reporters were busy at pay phones calling in their stories.

"We've been tricked!" the head warden snapped at his inferiors. This was a somber day in his career.

Then the phone rang.

"Hi. This is Harry. Listen I just wanted to thank you all for a delightful morning. And tell them from me that I think you got a great bunch of inmates. The best!"

He was calling from his hotel twenty minutes away while Bess goosed him in bed.

Bess called for room service. Houdini devoured a grilled

cheese sandwich doused in mustard and some tomato bisque, changed into clothes, and then they departed, with their dog, Shalom, for Capitol Hill.

Once there, Frank and Byron waited outside as the Houdinis entered the august Old House building.

Houdini's "miraculous escape" had made the front page of the *Herald* afternoon edition. It was a packed hearing. Bess removed Houdini's homburg. The magician was surrounded by dozens of congressmen, fellow conjurers, and three or four spokespersons for the mediums. In the gallery sat or stood hundreds of onlookers.

There were more than two hundred mediums in the city, who had obtained their licenses to deceive for a mere twenty-five dollars. The Copeland-Bloom bill before the Senate would prohibit fortune-telling, séances, mediumship of all kinds that were undertaken for fees. Houdini knew that passage of the bill would set an important precedent for cities elsewhere in America. His testimony was deemed crucial given his demonstrated ability to flush out frauds who had eluded less acutely trained eyes. "It takes a rogue to catch a rogue," Houdini was fond of saying.

A recorder sat near the congressmen, typing every word for the *Congressional Record.*

Shalom barked, and the key senator conducting the inquiry asked whether the dog was necessary.

Houdini stood up and passed around a rope tangled in knots for the congressmen to examine. All agreed it was inextricable.

Shalom freed the ropes within seconds, then went on to choose the correct card from a deck that Houdini had mixed up.

"My point, gentlemen, should be obvious. Even a terrier can accomplish supposed miracles."

There was great merriment.

"Mr. Houdini," Senator Rathbary began.

"Call me Harry."

"Harry, we want to thank you and your wife for coming here today."

"You bet," Houdini said.

"Now to business." The senator examined the paper before him. "Is it not true, as this afternoon's newspaper indicates, that you have enacted miracle escapes for the past thirty years, many of which have absolutely no rational explanation?"

"No, it is not true, senator."

"Well then how do you explain—"

Houdini cut him off. "I do not explain. I have my own proprietary secrets which insure my livelihood. As do the mediums and necromancers. Trade secrets, mind you, that have nothing to do with religion or miracle working. The difference, sir, if you will permit me, is that I work my wonders without pretense or promise or any possible harm. I am the first one to own up to the art of legerdemain. I'm a prestidigitator."

"A what?"

"I pull rabbits from hats, slip out of handcuffs. You know very well what I do. Those who pay to see me perform are entertained, not led astray by false claims of a serious nature. Nor do I endeavor to relieve my audiences of their savings, or send secret confederates out and about to dig up private information which I can then use later to deceive them."

"Are you denying that you inspire?" Congressman Bloomington broke in.

"Of course I inspire, or I'd like to think so," Houdini rebutted. "But so what?"

"The *point* is inspiration, Mr. Houdini, isn't it?"

"Call me Harry. No, that isn't the point at all."

The congressman was not worried in the least about concealing his bias. "Mediums inspire. Inspiration is a good thing. Whatever works to console the bereaved, the ailing, the perplexed."

"Are you telling me, or asking me?" Houdini stated,

annoyed. It was obvious to him that there was strong opposition to the Copeland-Bloom bill.

"Yes. I'm asking you."

"Well then I must tell you that I totally disagree, Congressman." Harry looked at Bess. She nudged him to get on with it. "Whatever works is a dangerous philosophy," he continued. "Mediums don't just claim to inspire, or to be inspired. They claim divine, spiritual powers. If you died tomorrow, they might take your wife aside, convince her that you were within grasp, and induce her to turn over your entire estate, everything you'd ever worked and saved for, in the futile hopes of speaking with you over at the cemetery."

"And don't you have divine or spiritual powers?" the congressman went on, totally ignoring Houdini's aspersion. Houdini thought he was being baited. Bess read the situation differently.

Houdini laughed. "You'll have to ask my wife about that."

"What about it, Mrs. Houdini—and remember you are under oath here," he continued.

"What about what?" she said, horrified that she'd been brought into this. Bess was as shy as she looked, in spite of having been up on a stage half of her life. She'd been raised in an insulated parochial family, with little exposure to the outside world. And even though her worldly travels and success had filled her head with new vistas and riches, she was essentially a modest, down-home country girl. What this meant was that she wouldn't let her housemaid do main meals, or clean Harry's clothes. At some feminine point in her pride she supplicated herself, laid down before him and invited a stereotypic role, which in her heart she cherished. Harry was worth it.

"Does your husband have spiritual powers?"

"No," she said with point-blank certainty. "He can't even drive straight."

The congressman lost his train of thought.

Congressman Hanson began, reading from a sworn testimony by two senators of the Lincoln administration.

"I have here a document of considerable interest. In it, President Lincoln is reported to have saved this nation as the result of a medium, Miss Nettie Colburn."

"Ridiculous—" Houdini started.

Hanson lifted his hand. "Please . . ." He continued. "Lincoln's wife had invited Miss Colburn to the White House, where she met with the President and was seen to have fallen into a spiritualistic trance, out of which she conveyed divine commands to Lincoln. The President listened for over an hour, followed the medium's instructions and proceeded to issue the Proclamation on Emancipation. The document is on record."

Houdini shook his head. "You may know that Al Heinberger gave séances at the White House for President Polk, too. Al was one of the shrewdest magicians that ever lived, so shrewd in fact that the President insisted he'd been aided by spirits. Belachini had the Kaiser Wilhelm eating out of his hands, as I did the Czarina of Russia and all of her aides-de-camp. And I can also attest from personal experience that whatever qualifications it takes to be a leader, detecting sharpies is not one of them. I know because I bamboozled Theodore Roosevelt several years ago. He swore I was a soothsayer, or some such. I'm not. I just do my homework."

There were sophisticated guffaws from the floor.

Houdini continued. "I read somewhere that President Harding left on his Alaskan odyssey because the dogs were barking so loud at night in the White House that he couldn't get proper sleep. About that time, his wife had called upon a soothsayer to diagnose his bad dreams. The report I read indicated that the medium seized upon those dogs, stating that they were howling out of grief because the President was going to die soon and his cabinet be plunged into disgrace over some teapot. Or maybe it was the teapot would be plunged into the cabinet. Whatever the wording, it certainly calls into question the wisdom of allowing these quacks to continue to prey upon innocent victims. Imagine filling Mrs. Harding's head with such hokum. It's criminal."

Senator Rathbary called on the testimony of a Mr. Mackenright. "Please state your name and occupation for the records."

"I am Douglas Mackenright, past president of the Commonwealth Council of Psychic Science. I was on the stage at the Grand Theater in Islington, London, two years ago, when Harry Houdini completely dematerialized in a tank of water."

"Could you explain that for the benefit of those who may not know the word?"

"Certainly. In a sitting room where séances are conducted, time is required normally for essence to be crystallized into psycho-plastic matter. The process is known as dematerialization and normally accompanies the appearance of ectoplasm which comes in black, white or off-white colors. Now, I watched that man"— he pointed at him—"Mr. Houdini, slip through I don't know how many bolts and chains and iron lids with locked hasps, reemerging before an audience all within three minutes. While he was inside the tank of water into which he'd been trapped, I saw his body turn into slimy ectoplasm. That's how he was able quite literally to ooze through the locks."

"The container was transparent?" Senator Rathbary asked.

"Yes. Two thousand people saw what I saw. I just happened to be standing four feet way. Believe me, it was the greatest proof of God I have ever known, since reading the Bible."

Houdini was shaking his head.

"Well?" the Senator asked Houdini. "What say you to that?"

"The cloudy ectoplasm was milk. I'd been placed in a container with twenty-two pails of milk."

The audience broke out in hysterics.

"Look, gentlemen," Houdini declared, taking out his pre-

pared speech. "The fact is, over one million people have
been driven into insane asylums because of this nonsense.
Countless hearts have been broken. I can't imagine how
many others have killed themselves. Why, just yesterday, I
read of a student at Cornell who drank arsenic so as to be reunited with his dead girlfriend. And you all must have heard
about the German man who killed off eleven members of his
family in order to be put back in touch with his deceased
three-month-old child up in heaven? This is outrageous! I
pity people like Mr. Mackenright and his fellow countryman, Sir Arthur Conan Doyle. I really do. These are desperate men, longing for answers, longing to be reunited. But we
make a mockery of justice and we perpetuate gross impos-
ture by allowing mediums to pursue such avenues of deception and indecency." He paused, pleased with the writing.
Then he thought to add, "Several mediums I've known of
personally managed to use disgusting sexual advantage in
order to exploit those who were religiously vulnerable. I myself, while seated in dark séance rooms, have felt hands in
places no hand, other than my own, and I suppose my wife's,
should ever be put." He felt awkward about this last part. It
wasn't part of his prepared speech.

Houdini looked around, trying to gauge the reactions of
others. Suddenly, someone hooted, "Houdini's just a Commie Jew Bastard Atheist!"

The voice had come from far in the rear. The standing-
room-only crowd did not yield up the person's identity.
Clearly there were others who felt in sympathy with the
heckler.

"Who said that!" Senator Rathbary shouted, striking the
table with his gavel.

"That's all right, Senator," Houdini stated. He addressed
the half-dozen key members of the hearings committee at
the long wooden table before him.

"The man proves my point. This country's slipping inch
by inch to the fundamentalist nuts. I mean you've got a
Texas dentist who rises to become Emperor of the Invisible

Empire, lynching negroes and arming hundreds of thousands of fellow Klan fanatics in a perverse effort to keep this country free of all ethnics—and that includes the Pope. And if Christ were here today, they'd probably try to lynch him, as well. This is spiritual war, Senator. And the mediums are part of it. Allow them to continue and you're simply kowtowing to insanity. I've come here today on behalf of the sane, the rational, the free. I support science, logic, not bigotry and close-mindedness."

There was mixed applause. The Houdinis thanked the congressmen, got up, shook a few hands and left. Bess was proud of her man.

"You did fine," she whispered, holding her husband's arm as they descended the steps to the car.

"How do you think the hearings went, Houdini!" a reporter shouted after him.

"Good," Houdini said, though he was unsure.

"Any comment on the *Scientifica Americana* contest?" another reporter fired.

"Yeah . . . the spirits don't have a chance." He laughed.

The Houdinis reached their car. "Bad news," Frank said. "Eunice Holstein wasn't even booked! That's going to mean trouble. She hates your guts."

"Huh?" Houdini said, bewildered. "How's that possible?"

"The Attorney General of New York got a court order to release her," Frank said with a deploring timbre. "She's got all the right connections."

The Houdinis were traveling light this time, as the visit to the Capitol had been their primary reason for leaving Brooklyn. However, Houdini had booked one stunt in Pittsburgh for the following morning, and they now headed there by train.

Thomas Weckstin was in Pittsburgh to meet them, waiting with a single suitcase and a knapsack containing a two-hundred-foot Manila hemp rope.

Thomas, twenty-eight, golden-haired, straight-jawed, homespun machinist, also from Houdini's town of Appleton,

Wisconsin, had been more or less adopted by the Houdinis after his parents had passed away.

Starting with his first winter plunge into Lake Winnebago, Thomas had studied from the master. Cold water was the worst. The first three seconds felt as if they would kill you. They never did, of course.

"Eat the pain," Houdini had advised him. "Just stand in the water and chant, 'I am not going to die . . . I am not going to die.' Within a minute—no matter how cold—you won't want to get out. It will feel warm."

"And that's your secret?" Thomas had asked him, incredulous.

"Yep."

For ten years Thomas had traveled with the Houdinis, fixed gear, prepared tricks and worked more closely with Houdini than anybody. Thomas had taught Houdini's two other engineering assistants, Joe and Royale, nearly everything they knew about the business.

The Pittsburgh exploit was to be straightforward. Near the confluence of the Allegheny and Monongahela rivers, overlooking the 'golden triangle,' Houdini would jump from a high bridge, in the usual shackles and straightjacket. This time, on top of the endless restraints, weighing four hundred pounds, the handcuffs, the hanging upside down, etc. etc., three tires would be securely squeezed over him as well. Houdini knew that he could use the tires to his advantage underwater.

"There's just one slight problem," Thomas announced as they drove out to the site on the way to their hotel. "You'll see what I mean."

Houdini examined the water from the banks. Spring had come slowly to Pittsburgh this year, as it had to the whole East Coast. Snow still lay in the shadows, black from all the soot spewing forth from the steel mills. In the river, enormous sheets of ice, drifters, floated on or just under the surface, many of them several feet thick. Their speed and the sharpness of their perimeters could easily slice a man in two.

Underneath the bridges, the ice was thick. Out beyond were the fast-moving currents and deadly drifters. It was an odd predicament. The local impresario predicted an enormous turnout. The weather was cold but not bad enough to keep people from the Great Houdini.

"Okay," Houdini said, after twenty minutes of careful reconnaissance. "Tomorrow, in front of the spectators, we'll chop a big hole through the ice. Ten feet across, on account of the wind carrying my fall. You'll stand by discreetly with the rope, Thomas, in the event of any problem. Same as usual."

"The conditions are weird," Thomas fretted.

But Houdini prevailed. He always prevailed. When he dove manacled into Berlin's Spree, into the Tay at Dundee, the Mersey at Liverpool, the Yarrow at Melbourne, where he chanced underwater upon a long-dead corpse, and into the Seine from the roof of the Morgue. At Aberdeen Harbor, against the better wishes of the harbor master, in a cold gale, heavy chains around his neck, Houdini vanished for four minutes underwater. Thomas threw the rope. Still no Houdini. He was playing, testing his limits. He reemerged only after four minutes, forty seconds, beating his old record, which he'd set in competition with the pearl fishermen of Fiji some years before. At that time, he'd insisted that they dive handcuffed. He was the only one to retrieve the pearls, undoing, then reaffixing, the cuffs underwater to make it look as if he'd snatched the pearl with his teeth.

"Do you want to come?" Houdini asked Bess.

"I've seen this one too many times." She hesitated, noticing a look of disappointment in Harry. "Okay, I'll come."

"No, stay here in bed. It's too cold."

So Bess slept in, reading, sipping a vanilla soda, listening to Fred Allen and Will Rogers on the radio, while her husband headed out early that next morning.

Houdini, Thomas, Frank and Byron arrived at the bridge. The press was there, along with a live radio announcer and the biggest crowd Houdini had ever beheld.

"I have no idea how many have actually paid," the local manager told him, above the cheering that accompanied Houdini's arrival. "I'd guess there's forty thousand turned out."

The weather was gray and cold, a wind out of the north at probably twenty knots. It looked like rain.

"Striptease time," Houdini joked to the radio microphone.

Bess heard it. They'd interrupted Will Rogers for a live local broadcast. Pittsburgh was big on radio. It was from a rooftop a year before and a mile away from the Houdinis' hotel that radio began. At that time, before tubes, the listener clamped a crystal set to the telephone. That's how folks first heard the live Dempsey-Carpentier prizefight in '21. Bess couldn't deal with it now. She got out of bed, as far away from the radio as possible and into a hot bath. She just couldn't handle the jumps anymore, especially after the death of Jimmy Boy Walker, the "Spiderman" who had plummeted thirteen stories to his death in New York emulating Houdini just one month before.

They chained him, strapped him, turned him upside down, "UPS" as Houdini always put it. Then, utilizing a portable winch, they swung him out over the river, which churned and rasped like sickly alimentation eighty feet below. Harry smiled.

Down on the ice, men were chopping away with firemen's hatchets. Finally, Thomas approved of the hole. He came back up the bridge, wearing the knapsack with the safety rope, and wished Houdini the best.

"Okay, men, do it!" the impresario cried out.

And with that, the winch dropped Houdini, whose nearly seven hundred pounds of manacled deadweight plunged perfectly into the receiving abyss. The crowd was remarkably still. The wind groaned.

Thomas held his watch before him. The seconds passed slowly. Four minutes were up.

"Don't tell me—" he whispered to Frank, who stood next to him, nervous as all hell.

"Just do it," Frank said.

The crowd was restless. Thomas held back no longer. He quickly tied a double bowline to a stay on the bridge and hurled the rope into the hole. He'd already practiced the throw the previous afternoon.

Both men and women were screaming now. The radio announcer was also shouting.

"Five minutes! Houdini's been under five minutes and four, five, six seconds. Nobody could survive that!" the announcer hollered.

"Go to the ice, Frank!" Thomas cried. Houdini was not grabbing hold of the rope.

In fact, Houdini was nowhere near the hole.

The water was thirty-seven degrees. Houdini found it thoroughly invigorating. But what he had not properly figured was the range and rate of the current. It had taken him over two minutes to free himself from the hundreds of pounds of constraints, which, by their weight, had dragged him directly to the bottom of the river, at a depth of twenty-three feet. The pressure hurt his ears badly, and by the time he'd pushed off the rocky bottom, he found to his chagrin that the current had carried him elsewhere. The universe above was white. There was no hole.

Houdini shot up to the sub-surface of the ice and there lay on his back, his mouth sucking oxygen from the eighth-of-an-inch of air space between the fast-moving river and the fast-moving drifter under which he remained trapped.

He had no idea where he was.

Up above, nine minutes had gone by. The press was pronouncing Houdini dead. Byron, a surging crowd and elbowing policemen stood by helpless on the river's snowy edge. Frank was kneeling next to the hole. He could see nothing. Up above, Thomas tied one end of the rope to the bridge and rappeled down onto the ice to save precious seconds. He joined Frank, and the two of them tried futilely to see some sign of Houdini.

Another minute passed. Up on the bridge the radio jockey somberly announced the likely death of the Great Houdini. "This will surely go down as one of the darkest days in the history of entertainment. . . . And yet, some will say, it was inevitable!" His words pierced Pittsburgh's scudding cold and moribund crowds like token sidekicks of respect, hyped and ineffectual.

Yet people wept and searchers began the dreary task of dropping hooks through the hole.

Meanwhile, nearly two miles downriver, Houdini crashed into an icy boulder. He clung on underwater to a large caulky depression with just enough quartzite to provide finger holds. The wall of ice kept going downriver past him, like a locomotive whose knife-sharp edges barreled away mere inches from his side.

Houdini scrambled to safety. Far up the river he could make out the enormous crowds and hear the commotion. There were sirens screaming. *Poor Thomas, poor Frank* . . . , he thought. But otherwise he felt fabulous, heading off into the woods in his bathing suit and top. It was good to be alive.

There was a knock at Bess's door.

"Who is it?" she shouted from the tub, out of the radio's earshot.

"There's an urgent phone call for you in the lobby, Mrs. Houdini!" the hotel manager said anxiously.

"I'll just be a minute," Bess called out. Her heart was pounding, one of the hardships of living with Harry.

When she walked briskly into the lobby, people were staring. The word had spread across Pittsburgh instantaneously.

"What?" she said in the direction of the front desk. "What is it!" she screamed.

"I'm sorry," the manager began, standing beside the radio, which was broadcasting the event.

Bess collapsed. The management converged around her with smelling salts.

In New York, the Doyles were following the entire incident from their car radio, as Captain Pushcart drove them in their white Cadillac back to the Ambassador from the offices of *Scientifica Americana*.

Sir Arthur looked at his wife. He understood from Houdini's writings that he had made some secret death pact with his wife and closest friends, whereby Houdini would return from the other side and speak to them if it were at all possible for him to do so. Doyle was feeling devastated. "Now we shall know," he said plainly.

Lady Doyle did not expect to cry, but there she was, dripping all over. Houdini had come the distance too many times in her mind by now. She felt as if she knew him. Indeed, the Doyles had lived with countless scenarios by now to account for the Houdini phenomenon. They'd studied him the way one analyzes the weaknesses and strengths of an athlete on the opposing team. Sir Arthur had his elaborate psychological theories. In her gut, Lady Doyle had sensed something further out in Houdini, beyond easy explication—some fiendishly elusive know-how that was primitive, and unsalted. Without recourse to theory. Now she felt betrayed. His loss hit her unexpectedly.

Thousands of men had solemnly taken off their hats, waiting for Houdini's body to be recovered.

The radio announcer was recapping the whole tragic affair. Pressmen were swarming around Thomas, Frank and Byron. There were ambulances from Mercy Hospital and dozens of squad cars. Flags were preparing to drop to half-mast. Another huge contingent of reporters was on its way to interview Bess, who lay on a cot looked over by the house doctor.

Suddenly, a cry rang out. *"It's him!"*

Within minutes, the vocal crescendo had assumed orgiastic heights.

"My God!" bellowed the radio announcer. "Houdini has come back from the dead!"

He'd jogged half-naked through the forest to stay warm, reemerging from the woods just under the bridge.

In New York, Sir Arthur Conan Doyle, hearing of this utterly spiritual turn of events, blinked twice, stepped out of the Cadillac, threw his hat high into the air and, in the middle of the crowded sidewalk before his hotel, began to roar with laughter.

8

Heartbeats Across New York

In which Doyle and Houdini first connect . . .

On this particular Friday night in New York a certain Shipwreck Barnaby was into his nineteenth uncomfortable day atop a flagpole. He was not fasting or making union or Communist demands. He was trying to set a record, and some thought they detected electric halos forming around him after dark. Meanwhile, over at Radio City, Jessica Dragonette was singing up the "Italian Street Song" blitz on behalf of Coca-Cola, live.

Live radio had become the thing. There were four hundred million radios broadcasting at, or around, 833.3 kilocycles, a fact the inventor Marconi interpreted as having something to do with millions of miles and communiqués from other life forms on planet Mars.

Sir Arthur Conan Doyle—busy this night initiating his American lecture tour debut at Carnegie Hall—tended to agree with Marconi. And radio, he added, not only enabled intelligent life forms on Mars to send us their best wishes and Christmas greetings, but also provided a means whereby our ancestors and dearly departed could reach us. Radio was a powerful catalyst linking life and death.

"Does that include Vincent Lopez and Guy Lombardo's radio show?" somebody from the audience asked Doyle, having just been subjected to the theory. "And what about Harry Horlick and the A & P Gypsies performing 'Two Guitars'?" another inquired.

Doyle loved the playing field, and he wanted the sellout crowd of thirty-five hundred Americans to like him. To love him. There were eight reporters present. In addition, the lecture was being broadcast live on radio. The concert hall was buzzing. Captain Pushcart had done his PR job.

"Perhaps the dead souls of other deceased musicians, like Stephen Foster or Mozart, are merely using the melodious hoots and tunes of Bix Beiderbecke and the Wolverines to reach their out-of-tune descendants. Who can say for sure, New York being what it is on a Friday night?" he concluded with an affable grin. Lady Doyle sat in the front wondering where in hell her husband got a hold of Bix Beiderbecke. Bix had definitely not made it yet to Sussex.

The audience loved Sir Arthur.

And whatever the real behind-the-scenes mergers between Martians and RCA, there was nothing like radio. Except, of course, the movie shows.

Up and down Broadway lines of people poured in to witness unbelievable lightning, the voice of God and all that miracle work of De Mille's *Ten Commandments*. Harold Lloyd's dizzying *Safety Last* and Charlie Chaplin playing an escaped convict-turned-minister in *The Pilgrim*, Hollywood imports, were competing with the local stage hit of the decade, *Abie's Irish Rose*.

Forty million Americans, one out of two, went to the movies at least once a week. They wore their Fair Isle sweaters and checked plus-eights, their bell-bottoms and raccoon skins. Women dangled long cigarettes and ceased to keep their knees together. They followed the speeches of Margaret Sanger, used coat hangers, knitting needles, swallowed poisons—whatever it took to produce a miscarriage. They got divorced in hordes unimaginable a decade before. "Everybody's doing it," they rallied free and easy.

Gone were the high-laced, ankle-binding shoes, the black cotton stockings. Suddenly, silk was the thing. Bobbed heads, these were the shebas. And the greased-down, high-talking fellas who ferried them from theater to theater in Hupmobiles or painted Model Ts, down the brilliantly lit avenues and boulevards, these were their sheiks. This ragtime joie de vivre had singularly put an end to the "dress for mourning and general wear" mentality that followed the war. The Doyles had spent most of the day observing bright, dark, uncanny, repelling, irresistible New York City.

For those wishing more discreet and understated European culture, John Barrymore was delivering the most depressing *Hamlet* in a hundred years.

And for those others who had wearied of the ten-minute-long radio commercials, or feared venturing out along crime-engorged city streets, there was of course an ample flood of American reading to be had. Requisite poems by Edna St. Vincent, Sinclair Lewis's big new satiric *Babbitt*, T. S. Eliot's latest sour grapes, *The Waste Land*.

Miss Amy Beckwell fell into none of these "absurd age" categories, as she listened intently to Sir Arthur's lecture, feeling increasingly stirred. This was the man, according to Ralph Harrington, who would help inadvertently to save *Scientifica Americana* in lieu of anti-pimple ads. He was the world's leading advocate for life after death. Amy had read her share of Sherlock Holmes and had expected a more severe and unemotional speaker. She was surprised to see so quaint and fatherly a man of letters addressing the eager crowd.

Doyle. Master sleuth, physician, rich and famous and English, with nothing to gain by such claims. Amy was more than a little curious. Perhaps because her dad had abandoned the family while Amy was still a child. Or perhaps because her one older brother had died in France. A report stated that the shell had literally separated his chest from the rest of him.

She felt guided toward Doyle this night, despite having carefully exorcised sentiment from her life in favor of a career nearly one year ago, when she'd left home in Hastings-on-Hudson for the city. Amy had no man in her life, only work. She'd tasted death at her brother's cemetery, meditated on the vanity of vanities, plunged into young professional despairs and plunged out again with renewed faith in the business of America, which was business. Her business, aspiring in the shadows of new skyscrapers, holding her head high amid the lunchtime stampedes. Lurking beneath this ripe confidence, however, was the sober Amy, the Amy of miracles, the Amy who wished upon stars and hoped, still, for Santa Claus. She'd had visions she'd told to no one, and she clutched the hope of a unique future, like a dazzling star ruby of certitude.

And the moment Doyle began to speak, she recognized that destiny, grew faint, found herself leaning forward, considering every one of his words.

Doyle stood where countless soloists before him had induced the tears of music lovers, in his plain-fitting cotton suit and heavy-handed style, his hands lugubriously forming ideas.

"Often, people have asked me, not unnaturally, how I can be so sure of this one fundamental assertion. When I tell them how my own mother, down to the wrinkle, leaned against me and let me taste the skin of her forearm at a candle-lit séance some years ago, or how my dear brother returned from the other side to request that a dispensation be made to a masseuse he'd known in Copenhagen"—not one chuckle issued from the hall—"and upon my inquiries I learned that in fact there *was* such a woman—my brother was quite a guy—and they'd been secretly in love, well then I must declare before such evidence that all those Viennese fancy-spun theories of psychology become picayune and irrelevant."

A reporter seized one of Doyle's pregnant pauses. "Excuse me, Sir Arthur: you tasted the forearm of your dead mother?"

Doyle nodded innocently. "That's a frequently tried test. If the materialization had been fake, I would have known it to be so . . . Like caviar," he said.

Oh Arthur, please! Lady Doyle blipped, using the "second sight" that she and her husband had between them.

The reporter started to write in his little notebook, then realized he didn't have a clue what Doyle was talking about. Sir Arthur caught the man's uncertainty and proceeded.

"I have sat in a darkened room and with the aid of my wife, a planchette, an open heart and open mind, been visited by spirits. They sang, vied with one another to see who'd speak first, played musical instruments, floated gently about the room in every conceivable shape and form. Sometimes they have taken my hand, or touched my face, rubbing cheeks lovingly, even stealing a kiss. Spirits have effected paintings no less masterful than those of a Turner or Rembrandt, filled up slate after slate, notebook after notebook, with verse that would honor Shelley or Browning, with profound commentary, in languages both known and unknown to my wife and me. In the company of other mediums, I have witnessed spirits who were compelled to imprint otherwise impervious photographic plates with their own unambiguous messages, or to leave chemical odors as redolent as Parisian perfume. Finally, these spirits have prophesized great events—"

"Like what?" a reporter shouted.

Doyle waited, physically manipulating the tension before him in the audience. "The day and very moment the war turned, then ended, for example. Beginning with the Battle at Piave."

"How can that be verified?" the reporter replied caustically.

Doyle examined his audience with a look of sympathetic cajoling. "What constitutes proof? Does Einstein's 'relativity' require proof? Did Galileo require proof? Lesser men require proof. Not apostles. And we are all apostles here. I'm talking about a new religion, ladies and gentlemen."

Lady Doyle closed her eyes, feeling suddenly ghastly of color. She'd hoped that her husband would just once manage to avoid his inevitable descent into evangelism. They'd disagreed on this point ever since she was first converted to the family cause. She disliked making spiritualism into public spectacle. Heaven was not for the masses, according to her. If it were, she might not care as much for it. This was a fact that had to be weighed. Nothing good could come of crowds, she insisted. But her husband felt that the Great War might have been avoided had more people been willing to talk about such matters, and the only way to talk was to talk, to institute large forums for the exchange of sentiment and expectation.

"These are great expectations," Doyle reminded her. "We are not alone the beneficiaries."

But Lady Doyle found the notion stuffy and insufferable, and they fought from time to time over strategy. In the end, she lost. Doyle's generosity of mind was contagious, as his Sherlock proved.

By now, the spring of 1923, Doyle had honed his energies entirely upon the gnostic fantasies and immortal ectoplasms that had prompted him to take up Ralph Harrington's offer of a contest in the first place. Christ's own swan song had become Doyle's mission in life: the reaffirmation of soul in a world gone mad. Despite whatever reticence she may have earlier conveyed about the subject, Lady Doyle was married to these goals.

Life had become for both of them a string of elegies and fecund sighs. There was poetry in such an outlook, which, in Sir Arthur's case, had swayed him from earlier whaling expeditions, military bloodletting and the conquest of nations. He had his own Scyllas and Charybdises to contend with, forty years of habitual machismo. But the war had softened him. And by now, he was all "tutti frutti benevolence," as she put it, totally respectful, unassuming. He had principles; he was fair. His heart was like one of those jammed subway cars beneath New York—filled with the whole world.

He championed the underdog. Doyle was haunted by what he perceived to be the innocence of the condemned Sacco and Vanzetti, and he appealed to the mean-spirited Judge Thayer, protesting the irrational miscarriage of justice.

Where other men in the public eye, driven to speak out by events beyond their control, might remain content to write letters to editors, or hold forth on podiums, Doyle went a step further with the unique gifts of his inventive mind: he suggested the one obvious piece of police work in the case of Sacco and Vanzetti that had been absurdly overlooked, namely, a ballistics report on Sacco's pistol.

Lady Doyle loved him for that ability to mix his life and art so effectively.

Sir Arthur glanced down at her. She was seated off to the side in the front row, making a face he understood at once. He'd strayed.

Now he got back on track. "How many here have lost someone dear to them in the past ten years?"

Nearly every other arm in Carnegie Hall was raised.

Doyle of course knew that he had his audience with him. "And who among you has not sensed the strange, rapturous return of those we have loved, in some unexplainable form or another? However momentary, hidden or shy? A lingering spirit, an intuitive calling in your gut, something unclear but wondrous; a psyche that has lived in you, guided your memory, calmed your grief?"

Hands all over the auditorium began gingerly to go up. Doyle kept speaking, acknowledging his hundreds, tens of hundreds of allies.

"I will not presume to tell you what death is or isn't. But I can assure you, death is no gangplank. What we have all felt—though many may still fear to come forth—is a universal truth, cloaked in private hesitations, incessant yearnings, deepest secrets. What is that truth? Say it, say it so that all can hear. Isn't that what your inner voice calls out? That truth, ladies and gentlemen, is known by many names. God. One's trust in Christ, or in the spirit of Mother Nature. For men like Isaac Newton, that truth could be reduced to the principle of thermodynamics, that is to say, the conservation of all things, be they of rock or of cherubic flesh. And, as a consequence of that preserved state, the eternal reincarnation of souls, such as the Hindu has known for five thousand years under the name *samsara*.

" 'Lacking proof!' the journalists scream. *Samsara*, or whatever it's called, is religion. Thermodynamics is highfalutin' theory. 'We want solid, everyday proof!' So you shall have it!"

Doyle looked at the reporters. "There is no proof required, my friends, for the truth inheres in the life force itself, without boasting of its powers."

He looked around the audience toward the first sniveler he could detect. "Raise up your child, madame," he requested.

A young mother, understanding that she had been singled out, blushed, made a vague clamor, then, with the help of her husband, lifted a baby high above their heads for all in the audience to see.

Doyle continued. "Does the newborn have to boast and prove to its parents that it is alive? I was a doctor; I smacked my share of infants' behinds."

There was general laughter.

"Why don't you put your child down now," he said conscientiously. Then, "I have elicited the gargled shrieks from babes just seconds into this world. If a hearty cry is proof that oxygen has reached the infant's blood and guaranteed its precious little life, what is one to make of even fiercer cries, more urgent voices, groping telegrams, conveyed by even stranger means than a birth canal, in the stillness of a crowded room, across the unfeeling surface of a Ouija board, or etched into the naked slate?

"There are those who will argue that no bona fide spirit would waste his time and energy coming down from Heaven in order to move a mere penny, shake a tambourine, raise a table a few futile inches, stop a clock for no reason, crack a cheap mirror or howl in the night. But what better way to seize hold of our collar in the midst of our busy lives than through such unexpected minor distractions. Existence, after all, is fraught with mundane details which assail us, mostly, at home. Those things we never overlook, however minute: the little things, mosquitos of recollection and chimes of recognition; déjà-vus, faint signals. Has not Einstein insisted that there is the compressed power of one hundred billion horses in a smidgen of dirt? A little spout of steam succeeded in moving a whole locomotive. And who could have predicted that the same nervous impulse which twitches a frog's muscle would light up the streets of New York on a Friday night?"

Doyle spoke with mighty confidence, slowly, empathetically, firmly. He looked at every set of eyes in that large hall, which was a rare talent. Hundreds of thousands of lecture-goers had been similarly "inoculated" by Sir Arthur Conan Doyle on four continents. After America, he and his wife planned to crusade throughout darkest Africa.

Lady Doyle could not help but swoon to her husband's eloquence. This was the man she had married, giving up a more comfortable life, perhaps, and getting in the bargain enviable travel to parts unknown, great expeditions and a partner who was willing to extend the limits of what was known and familiar.

Amy Beckwell also swooned. Here was the inner voice to match her own. It was undeniable. A pity he was old, she thought.

Doyle's eyes all of a sudden squeezed inwardly and watered as if he were trying to repress an enormous yawn, which he wasn't. He withdrew a hankie without to-do and silently jettisoned some slaver as a reporter asked him a question.

"Sir Arthur, what have the spirits actually told you about life after death?"

Doyle hurt, unexplainably, caught his breath. Lady Doyle noticed that her husband's cheeks were flushed. He wasn't answering the question. *Arthur*? she whispered in second sight, too far away for Doyle to hear her. Nevertheless, his eyes strained toward hers.

Now, something hit Doyle's chest, hard! He choked, frantic, staggering back away from the microphone.

The audience rose in alarm. He fought to catch his breath.

"Is there a doctor!" Lady Doyle screamed, fully attuned, running up to the stage.

The audience whirred, stood up, waited.

My god—a heart-attack! Doyle thought. His legs grew weak.

Two miles away, Harry Houdini had just punched his own chest with exceeding force. It was a ritual he frequently employed to stimulate his insides. Now he took six exaggerated breaths to flood his bloodstream with oxygen, and proceeded.

He was standing in his bathing suit, on the gigantic stage of the Hippodrome on Sixth Avenue, New York's largest playhouse, stretching from Forty-third to Forty-fourth Street.

Moments before, so as to convey dramatically the difficulty of the trick he was about to perform, he'd asked his audience of nine thousand people to try and hold their breath for even sixty seconds, while he in turn held a stopwatch.

"Starting . . . *Now!*"

Thousands of faces puffed up, eyes bulged, brows poured sweat, lips puckered. Houdini's lawyer worried about liability.

Gasps issued in a rapid volley from all over the auditorium. There was laughter and various cries of incredulity.

"Now: just imagine what it will be like for me, holding my breath as you just did—but upside down, *straightjacketed, banded, locked* in the toughest handcuffs, *trapped* in New England stocks—used for witches in centuries past— *bolted* down, *clamped, nailed, chained* . . . and all *underwater*, in *sewage!*" He took sadistic pleasure in enumerating the multiple manacles.

"You're crazy!" came the shouts.

A few people got up and left. They couldn't take this. But that always happened at Houdini's performances.

He climbed up a foot ladder to the top of the ten-foot transparent "torture cell." As the theatrical handbills, billboards and illuminated marquee all implied, inoffensively of course, the mucilaginous liquid into which he was to immerse himself was like sewage.

Thomas Weckstin, Joe and Royale together clamped Houdini's feet and head in stocks.

"Now for something never before tried," Houdini said loudly, with a dramatic clenching of his teeth. "On top of everything else, an unbreakable diving mask of steel shall be bolted around my face. Once it is sealed, my unwilling assistants will pour slimy fecal matter from New York's subway down a tube. Any breathing will be impossible, and the pressure of two liquid containers shall not only be painful but further impede my feeble efforts at escape."

He made it clear by his gestures that he, too, was horrified by the new addition.

He squirmed into a straightjacket. His assistants applied the numerous shackles (window dressing for Houdini).

Thomas stood near by now. Joe and Royale winced, turning their heads away as they poured the sewage from a large pail down a tube into the awkward-looking headgear. The audience moaned. Houdini had modeled the headpiece after his reading of some Jules Verne.

All eyes present could make out the malodorous sludge drooling over his face, fibrous and unimaginable, filling up the mask.

His oxygen supply was now cut off, the incoming tube removed, the hole sealed with a steel inset. Audible gagging could be heard from the audience. Houdini now crawled head down into the tank, his face covered in the latrine stuff. Joe and Royale lowered him by the stocks, clamped the heavy iron lid over him, removed the ladder and their two standing chairs and walked off the stage. The lights dimmed. Houdini remained alone, a single spotlight illuminating his torture cell.

Eyes everywhere darted from the spectacle to their watches. Houdini had been holding his breath for three minutes.

Four minutes.

Five minutes.

In the murkiness of the water, his death struggle was not visible.

Six minutes.

There was screaming. "Somebody save him!"

Thomas ran out. Now Joe and Royale followed him onto the stage with axes, poised to break through the glass container.

"Do it!" the Hippodrome manager begged, running out onto the stage as well.

"Not yet!" Thomas insisted. "I can see he's still working!"

The audience was bursting with helplessness as they watched their hero condemned to death by drowning.

"You gotta save him!" a woman cried.

"For God's sake, do something!" others bellowed.

A general roar of indignation rose up. Nine minutes had transpired.

"Thomas, he's dying!" Royale screamed.

Thomas raised a hand, still resisting. He had orders from Houdini to play it out.

A woman fainted in the audience. "Somebody, please . . . help us!"

Ten minutes.

"No more goddammit! This is suicide! Break it open, Royale!" Joe shouted. "Christ almighty, *hurry*!"

Royale lifted his ax. Thomas didn't interfere.

One second before the downswing of the ax, lo and behold, the iron lid slid from its bolts, and Harry Houdini, drenched in New York's subterranean castoffs and bowel movements, as thick and clinging as seaweed, exploded from his containment, falling down the ten-foot wall of glass, water splashing around him. He crumpled onto the stage and discreetly winked at Thomas.

Royale dropped his ax, aghast. Thomas rushed to his boss's assistance. Joe stared up at the lighting grid and made the sign of the cross. It was all executed with precision flare. Of course, the so-called sewage was merely dyed water with pieces of sponge floating in it.

Houdini then stood up, stern, grimly serious, like a Zen master.

People howled with hysterical relief, threw up their hats, and the clapping went on for longer than the trick had even taken.

The manager would admit to Houdini that in ten years at the Hippodrome he'd never seen such a thundering applause, such palpable adrenaline, such wild and uncontained exultation.

There was a brief intermission. Frank and his assistants continued to move throughout the audience, watching for any would-be assailants.

Joe, Royale and stagehands meanwhile prepared for the next trick: Max.

Max was from the Bronx Zoo, via India, *Elephas maxi-*

mus, a sterling, gentle, ivoried giant, his tusks extending six feet.

The trick astonished everyone, including the Hippodrome manager. One minute the elephant was there, standing happily before the crowd, munching on a bushel of cotton candy, the next minute, Max was gone.

Everyone knew there was a swimming pool under the stage with a small air space between levels. He couldn't be there. So where on earth was he? And how had Houdini pulled it off?

"Not even the elephant knows how it's done, or where he is!" Houdini quipped. He had a face that did not admit to a smile, even when he did smile.

In Houdini's entire repertoire, the elephant trick would go down in history as a marvel of the unexplained.

Next, a group of volunteer masons, solicited from various unions in New York, rolled a large brick wall onto center stage, atop a double rug from Persia. The masons had built the wall on a narrow steel platform that was raised two inches upon casters.

A scrupulous committee was called from the audience to stand by. Three white screens were placed around the wall. The configuration was open to the audience. Each member of the committee felt, and kicked, the bricks, vouching for their durability.

Houdini then said to everyone, "Now watch."

And with that he walked right through the wall, appearing on the other side.

It was as miraculous an effect as had ever been produced. The audience was bowled over. The combination of stunts and magic left them dazzled. Houdini was at the height of his career.

Reporters flocked back to their papers.

Houdini left the Hippodrome by special police motorcade for Hammerstein's Victoria Theater and Roof Garden. The City of New York, which prized its resident star, had offered its assistance in the matter of protection from one hall to the other. Frank Lattimer wasn't taking any chances. Eunice Holstein was free. The last thing she'd grumbled before being handcuffed was something about revenging a murder in Budapest. Frank didn't understand and didn't think to pursue it.

Holstein's accomplices—at best, guilty of easily paid-off misdemeanors for discharging firearms in public—had vanished. And while Frank suspected that sexual perversion had occurred behind those curtains onstage, there was no evidence. Nor had the medium taken money for her said services, or none that could be traced. Frank knew there was more to it than that: Holstein had a huge clientele. However obvious her ruses were to Frank, people like influential widower Judge Newcombe of the Superior Court of New York—a favorite candidate for the upcoming gubernatorial—had been taken in.

Frank had already calculated how he intended to infiltrate her operation and hopefully obtain a confession from Ginger Riddles, admitting that she had indeed paid Holstein for services offered. Frank also had an ulterior motive in seeing Ginger again.

But for the time being, he had other matters to contend with. Frank was now automatically checking the Stutz for car bombs. He and Byron had taken on three additional gumshoes to scope out any hidden snipers along the motorcade route, in every audience before which Houdini performed and round-the-clock outside the Houdini brownstone.

Upon reaching the Roof Garden, Houdini entered by the back way and repeated his entire performance again, murky water and all, with the exception of the elephant. The Roof Garden was not large enough to contain Max. Instead, Houdini worked his enhanced needle trick. With a doctor present, he would pull out of his mouth one hundred feet of thread, larded with two hundred needles which he'd washed down with three glasses of lemonade. How he accomplished it remained an inescapable mystery, like all the other enigmas in his routine.

The escape artist was doing two shows a night in New York. Bess was frantic, but Harry had his reasons. Two months before, in Cleveland, he'd struck bottom. His act could not draw crowds away from Douglas Fairbanks's newly opened *Thief of Baghdad*. The Cleveland crowd had not for a moment disputed Houdini's supremacy in the realm of stunts. But stunts, they seemed to say, had become boring.

Houdini panicked, and came up with new tricks, and then he got the hell out of Cleveland.

"What are you proving, two shows a night? Harry, we haven't made love . . . you haven't sat and read a book, or even seen your brother . . . you've hardly slept in weeks."

He remained immune.

She was exasperated. "Who do you expect to bury you, me?"

He said nothing.

"And tomorrow this contest. On a Saturday! I'll bet your father would never have stood for it . . ." She wouldn't let up. "I thought Jews didn't do contests on Saturday."

"Shut *up*!"

"Fine."

She stormed to bed.

Harry went and sat in his electric chair, ice cubes in his hands. The chair had been used to execute the mass murderer Kimblor at Auburn Prison decades before. Houdini had acquired it at an auction for what he termed "sentimental reasons." Bess deplored their having it in the house.

Houdini sat contemplating a photograph taken of him and Doyle together in England a few years before. It was the night they'd met backstage at one of Houdini's performances in London. He kept the photograph on a wall between a George Bellows gouache of a boxer and a canvas depicting a factory done by Thomas Hart Benton. Houdini collected paintings.

He stared at the bushy-browed eyes, the solid hands, the innocent, fireproof expression. What was it about Doyle?

Houdini craved knowing him. To know what he knew, if anything.

His heart was pounding. He closed his eyes. There, in the darkness, he detected a shadowy bulk, lying on a floor. In the background, there were cries. It was a man. The distant cacophony seemed familiar.

And the shape of the man tormented Houdini, yet he could not say who or what it was.

Houdini looked again at the photograph. He had read some of Doyle's nonfiction, his voluminous letters to newspapers, and had perpetually come into conflict with Doyle supporters at one séance or another.

The ghost-buster in Houdini had no quarter for the gullible Scotsman. But the hidden one, who'd left no trace, no intimation in thirty years of diaries, who had not even betrayed himself to his wife—Ehrich Weiss, Houdini's real name—aware of something, adamant about concealing it, deeply feared what he might discover there. In Sir Arthur.

"He's coming around!" Lady Doyle said.

It was days, weeks later, Sir Arthur thought.

"How long have I been out?" he mumbled to his wife, who kneeled beside him. A house doctor kneeled as well, placing a stethoscope to Doyle's heart.

"Less than a minute, darling," Lady Doyle said.

"But that's impossible . . ."

"You just fainted," the doctor said with a kindly smile. "Your pulse is a bit rambunctious. A little rest should do the trick."

Doyle's face was streaming with perspiration. He uttered something about "being underwater . . . it was dark . . . I couldn't breathe, and then—" He forgot, as he would a bad dream.

Lady Doyle heard something else, shadowy commentary, commingling with her husband's distress, coming up through the same vocables, adopting their shape, the concussion of his lips, the phoneme-after-phoneme of recall and agitation.

"It's him!" the voice of Pheneas revealed, susurrating like an admonitory echo in her gut.

She thought back to the meeting in London . . . with Houdini! It was the only other time her husband had ever felt the palpitation, the faintness, and he'd ended up on the floor of their hotel room.

She stared at her husband, seeing through to the dangerous stranger beneath Sir Arthur's perplexed coming-to. And it made her angry. This contest was too much strain on both of them. Sir Arthur should never have accepted Harrington's invitation.

Doyle stared up. From where he lay, it seemed a towering figure loomed overhead, beyond the comfort of his wife. He looked directly into the eyes of a beautiful young woman. Her face was full, Botticelli-like, outlined in a glaring golden light. If his wife hadn't been there with her garlic breath, Doyle might have had justifiable cause to assume he'd just made the great crossing into the beyond.

Amy Beckwell, who would be accompanying her boss the next morning for the first audition of the contest, had felt impulsive concerns over Doyle's well-being and taken the liberty of running up onstage to lend support. She didn't need to say a word. Lady Doyle appreciated her obvious sensitivity and heedfulness. She was beyond the slightest feminine suspicion. There had been scores of spiritualist admirers, particularly among young women widowed by the war. But Lady Doyle knew very well that Sir Arthur was as straight as a croquet mallet, far beyond the baser distractions in life. And he was.

"He's all right, folks," the doctor announced to the audience.

There was a round of applause. The live radio announcer was reporting the incident as if Firpo had just been knocked out in round one.

"It's that question which got him!" the reporter who'd asked about the spirits and the afterlife said to an associate.

"Ask it again," his friend goaded. "Obviously a sensitive issue."

Doyle stood back up, brushing off his jacket. He regained his composure, not a little embarrassed, thanked his thirty-five hundred visitors for their forbearance, and assured his wife, the young woman and the doctor of his well-being. "I will go on," he insisted to Lady Doyle.

"I'm all right, I'm all right," he shouted into the microphone. "It was a vision!"

The expectant crowd cheered and was by all appearances spellbound. They'd seen it for themselves. This was an authentic visitation.

"About the afterlife, Sir Arthur . . . I was asking you?" the reporter rephrased it, a little more reserved on account of Sir Arthur's weak heart.

"Yes, yes, of course. I remember now." And Doyle stared out toward no one in particular, stunned by what had happened, recalling decades of evidence he had gathered, confessions, revelations, firsthand accounts, the voices of Innes, of Kingsley. The memory of that water, swirling, death-reeking water, filled him with trepidation. Something had happened. It was not medical.

The audience sat expectantly.

"We have information," Doyle said, rallying, "that depicts a world of art, science, flowers and home circles. There is wide travel, the mating of souls, complete harmony."

"That is what you personally have heard?" the reporter pressed.

"That is what our 'dead friends' have actually described," Doyle propounded. "We are out of the canyon. The view is clear . . . Now I must thank you, and say good night."

Amy Beckwell, who now sat next to Lady Doyle in the front, had found her male mentor. She held Lady Doyle's hand.

Across town, Houdini went back upstairs and slipped

under the covers. Bess kept her distance. Harry nudged closer. She inched farther toward the edge of the bed. Harry nestled her like a spoon.

"When this contest is over, we're going to finally take that honeymoon we never permitted ourselves," he whispered.

With a little more coaxing, she turned and clung to him.

9

The Reverend Z. Massy

The contest gets under way . . .

Very early Saturday morning, Frank accompanied Houdini to the Barbie Pecker Middlestein Memorial Sanitarium in Connecticut, where the nut case Baker T. Massy had recently been transferred from Sing Sing. Massy, who previously had run a large mail-order enterprise, had been arrested on charges of recklessly endangering the public, and of fraud. The younger brother of the notorious Reverend Z. Massy, Baker T. had sold an estimated three hundred thousand defective Ouija boards, as well as millions of shares of worthless stock in the company. "A most senseless and perplexing sort of crime that admits to no compassion," the court at first decreed.

At the appeals hearing, medical officers for the prosecution representing several eastern states had warranted that the phrase "Massy Ouija, or Massy Fever" had been entered into the 1923 Annual of Psycho-Motor Ailments. An estimated ninety thousand cases had thus far been reviewed, and of those, more than half were judged to be insane, the sinister, perhaps permanent result of purchasing one of Massy's Ouijas and carefully following the printed directives.

"Those were typos!" Massy had pleaded, demanding a mistrial.

The defense had proved that Massy himself was the tragic victim of one of his own boards and was entitled to the same therapeutic environs as were freely provided other such victims. The plaintiff—in this case eleven states, the court recorder registering it as "Eastern seaboard vs. the Massy Board"—conceded this point and Massy had been tossed (with not a little judicial relish) to the dogs.

Frustrated by his inability to nail Eunice Holstein, Houdini looked forward to seeing the likes of Baker T. Massy confined to a padded cell. But he had an even more urgent motive in visiting Barbie Pecker Middlestein at 7 A.M. on the Jewish Sabbath. He needed a couple of phone numbers, and Baker T. Massy was the only man alive who had them.

According to Frank's detective work, Baker T. was definitely in collusion with his reverend brother, who was expected to top off the first round of medium auditions at the *Scientifica Americana* contest this day. Reverend Massy was as slick and consummate a con artist as Holstein. Expose his fakery and the spiritualist cause would be a laughing stock, while Doyle and his muddle-brained disciples might be demolished.

The Reverend's own method of religious fraud involved nothing so seedy as plaster molds from dead people, but rather what a scientific consultant hired by Frank termed "complicated telephotography." The FBI had only worked out the system a year before, for transferring fingerprints via wireless from one station to another. The technique had even been written up in *Scientifica Americana*, which was no doubt where the Reverend got it, Frank assumed. Houdini intended to destroy Massy. It would be a major, preemptive coup. Harrington's contest might be concluded in a single swipe. *Harrington ought to appreciate that*, he reckoned.

Telephotographic fraud was no easy business, as it required ingenious helpers and two pieces of expensive equipment. Frank's consultant figured that Massy could have had them built for three thousand dollars each. He could recoup that in a single séance if he snared the right widow.

The machines cut through light with a revolving disc that contained numerous minute mirrors. Those mirrors converted flashes of light, first into photoelectric cells, then into waves, and the waves were transferred by wireless. The first apparatus encoded and sent, the other received and decoded. The decoder, with its colored ink roller and minute printer, was contained in the Reverend's levitation table.

"It's just incredible to me that a religious fellow would go to such lengths to pull off what he could probably have accomplished with much less effort," Houdini said.

"He's trying to be the best," Frank suggested. "There's tough competition out here. I don't have to tell you!"

They continued to drive through countryside. It was a Hudson River School kind of day. Houdini stared at the dappled light through the oaks as the Stutz sped up the parkway, past granite boulders and rushing streamlets. He was watching for bear. They'd have just emerged from their winter dens and would be lumbering toward New York's outlying cornucopias in search of chocolate sundaes.

"Our consultant went to one of the séances. He figured it out," Frank explained.

Houdini could appreciate Massy's labor, given his conspiring anticipation of another kind of payoff. At a Reverend Massy séance, as Frank went on to describe, the seeker after eternal truth received something more than vaguely recognizable, ephemeral cries in the dark, spirit kisses, a silly jingle of music or the easily faked sensation of a passing hand over one's face. Massy ingeniously provided solid evidence, stuff that could be taken home, framed in an altar, or placed under one's pillow forevermore: printed pictures of loved ones who had passed away, and elaborately written messages, all coming out of that miracle table that looked so ecclesiastical and austere, on the surface.

Massy simply sat quietly before his table, reciting Oriental humbug. A hidden little speaker in the table was actually a telephone, Frank's scientific consultant had determined, and it must lead via ordinary wire into a wall outlet. It would take Massy's humble assistant, also cowled in the Zurbaránish monk's robes, about two minutes to set up the device once the heavy table was rolled in.

The consultant, who used to date Frank's sister in high school, was a former whiz-kid associate of Edison's and Samuel Insull's turned undercover agent. He figured out that Massy must be getting advance dope on the customers, sending confederates out to secure photographs and other kinds of evidence. That was not always possible, of course. But once into the séance, with the phone line open, *anything* was possible.

The phone line presumably came from Baker T. Frank checked out any calls from Sing Sing. Baker T. had been in the prison two months while his lawyers worked the system to get him out, and he made not one call the whole time. Clever. Very clever. And so far, he'd not placed a single call from the sanitarium either, though—presumably for effect, like a child with his blanket—he clutched his portable telephone and kept it on his person at all times, a fetish that hadn't led to any suspicion since Massy was now a bona fide *crazy*.

Any phone would do, however.

"So the Reverend Z. calls Baker T., tells him when to return the call, that is to say, when the séance will get started. His brother phones back at the appointed hour, but nobody hears it because there's no ringer on the phone in the levitation table. Now the channel's open—Baker T. hears every-thing that goes on at the séance, separated by long distance. And he's able to speak into the phone in the guise of spiritu-alist voices, reading Arabic text, screaming like an Apache from the dead, whatever. And those at the séance hear it through the speaker hidden in the table, while the Reverend lends his innocent commentary.

"Here's the clincher. Baker T. stops hollering, hangs up, which is the signal for the Reverend to prepare his seekers to receive more tangible evidence. Because of the special na-ture of the hidden phone in the table, it's dedicated to Baker T.'s line. He can hang up and get back on at will.

"Once Baker T. gets his provocation from the séance—say, somebody mentions a mom or a dad or a pet dog that died, whatever—Baker T. calls some other number where you can be sure an accomplice is working the encoding/sending machine. He gets to work, and within a very few minutes has wired the hard copy evidence from the spirit world.

"The wire starts to come through, photographic paper slowly squeezing out of a razor-thin opening under the table, into the Reverend's lap. Meanwhile, Baker T. has called back to the séance and is hollering in distant trance voices, and it's so loud and annoying that the sitters don't have a prayer of hearing any part of the printing apparatus inside the table. The Reverend's also creating his own ruckus. Be-tween the two Massy brothers, it's all hell breaking loose in there. That's how they do it," Frank explained to Houdini.

"The paper evidence from the other world has given Massy innumerable disciples. He turns up in the society col-umns. It's big business."

"So the sending machine—the alleged 'beyond'—is acti-vated by a few phone calls and those so-called psychic voices are thereby converted into picture," Houdini conjec-tured, confused, but trying to work it out.

"I guess that's what's going on," Frank concurred.

At some level it was the most simplistic ruse. A telephone. But who could see it? The gullible yearners, the bereaved, the worshipful, would be easily impressed by the unfamiliar tangle of fancy widgets. They were no match for the controlling clairvoyant/engineer, who, meanwhile, sat passively, with nothing to hide—other than the insides of his table.

Houdini had been around the Holsteins and Massys of this world since he was a kid. They had populated the freak shows, vaudeville alleys, the rural circuses. He'd seen them hanging around the boarding houses in New York, when Houdini and Bess were down on their luck and prey to endless schemers. He, too, felt the allure of their promises. Houdini worshiped his mother, who had died several years before. He would give anything to know that she was safe, on the other side, happy, unafraid, fulfilled. If he could only speak to her . . .

He had tried. Hundreds of times, in the early days. The Holstein and Massy types had humiliated him, bled him dry before other rapturous yearners. Houdini now fed on the taste of revenge.

Frank and Houdini drove up along the unkempt lawns to the large red-brick colonial main house. The plaster was peeling off the Doric columns. Frank noticed several broken windows behind the bars. As they came through the main entrance, where an orderly greeted them and escorted them to the head office, they could hear the screams. It was a zoo.

Houdini had an appointment with the clinician Seyberts, who'd taken part in the first brain surgery done with only a local anesthetic. The patient had been fully awake and spoke with reporters while his head was being fixed. Seyberts had been experimenting with various new drugs and invasive brain surgeries on the patients at Middlestein.

"We get real animals here," he admitted. "Sing Sing's our biggest supplier."

They'd arranged, with the County's blessings, to inject some fancy new truth serum into Massy's neck veins this day. He wouldn't have much of a chance to object on account of the new straightjacket he'd been given.

"You should have seen his expression," Seyberts said.

Houdini had come to interrogate Massy. The drug was expected to take all of a minute to set in.

"Nice thing about my work here," Seyberts explained, "I don't have to try to cure these people, or thin their brain colloids with carbon dioxide and manganese chloride. We're not tracking lucidity. We want to know how to *make* them insane."

"What on earth for?" Houdini asked.

"It's a different approach, I guess. If you know where the sun sets, you can easily deduce from whence it rises."

They walked down the corridor. If Baker T. had not been truly insane at the time of his appeals hearing, he certainly was so now. The poor bastard was surrounded by wails and lamentations and excrement. Middlestein housed over twelve hundred patients. Most of them, it seemed to Houdini, had come down with Massy Ouija.

Ever since his first visit to an asylum, in Nova Scotia two decades before, where he watched an inmate struggle for hours against a shackle belt, then tried it himself, Houdini had returned countless times to sanitariums all over the world. They were the best place to keep up on all the latest straightjacket technologies. Nowhere else could he get a bird's-eye view of desperate muscle, flailing disorder, the human body entrapped and struggling. Like a painter examining his nude model, Houdini had detected subtle pitfalls in the manipulation of his own joints, as well as leather and steel. He'd watched the horror of exhaustion creep over the victim, seen tears reduce a man more quickly than his physical exertion.

As they continued to the padded cell area, Houdini looked through reinforced glass into the claustrophobic bull pens and cubbyholes. The joint was in dire need of overhaul.

"Middlestein was privately endowed," Seyberts acknowledged, catching Houdini's look of disgust at the surroundings.

"No one to blame. Interest on the principle just hasn't kept apace of inflation. Since only the hardened dregs and terminal brain dummies are let in, there's little government support here."

Or supervision, Houdini imagined. Seyberts was free to play god. And that didn't bother Houdini one bit, not today, anyway.

"What is it, exactly?" Frank asked, as Seyberts took out a vial from an ice chest, pierced it with a needle and drew liquid into the syringe.

"A delicate brew of scopolamine and sodium cyanide," Seyberts replied. "Comes from poisonous alkaloids like nightshade and henbane. At San Quentin, they got the subconscious to slip out like a hooker from her panties.

"You wouldn't believe the confessions we've gotten! Of course, you can't use them in a court of law because of the self-incrimination business." He paused. Then, "But I gather that's not the point of your visit."

"Right," Houdini averred.

They reached Massy's cell. He lay helpless on the floor, like a grumbling sarcophagus. His portable telephone lay next to him, lifeless and out of his reach.

"How *are* we this morning, Mr. Massy!" Seyberts chirped with a big smile, unbolting the door and swinging it wide open. "We don't need any water, do we?"

The three men entered, and Seyberts raised the syringe in his hand to give the convicted fruitcake a thrill.

This was too much for Massy. The bunched-up hulk writhed and wriggled, supine and clumsy, like a crippled grasshopper making toward—where? His phone? The door? The window?

His face was all contorted under the heavy reins. This was the most abominable-looking jacket Houdini had ever seen. Later, he'd *have* to try one on!

"Look who's come to visit you today, Baker T.—why it's

none other than Harry Houdini and his friend Frank. You've heard of Houdini?"

Massy started screaming at the top of his constricted lungs, feebly jerking like a fully revved automobile engine with no wheels on which to get anywhere.

A nurse appeared at the entrance to Massy's cell, looking horrified.

"What is it, nurse?" Seyberts demanded, above the din of Massy's tirade.

"Nothing." The woman turned around and carried on with her duties elsewhere.

"Don't mind her," Seyberts said. "She's pretty mixed up herself, frankly. Part of our working convalescence program. A disciple of Massy's brother, I understand . . . Here, hold him down . . ." He then applied the syringe to Massy's throat.

Back in New York, Ralph Harrington greeted the arriving multitude. The Masonic Hall on Fifteenth Street near Third Avenue, where Harrington's Manhattan Liberal Club frequently met, was the chosen site for today's, and Monday's, marathon of testing. Nearly a dozen prescreened mediums were waiting in various rooms upstairs. They all had their crates of equipment with them.

The main floor was bustling. Amy Beckwell said hello to the Doyles. "Remember me?" Sir Arthur was quick to thank her for her solicitude on the night prior and might have elaborated on the sense of universal kindred spirit she'd set off in him had there been any time. But there were two hundred reporters who were prime for conversion.

Amy sat next to her boss, Harrington. Her eyes avoided those of a handsome young man who came up and sat beside Bess. Bess introduced him to Harrington and Amy as Thomas Weckstin. He was charming, Amy thought, and she was glad when Harrington took Bess aside.

"He should have discussed this with me first," he whispered tactfully to Bess, who had explained why Houdini was late.

"So what am I to do?" he asked painstakingly.

"He'll be here by ten, he promised," she said matter-of-factly. Bess had no appreciable interest in all of this. She'd been bored or, at best, amused too many times at séances. They all amounted to the same gag, in her estimation. And her husband could usually get to the heart of that gag, as with everything else in his life, within minutes.

Houdini and Doyle had not yet been officially introduced, which was part of the big publicity stratagem, and now it looked as if Harrington would have to commence the proceedings in Houdini's temporary absence. He could manage it.

Harrington quietly introduced the Doyles to Bess.

"We are *so* pleased to meet you!" Sir Arthur waxed enthusiastic, taking her hand with fervor.

"Charmed," Lady Doyle affirmed.

"Well I know Harry's also looking forward to this," Bess said with a spark, feeling the first wave of excitement in the presence of one so genuinely famous. "He's read many of your books. I have also."

"Really? I am honored."

"No, I am honored."

Lady Doyle turned away.

Harrington stood up and called the proceedings to order.

"Sir Arthur Conan Doyle, I want to welcome you to America. You and Harry Houdini, who will be here a little later today, have a lot in common," he recited, for the benefit of all assembled in the presence of *Scientifica Americana*'s star adjudicator.

Doyle had been bolstered by the enormous success of his Carnegie debut the previous night—front-page stories in all the major dailies describing his otherworldly visitation, the stunned audience, weeping women, hard-boiled men reduced to devotion. He thanked Harrington and expeditiously suggested they press on, there being much work to accomplish in little time.

People took their seats in the many rows of metal folding chairs.

Harrington read off his little note cards and introduced the six august members of the official committee whose task it was to judge the contestants.

"Welcome if you will Dr. Henden Grundranvodst, a visiting physicist from the University of Reykjavik, famous for his psychic laboratory."

Grundranvodst took a bow, his pince-nez jingling. Bess noticed that he had the most enormous ears.

"Now much of his gear has been shipped across—it's what all that rococo high jinks is about." Harrington pointed to the stage. "Thank you, Doctor.

"Then there's Professor Shleihauffen. Shleih—"

Harrington gave the Professor the moment. Nobody clapped. The Teutonic fellow, twice profiled in Harrington's magazine for ground-breaking touchy-feely sort of research, smiled iffily. Harrington closed up the gap. "You've probably all heard of him—outstanding biokinesiologist from Monchen-Gladbach here on sabbatical with his mother at the New York Academy of Behaviorism . . .

"And Dr. Morris Abraham, from Fort Wayne, Indiana, most noted, of course, in the field of etheric lactations—"

"Vibrations," Abraham inserted shyly.

Harrington mumbled over the slip and pushed on in his baritone manner. "A world-leading psycho-metrist, and inventor of—don't need to write it down, fellas—the ectoplasmic-biodynamic-corroborator, or EBC machine, used, most recently, you'll recall, to correctly analyze that suspicious ooze detected in the bathrooms at Penn Station. Abraham rightly judged it to be a mixture of cement grease and pine sap, not spectral manifestation. A major blow to spiritualism."

Abraham bowed.

"Then there's Dr. Shannon O'Nearly, renowned admirer

of Nobel Laureate Richett. He needs no introduction. Shan—Take a bow . . .

"And not least, Timothy Crowded. You've heard of him, some of you've even printed stories about his lightning machine that burned up thousands of acres of Maine some years back. A real maverick, stand-alone inventor, lecturer on topics as diverse as physiological engineering and gravity. Honored everywhere. Formerly of MIT, most recently operating from the SSSOL." He pronounced it Soul.

"For the record, Mr. Harrington—the soul?" a reporter queried.

"Let's see here, it says, 'the secondary school system of'—"

"Lubbock," Crowded interjected.

"That's Texas," Harrington clarified. "Since his spectacular successes in New England, Crowded has been taking his theories to the younger generations all over America. He did Oklahoma, Kansas, hopes to reach Mexico soon." He looked at Crowded. "Isn't that right, Tim? And by the way, he's also Eugene O'Neill's fourth cousin. Will you please welcome Timothy Crowded."

Still no applause.

"And then our very own Mr. Barkwaithe, associate editor of *Scientifica Americana*, a known sensitive. How about a rousing hand!"

The reporters dumbly slapped palms against pads, or made more supreme efforts, suspending their cameras under their arms and clapping once or twice. The appeal had missed its mark. Harrington's showmanship felt out of place, at least to Lady Doyle. Bess was more accustomed to such hype. But Amy Beckwell, Houdini's assistant Weckstin, and several others, wondered about the whole approach here. Lubbock? Reykjavik? Monchen-Gladbach? Where was Harvard, Yale, Princeton? Who *were* these silly-sounding people?

Like Bess, Bertram Fennell, Harrington's senior editor, was not troubled by the carnival flare, though for a different reason. He knew very well who these men were: scientists of admittedly eccentric renown, but perfectly chosen from around the world. Men with the singular thingamajigs and doodads to foil fraud, or detect Heaven.

Harrington blew his trumpet a little more, trying to steal time in the event Houdini arrived early. "Now, add to this unprecedented weight of authority the magisterial advocacies, for and against, of Sir Arthur Conan Doyle—sleuth, scientist, man of the world, a medium's medium—and the Great Houdini, whom we all know to be as elusive as spirit, an artist extraordinaire—who'll be here any minute—and you have what promises to be the most ferocious and decisive scrutiny ever applied to those alleged psychic phenomena."

Now there was a more generous ovation from the reporters. Doyle stifled further to-dos and sat back down at the long table where the assemblage was gathered, before the press.

"What can you expect to prove in two days?" a reporter fired out.

"Evidence, one way or another," Harrington belted back. "We've got state-of-the-art measuring devices, great minds, proven methods. The whole world's been waiting for this moment. Soon we will know. If the answer's yes, we can all relax. Death is meaningless. If the answer's no, then it's back to dog-eat-dog business-as-usual. High stakes. The ultimate scientific and philosophical questions. Five thousand bucks in the offing. I'm counting on all of you to write it up with the gusto it deserves . . ." He looked around for a show of support. Feelings were mixed.

"What happens after Monday?" another reporter asked.

Harrington explained the open-ended nature of the competition. "We're going in with no expectations," he admitted. "We may not find a single medium. Or we may find ten of them that pass the stringent conditions set forth. The Doyles and Houdinis will be heading west on respective tours, and the contest may well continue in Denver or Los

Angeles. When we've chosen *the* one, you'll be among the first to know. Because you're all invited to watch, and I certainly hope you will!"

"Hey, that's great!" the pressmen yelled. They hadn't counted on actually *seeing* anything.

The committee stirred uneasily with the news. Bess was delighted.

"I'm nervous with that, Ralph," Sir Arthur intervened. "Mediums need a certain hospitable atmosphere to carry on their work, as you probably know. Two hundred reporters, cameras flashing—"

"Not to worry, Sir Arthur. These men are professionals, no different from those in your own country."

"That's precisely my fear," Doyle stated, in a not unfriendly, but firm, manner.

"Sir Arthur, as long as everybody respects everybody else, I see no problem with a few hundred additional onlookers. The doors are barred, obviously, to the general public. But the press is fundamental in this country. It's their right to know, and our responsibility to let them know. And anyway, either the medium is for real, or he isn't. An audience of professionals shouldn't make a difference."

The committee members were not prepared to publicly argue this issue. And Doyle was too much the gentleman to fight American ways. So the contest got under way.

It would take an hour for the committee members to finish setting up and fine-tuning their gear all across the stage. In their far-reaching investigations and esoteric tests, these adroit men of science had seen it all, from serenading snake oil to the unexplainable swamp things. They carefully erected delicately mirrored galvanometers, useful in capturing the ever-so-faint illuminated entry of a spirit into a room; a chair, poised by a spring balance so as to gather and record any spiritual vibrations apart from the normal shifting of buttocks; red, white and blue flood lights for capturing the *bon gre, mal gre*, the fleet, the shy, the indecisive spirit; a seismographic recorder with paper tape and printer to detect the slightest burp or tremor occasioned by anomalous beings; a uranium counter to sense any isotopes or radioactivity; gas chronometers for registering astral flatus; spectroscopes for measuring haloes according to color and wave length, indicative of the chemistry of the visitation; photometers for analyzing the luminous intensity of any manifestation; and a high-tension electrified wire cage with medieval dungeon-like toys inside for analyzing levitation.

There was a medium's closet of balsa, ready to receive the slightest soul print, and outfitted with impermeable silk walls, "to insure the integrity of any volatile being," as Shleihauffen put it; and pitot-static tubes to collect any conceivable ectoplasm that might drool here and there. Sound recording machines of different resolving powers were attached to large box cameras with trip flashes. Also present were devices to record ferro- and vital-magnetism, in case objects started flying around the room. This was the greatest convergence of ghost-catching wizardry in the history of science. Puke collectors, rainbow snatchers and a treacherous long-haired pedigreed bichon frise capable of sniffing out paranormal mischief. Amy liked the little dog. Ludwig was its name.

Meanwhile, as the investigators busily continued assembling their bugging devices, the many mediums, or medium's lawyers and representatives, waited for their moment in the sun upstairs, in the spiritual emporium of lounges and dressing rooms scattered around the old stone edifice.

The waiting period was less than tranquil. Much to Harrington's horror, the Scottish Rite Secrets of the Empire Club, as well as the Temple Beth Jerusalem's Aliyah Girls, were also availing themselves of the Masonic Hall this day. Harrington's Liberal Club had no overriding sphere of influence on the rental policies of the building. While *Scientifica Americana* controlled the main floor, there was confusion upstairs, silly teenagers and paranoid stuffed shirts shuffling to and fro, running into the wrong dressing rooms and pissing off the mediums, making a commotion. They had their own, smaller rooms in which to congregate elsewhere in the building. The noise carried.

Mediums like the albino Mutzel, of the Bronx, who'd been buried by physicians for four days in March, then risen from the grave to much Bronxian fanfare, demanded a rescheduling. He could not talk to spirits, he insisted, if there was competing noise from the living. Harrington appeased Mutzel by promising him the last place on the presentation list. By then, the Temple girls and Masons would have gone home.

Lewis Hegdish secured a similar promise. Hegdish was a failed Yiddish playwright from St. Louis who had discovered that he felt no pain whatsoever. Nor did his body evidence injury. No blood ever flowed from a wound. You could burn him, drive nails through him, slice through his fingers, pour cayenne pepper down his throat, ammonia up his nose—nothing seemed to bother him. But there was even more to the rumors than mere physical anomaly. Both Hegdish and Mutzel—friends who conducted their séances together—were alleged to have communicated with the dead.

In the Hotel de la Republic, across the street from the Masonic Hall, the great "air gusher" Nina Rafaella waited confidently. This willowy Neapolitan peasant girl had discovered her ability to lift good-looking men off the ground about the time she came into her menarche. Nina's parents had the village priest perform an exorcism. But her condition only grew worse. The lifting spread to other things—tables, horses, automobiles. Soon Nina herself was rumored to be floating across Italy's outback, no longer happy with her village or her parents. She floated all the way to Rome, where a university psychologist made her famous.

Nina was in possession of a continuous flow of air from her head, a "physical agitation of the ether" that all who came near her could feel. Nina was able, under the right conditions, to concentrate that gusher of air so that a veritable geyser of pressure issued from her person. There was no telling what she might be able to do with it. Her transports were rapturous and internationally celebrated. But for the time being, she was languishing in a ginseng bubble bath in her two-hundred-dollar-a-night suite, awaiting the phone call from her lawyer at the Masonic Hall.

Johnny Koulots, a one-time bantamweight champion, had acquired, since retiring at twenty-five, the much ballyhooed ability to defy gravity. He'd blown their minds in Madrid. Now, he bided his time in a lounge upstairs, punching pillows and greasing down his muscles. Two pretty Temple Beth Jerusalem girls, newly Bas-Mitzvahed, stumbled onto him, and he soon had them hanging flirtatiously from his outstretched arms, swooning over biceps, and succumbing rapidly to his idea of a cozy threesome. Johnny was the only medium in town who didn't take himself too seriously.

The sinuous Madame Vastayana, endowed with a heaving bosom, came from the British hill station of Nainatal, where she had allegedly demonstrated an ability to take photographs with her body. "Her breasts are a new kind of camera," the *Times* of Liverpool had reported. All over the world she'd won approbation for her mystical portraits. Prime ministers, viceroys, distinguished men from many countries, insisted on private sittings with the Madame, who was now busy down the hall from Johnny, gussying herself up in a sari and Burmese jewels.

Douser and De Angelo had grown up at the Lily Dale community of spiritualists. By the age of nineteen, they had appeared in the ballroom of the New York Waldorf-Astoria before one thousand true believers. Douser and De Angelo were Siamese twins and had four-dimensional X-ray vision between them, or so it was said. They had convinced at least one scientific man of eminence of their power to read fossil bones and make otherwise unheard of medical diagnoses. They attributed all of their aptitude to a spirit infestation in their hemoglobin, as well as the benevolence of certain New Yorker ghosts, with whom they claimed to be in daily contact. The jury was still out on these two.

And there were others. An Amish slate writer of humble origins. A University of Chicago mathematician who was alleged to be able to "divine" the hidden identification of all the cards of a deck, in a row, a chance of 623,360,743,125, 120-to-1. He did it, or so he stated, with the help of the spirit of Leibnitz, monad king, gambling fiend.

And there was a parrot-keeper whose Trace Marie was actually the stated medium. This remarkable little bird could describe in detail its peripatetic journey from a remote island off the coast of Mexico, its incredible love affair with a Brazilian scarlet macaw—against all odds—that finally ended in tragedy when the larger Amazonian fell beak-over-claws for a drapery designer in Yonkers. "Josey" did not mince words and showed a grave concern for the future of mankind, which it described as a species of "bullies." The parrot had made a sensation on several radio shows.

In keeping with the animal turn of events, the committee had also expressed interest in a French-speaking cow ("*moi*" for "moo", for example, not to mention a rousing rendition of the "Marseillaise" and the tune "I Have Good Tobacco in my Pouch") from the Burlington, Vermont, area, but due to its milking schedule, the fourteen-hundred-pound "Louisa Margarita" (as she apparently called herself) could not be present at the Masonic Hall.

And finally, there was Baker T. Massy's brother, the Reverend Massy, Vicar of Wilmington, born in the famed medium's town of Cassadaga, Florida, a once noted telecommunications engineer turned guru, distant disciple of Madame Blavatsky, with enough dubious misadventures crammed into his past (according to his official hagiographer) to doubly recommend him for Barbie Pecker Middlestein and Dr. Seyberts's care.

He was said to have walked naked across the Gobi Desert in search of either a rare Mongolian poppy, or a distant cousin, or both (his official chronicler was unclear on this point according to Harrington's wife, Dalores, who had read the book and made special arrangements to have Massy at the competition). Months later, upon reaching the Great Red Mosque in Lahore, he fell to his knees before thousands of praying Muslims, and began flagellating himself unmercifully with leather thongs. He gained a few disciples by it. Later, he was laid waste by cholera at Ephesus, where he communed with Aphrodite and took on a number of Turkish subordinates.

Massy subsequently walked across Luxembourg in his underwear, though his chronicler—who was currently auctioning the official biography of Massy to New York publishers—omitted any rationale for this action, according to Frank, who'd managed to get a copy of the manuscript from an insider at Massy's church.

A handsome man in his late forties, Massy had a congregation of several thousand who had taken communion, on a first name basis, with the dead, with past lives, even with Arab ghosts. He was a unique medium, they swore, able to produce tangible proof of the hereafter.

Lady Doyle, having heard of this contestant, was considerably worried about exposing Pheneas to the Reverend, especially in proper Arabic.

Presently, Massy sat in a solitary room, dressed in habit, staring from the open window that looked out on a blackened fire escape, awaiting his time, reciting pan-Asian mantras, while his assistant prepared the equipment.

Massy's brother fared less happily. Houdini and Frank had left Baker T. in a lamentable condition, frothing and incoherent, slithering about the floor of his padded cell in that monstrous metallic getup, which threatened to cut off his bristling circulation entirely, shouting for his telephone, which had been denied him.

The truth serum had done the trick: Houdini exhibited an uncharacteristically loud display of exuberance at having wrestled the two numbers from a blurry-mouthed Baker T. The poor Massy's nurse happened to be standing there at the time of Houdini's gloating. As he and Frank hurried out of the sanitarium for New York, she called the next of kin, her guru, as it turned out, with whom she had maintained a confidential relationship ever since the Reverend Z.'s brother was transferred to Barbie Pecker Middlestein.

By mid-morning Frank had driven them back to New York, and they soon pulled up in front of the Masonic Hall. Byron was there keeping watch for trouble outside, like Holstein, or any of her gun-toting ghouls. Houdini figured he'd work his intervention from a telephone at the hotel across the street.

Byron got Bess, who slipped outside and gave her husband the rundown. There was a pay phone at the front entrance, and Bess was instructed to call Harry the moment the Reverend Massy had commenced his séance. Houdini would be in the hotel lobby. Bess kissed Harry and he winked.

"What do you think of Doyle?" he asked.

"I like his wife, though she doesn't say much." The two of them had exchanged a few additional courtesies, pending a more intimate or at least sustained meeting, which only Houdini's arrival could finally facilitate.

"What about him?"

"He says too much."

"Is he . . . confident?"

"Yeah . . . I s'pose . . ."

Houdini savored the scenario. Then, "This is going to be great!" he said, sipping the air with a whistle of victory, patting Bess.

The contest was already in progress, a medium busily writing upon a slate, while the committee sat scrutinizing, their myriad machines ticking and clicking, whirring and recording.

The entire floor of the hall had been darkened. On the center stage, at the head of a table around which the six committee members, and Doyle, were seated, Yon Blennoit, a large Amish corn syrup distributor, selected from among two dozen similar slate writers, scribbled out messages that he said were coming from Barkwaithe's recently deceased aunt, Medalia.

"Can we see the slate now?" Barkwaithe requested, betraying an eagerness that was contrary to the singularity of restraint marking his fellow committee members.

"Not yet," the medium responded, in a tone of utmost quiet and suppression.

Feeling the weight of the beyond cramping a burning curiosity, Barkwaithe could no longer resist. He hit a switch, controlled by a portable panel in his hand, thus flooding the séance table with white light.

Blennoit went wild. "You idiot!" he screamed, lunging upward and striking out crazily with his special pencil, just missing Barkwaithe's face.

Barkwaithe returned the hostile act with a well-placed kick to the man's genitals. In Blennoit's urgency to flee, he shoved the slate table forward, knocking over three of the committee members. The slate crashed to the floor and shattered. Doyle tried to grab the Amish charlatan, but the man was too fast and disappeared out the back door.

A hundred cameras flashed; the radio announcers boomed with excited commentary.

Harrington was positively delighted with the first test. He could see the headlines. Reporters were eating it up.

Committee members examined the pieces of Blennoit's deception: he'd employed nitrate of silver and a secret wedge of hardwood separating two slates, which the committee had missed. For all of their expertise, they were not skilled in the art of frisking. Blennoit had managed to conceal a long, stiff wire with a piece of lead attached; powdered soapstone, iron filings, water and glue surrounding an electromagnet; all hidden under the bottom flap of slate and connected by a second wire to a copper plate. The magnet guided the fake pencil. Such trickery had been used for decades.

Doyle was as eager as anyone to expose the fraud. "For every verifiable mystic, there are one hundred fakes," he quickly acknowledged to the press. "I have found this to be the general rule. But I have also found that one bona fide medium may be enough to save the world."

One after another now came downstairs to be tested, beginning with Johnny Koulots. Try as they might, nobody could lift him off the floor when his muscles were clenched. The moment he slackened them, the former champion was a light one hundred thirty pounds. Doyle was not impressed.

"He's using powdered soapstone. Rinse off his body and you'll catch his methodology!"

Koulots congratulated Doyle, the first one to see through his trick in two years.

Harrington also congratulated Doyle, surprised by the degree to which Doyle had cultivated a sharp eye. Everything Harrington had heard about the Englishman had led him to assume a temperament so generous and yearnful as to be blind. Harrington could see subtle lines of battle emerging between his two advocates that he'd not counted on. He didn't quite know whether this development made for possibilities or was a liability.

The Siamese twins came on stage, striking a most bizarre pose between them. They sat akimbo before the scientists, back-to-back, which is how they came into this world, and proceeded to diagnose every member of the committee, whose names they'd never been told. The committee selection had not been made public until this morning, though as would be discovered, there were plenty of ways for the contestants to do homework.

"You're suffering from rheumatism . . . you from a heart condition . . . You've got cataracts and calcium deposits . . . four days of constipation . . . incipient cancer . . . You'll be dead this time next year . . ." and so forth.

Doyle, one-time medical man himself, was infuriated. "And what about me?" he asked scornfully.

"You'll die of a heart attack, by the end of the decade," they both concurred.

"How do you know that?" Doyle went on. His wife was intently attuned, down among the audience.

The twins stared at him with all the potent brunt of their alleged X rays.

"I'm picking up something!" Shannon O'Nearly said, monitoring his electromagnetic counter. "A field interference!"

"That's not possible," Timothy Crowded whispered loudly.

Doyle started to feel something, an ache in his chest, reminiscent of what had happened the night before at Carnegie Hall. The feeling passed. "Turn on the lights," Doyle said, uncomfortable with the proceedings.

By the time Crowded, Shleihauffen, Grundranvodst and Abraham had gathered around O'Nearly's device, the force field had resumed its stable setting. The twins sat with their eyes closed.

"We're tired now," they said, getting up and wobbling out in their excruciating, gunnysacklike manner.

"What was it?" pressmen yelled out.

"There seems to be real uncertainty up there!" a radio announcer hawked from the back of the hall.

Shleihauffen was first to offer an explanation. "Exteriorisation of motivity, that's my guess."

"It could be a number of things," O'Nearly stated in a diagnostic mumbo jumbo that left everyone yawning. "Ectenic, dynamic, pathotelluric, even subconscious. Any of those might have accounted for it."

Doyle weighed in with his own orthodox reconciliation. "Nothing's too amazing to be true. Michael Faraday said it."

Harrington sized up the disarray. "Then the consensus of the committee is that, while the two of them may be strange, they didn't *do* anything strange . . . Is that correct, gentlemen?" Harrington inquired in a voice that the press was privy to.

There were nods all around, though Doyle looked aggravated. He took a moment to speak with his wife.

"That was interesting," he confessed.

"I think they're fakes," Lady Doyle insisted.

"Perhaps."

"Even if they're legitimate, all the gadgetry in the world might not prove it."

"I realize."

"It's a no-winner," she went on, whispering in his ear.

"Let's talk later. I have an idea," Doyle said, returning to the stage.

The lingering indecisiveness in the room evaporated with the arrival of Madame Vastayana, her methylene-blue-saturated body paint visible beneath her loosely draped sari. Her black braids were waist-length, tied in colored ribbons.

"No cameras! That is the condition the spirits have requested," the Madame said in a masculine voice to all the reporters.

Her young male assistant, also Indian, arranged her private cabinet onstage, made of bird's-eye maple from Cuba. He requested that all lights be extinguished and gave the go-ahead to the Madame, who reemerged from behind the wooden chest, wearing absolutely—nothing!

Gasps went up in the audience.

Among the committee, there was repressed, scientific ogling, a palpable weakness that circumgyrated around the table, from observer to observer, as the Madame strolled in circles, stopping here, resting there, letting the spirits guide her. For a paralyzing moment, she halted behind Shleihauffen, whose eyes strained not to see the Himalayan nipples at his ears.

At a distance of eight feet, the Madame aimed her voluminous coconut breasts across the table at the one man who suddenly drew in her concentration—Doyle!

"Don't move, you!" the Madame commanded with an imperial resolve.

Doyle didn't so much as quake, though his wife showed considerably less equipoise.

"Pheneas, are you there?" Lady Doyle whispered to herself. "Pheneas, I want you to get that bitch!"

There was a flash—electrostatic—people's hair stood up, a crashing sound, a puff of smoke. Then it was over.

"My God!" Doyle burst out. "Incredible!"

Lights poured over the arena of activity. Pressmen went wild.

"I've never seen anything like her, it!" the radiomen blurted.

Dr. Morris Abraham was first to notice the stigmata on her back. It was bleeding, smoke rising from the epidermal fissure.

The Indian confederate threw the sari over his guru. She sat down, eyes wide, breath telling of her exhaustion. A faint smile of success brimmed over her body. With a single yank, she ripped free of her chest a strip of light sensitive material, like flesh.

There, looking dumbfounded, was Doyle, no mistaking the likeness.

There was general pandemonium. "She's one of them!" a reporter from the *Tribune* hollered. "She's for real!"

"Not so fast, boys!" Harrington yelled. "Well?" he said, directing his earnest concerns to the committee. Five thousand buckaroos—the fate of his magazine, probably of his marriage—hinged on their decision.

The men examined the photograph. Grundranvodst applied a microscope.

"What's the problem?" the Madame asked, unhappy with such close study.

"Ahhh!" Grundranvodst said, pointing out the leaves of a tree in the background. "Have you never seen this photograph before?" he asked Doyle.

"Let me see that!" Lady Doyle hastened onto the stage.

It took her all of a second to recognize it.

"You barbarous phoney!" she declared, making a priceless face, for a lady, that is, which sparked tears of hilarity in Bess. "Arthur, she got the photograph from your fairies book, see! Now get this vile exhibitionist out of here!"

Bess applauded, impressed by Lady Doyle's acumen and

loyalty to her husband. These were not the gullible flakes Harry had led her to believe they were. In fact, she knew with certainty as of that moment that she and Lady Doyle could be good friends. And she'd like that, because Bess had virtually no female friends. Her lifestyle had never allowed for it.

Madame Vastayana was outraged. Her temper flared. She smacked Lady Doyle across the face. Sir Arthur tried to restrain the two from utter fisticuffs. In the process, either he or Lady Doyle managed to rip the sari from the Madame's body. Hundreds of pictures flashed from the shooting gallery as the Indian princess fled for the high mountains in disgrace.

Harrington was bowled over. They all were. Amy gazed at Thomas. He turned his face away from the Himalayan sex goddess.

"Next!" Harrington shouted, with a hearty good laugh. "And don't be so easily fooled, gentlemen. Journalism, like science, is about restraint, not euphoria." He winked at the laughs-mongering press and coughed a smoker's cough.

It was one o'clock by the time Hegdish and Mutzel, Josey and Louisa Margarita had been devastated onstage. By this time Houdini had already had lunch at the hotel and fully gone over in his mind the prank he was about to perpetrate. The reporters and committee members had also broken for a meal, deli takeout for the scientists—pastrami on rye, pickles, chips, all wrapped in newspaper, and jugs of root beer.

At the Hotel de la Republic, Houdini took his call, relayed by the concierge in the lobby.

"Okay. Massy's just walked onto the stage," Bess said, speaking from a phone in the lobby of the Masonic Hall.

Houdini went to work. First he called Massy's accomplice, feigning his best insane asylum voice.

An older man picked up. "Hello, Baker?"

"Yeah, it's me. You got the apparatus all set?"

"She's hot."

"Okay then. Here's the message the Reverend wants tele-photographed. Got a pen? Good, write it down, as follows, 'If there's a hell, I guess that's where I'm headed, thanks to Houdini.' You got that?"

"You sure about this?" the man asked, seeming to be perplexed.

"That's what he asked for. And one more thing, you got a picture of Houdini, don't you?"

"Of course, right here."

"That's what I figured. Well, make sure you send it, but sign it first—write, 'All the best, Harry.' Got that?"

Houdini then called the direct line to the Reverend's special table. He heard a click, then could make out the background sounds of the preparation. A reporter had asked Harrington a question; there was the shuffling of casters, the scraping of table legs, seats gathering round, then, "Now we will begin by singing the Lord's Prayer." Houdini put the phone at a distance. The reporters had all opted to take part. The whole Masonic Hall was bellowing with the out-of-tune psalm, the Reverend Z. Massy at the helm.

The Reverend had had the hall completely darkened, following a willful strip search upstairs. He was clean. His table was assessed to be clean. During the loud singing, a message had come to him through the concealed slit on the underside. The photographic paper was of a papyrus sort, ancient-looking. On it read the words *"Ehrich, vielleicht wann du zuruck kommst, bin ich nicht hier."*

The Reverend threw up his hands, admitted to a revelatory sensation, then dropped the message, which—he emphasized—had come to him from the spirit of Harry Houdini's dead mother.

Without hesitating, the Reverend turned over the message to the committee and thanked them all, explained that he was confident about winning and that the prize money should be sent to his legal representative, whose address Dalores Harrington had been given. Then he bid a hasty departure.

A car had come behind the Masonic Hall to fetch Massy. All this time, Houdini was shouting unconvincing obscenities into the telephone, but to no avail—the Reverend had disconnected his table, and his assistant had already rolled it away into the waiting vehicle.

As Houdini ranted and raved in the pay phone at the hotel, Nina Rafaella, restless for her turn to begin, had wandered downstairs on her way over to the hall, having just consumed two bacon, lettuce and tomato sandwiches heaped in mayonnaise, and a goodly portion of chilled Vodka.

She immediately recognized Houdini, grasped that he was up to his usual no good—for such no good was famous among those of her kind—and proceeded with a little help to work her own mischief by causing the phone booth to rattle. There is no telling how she managed this, and no witnesses actually saw her do it. Let it be known for the record that she *concentrated* on the booth. But this was no ordinary concentration. Rafaella had not become a world-class medium through mere wile and cabal. She most definitely had a way with unseen forces.

Staring from twenty paces, as Houdini carried on oblivious to all but his own delighted trickery, Rafaella somehow managed to get the phone booth to start shaking. It rattled so hard that the glass exploded. Houdini dropped the phone, ducking hard, thinking he'd been fired at by one of Holstein's associates.

"Frank!" Houdini hollered. "Frank, can I come out?"

Frank, surrounded by flushing toilets, his pants down, had heard nothing. By the time he strolled back into the lobby, the "attack" was over, the screaming had died down, Houdini had crawled out of the demolished booth, and Rafaella had moseyed on across the street, dressed to kill. Houdini had never even seen her.

Frank could find no bullet. Nor had anyone on the first floor heard a shot. While the hotel staff swept up the rubble, Frank conferred with Byron and Dexter outside. They'd seen nothing. Then Frank escorted Houdini across the street.

The committee, meanwhile, was baffled. Doyle, a student

of medieval letters—having written several historical romances—vouched for the authenticity of the parchment.

Houdini made his triumphant entrance at last.

"Ahhh! Houdini!" Harrington roared. "Welcome, the Great, the Only Harry Houdini!"

There was cheering.

"Sir Arthur Conan Doyle . . . Harry Houdini!" Harrington said, by way of formal introduction for all to see.

"Nice to see you again," Houdini uttered sharply with a hint, missed by all but Lady Doyle and Bess, of derision. "How's business!"

The press laughed.

"Business was never better!" Doyle replied with a hearty pat to Houdini's shoulder.

"Smile, you two!" the pressman Simpson said.

It normally took something like boiling water to get Houdini to smile. But there it was, devilish, exaggerated, sure of his success. He was about to rub Doyle's nose in defeat.

Cameras flashed as the two celebs stood side-by-side, Doyle's arm around his compatriot, whose own monkey appendages hung wanly and unaffiliated. Doyle was clad in a dark, conservative, Saville Row twilled fabric. He could not have struck more of a contrast, a colossus of a man beside Houdini, who came up to his shoulders. Appareled in badly wrinkled, nondescript white cotton jacket and pants, both too short for him, city-slicker black shoes, shiny black socks, also wrinkled, and a dented Panama hat, Houdini looked better suited for strutting down Coney Island with his girl than the present situation.

"Hold it one more time now . . ."

The flashes ricocheted like fireworks, to punctuating puffs of smoke, snapping and clicking Kodaks, harried, scoop-driven pens racing and digging against pads, as the mass of reporters and the three radio announcers, still going strong, bombarded those seated before them with coverage.

"Well where is he?" Houdini asked.

Everyone looked at Houdini. Bess was not sure what to make of the goings-on.

"I suppose you're referring to the Reverend Massy?" Doyle said with an odd note.

"That's right."

Frank, who'd come in with Houdini, was peering around, searching for the table.

"You must have gotten the message," Houdini continued.

"They got a message all right," Harrington said, his nerves wearing thin in the discombobulation of the moment. "Show it to him."

Doyle handed Houdini the cryptic message. It was not what Houdini expected.

"Ehrich, vielleicht wann du zuruck kommst, bin ich nicht hier." He pronounced the words out loud.

Bess nearly fainted.

Houdini's voice cracked. "But I don't understand . . ."

"It means 'Perhaps when you come back I shall not be here,' " Shleihauffen said.

Houdini knew what the words *really* meant. They were the last thing Houdini's mother had ever spoken to him, on the docks in New York harbor, as he and Bess boarded the *Kronprinzessin Cecilie* for Copenhagen, July 8, 1912.

He'd afterward written that fateful sentence in his diary. Nobody but Bess could have ever known . . .

Doyle, with his overbearing trenchant gaze, sensed that something extraordinary had occurred.

10

The Breaking Storm

The Harringtons throw a party and lightning strikes . . .

It was 5:30 in the early evening. Bess finished getting dressed. The knockout touches were harder to confirm at her middle age, but she still commanded attention at parties. Her blue eyes and fair skin lit up beneath the diaphanous veils and satins, and her physique still drew in the younger male lookers.

Houdini checked that his diaries were safely concealed in the vault. It had a lock that only Houdini would ever know how to open. He thumbed through the pages of the 1912 volume, to July 8, to see if there had been any monkey business. He could detect no invasion. Houdini rarely moved the dated volumes, of which there were over two dozen, out of the safe. His working volume he usually kept under the bed.

Bess turned from her makeup table, perplexed. "What do you make of the Reverend?" she queried her husband.

Houdini motioned for Bess to join him in the bathroom. She got up and came over.

"Close the door."

"Why are you whispering?" she asked.

"There could be a spy. Sweetheart, we've got to be careful. Massy had to have gotten that information from someone close in."

"Who?" she pondered, glancing all around the bathroom for some hidden eavesdropping device. There were a dozen "close-in" associates—detectives, bookkeeper, lawyer, engineering assistants, the librarian, cook, driver . . .

Houdini didn't even want to commit to speculation out loud. "I don't know . . ."

She silently mouthed the word "Frank?"

Houdini shook his head with a pang of incredulity. "No."

They went back out into the living room. Dexter was there, sitting quietly on one of four white velvet sofas, going over the upcoming schedule. It couldn't be Dexter, Houdini thought, hardly glancing at the young man, uncomfortably aware of his manifest suspicions. Dexter, who couldn't even grow a beard yet, had worked his way up the Houdini hierarchy devotedly for several years. Someday it was his goal to manage the Waldorf-Astoria. That kind of aspiration was not given to stealth or to crime.

Houdini was leaving for a three-week western tour in two days, to California and Colorado. Dexter was chiefly responsible for all of the personal details, coordinating local managers, hotels, performance times, the leasing of cars, the prebooking of train seats and excess baggage space. There'd be eight people going—Houdini and Bess, Thomas, Dexter, Frank and Byron, Joe and Royale.

"You ready?" Houdini asked.

"The big car's out front. I went and filled it," Dexter said.

It was the boat-backed Opel 8, Houdini's special evening car. Three years old. Painted silver. Dexter loved to drive it, with its 2.2-litre side-valve engine, four-speed gearbox and transmission brake, and shaft-drive. Houdini had shipped it back from London.

"Frank and Byron go home?"

"Frank's still pursuing that Ginger Riddles dame. I think he's interested in her. And Byron—I don't know where Byron went."

It was Byron's night off. The other detectives, chosen by Frank, sat in two respective unmarked black vehicles out on the street, on either side of the Houdini estate, keeping twenty-four-hour watch. It cost Houdini a total of sixty dollars a week for the extra security. He could afford it.

Neither of them ever came in the house.

"Sal, make sure you give Shalom lots of scampi. It's Saturday night," Houdini reminded her, passing by the kitchen, where their black housekeeper stood preparing food for herself and the librarian, MacIntosh. She knew, of course, that the Houdinis were eating out tonight.

Houdini discounted the possibility of treachery on the part of MacIntosh. The elderly librarian was as faithful and nose-to-the-grindstone as his Harvard pedigree suggested. He was an archivist with a knowledge of cuneiform, as well as the *Egyptian Book of the Dead*—in the original.

But Sal was a different kettle. Houdini paid her ten dollars a week, plus room and board. She had full access to all parts of the house. Though he could think of no reason why Sal of all people would double-cross him, he now realized that he and Bess would have to watch her.

Dexter drove the Houdinis and Thomas to Ralph and Dalores Harrington's penthouse apartment east of Central Park, near 72nd Street. Harrington was throwing a small dinner party to inaugurate the contest. Jet-black clouds gathered around the skyline. Houdini heard on the radio that storms were gathering all across America, twenty-two hundred lightning bolts counted in one day in the state of Missouri.

And in Beaumont, Texas, telephone girls had gone to work in bathing suits when nearly fourteen inches of rain fell in just three hours, a new U.S. record.

Stanford White had designed the elegant edifice adjacent to the Harringtons' building, whose scenery had, in turn, been long before implemented by Frederick Law Olmsted. Compared to White's restrained and classic architecture, the semi-skyscraper in which the Harringtons dwelt was retrograde and freakish, combining the High Victorian picturesque of the turn of the century with a little bit of fake Moorish, fake Gothic and poorly done Jugendstil.

The park, which had seen three brutal rape-murders just that month, all three victims non–English-speaking girls, was littered with debris, as well as signs commending chewing gum, "Cheap Eats and Drinks," "Why Not a Kelly Car?" "Best Sausage From Wiecskesza," "Syrup of Figs" and Equipolitan Insurance. The signs blew and whinnied in the fast-arriving storm. Rain now pelted the street. The Houdinis slipped out of the car under the protection of the frayed awning at the entrance to the Harringtons'.

The doorman pointed to the elevator. The ornately configured glass box allowed for few people, who were shut in by an accordion of bare steel bands. Professor Shleihauffen, Amy and Barkwaithe had also just arrived. Amy and Thomas, who had rather noticed each other earlier that day, greeted, shook hands professionally and stood close together.

"You two've met," Houdini said, managing a fatherly grin.

Thomas tried to breathe silently. Amy fiddled with her heel in her shoe and tried not to focus on her perfume, which was possibly too heavy.

The box lurched, then slowly rose, with a creaking lack of resolve, via cables and pulley to the sixteenth floor. There was thunder outside.

The Harringtons' butler took coats. Dalores Harrington, in sequined, slinky, emerald return-to-Nature lizard, smoking a long Belgian cigarette in a platinum holder, two days back from her upstate nudist colony, where she'd taken hydrostatic and mud cures, and a little coal-tar derivative, greeted them.

"Why *there* you are, darlings! The Houdinis, yes? How glad I am to see you! I'm Dalores, of course."

Hands were gingerly touched and Thomas Weckstin introduced.

"A pleasure, Thomas," Dalores said, her eyes taken in at once by his strapping youth and good looks.

Barkwaithe, whom Dalores had known for years, introduced the professor.

"Good to see you too," she said courteously, gliding along, ever the attentive hostess, graciously bypassing his impossible Germanic name. She turned her back on Amy, Ralph's ill-concealed obsession. Amy wore a navy blue evening gown of lamé, fitting as snug as a bolster-case. She was used to Dalores's snubs.

The forty-year-old matron now led Bess by the hand, which protruded from a suit of modest white foulard, and left the entrance vestibule for the living room, where the rest of the dozen odd guests stood snacking on a peculiar concentration of Liederkranz canapés, pickled shrimp, log cabin cheese straws, tongue in spicy aspic and the usual party assortment with pâté de foie gras, pimento, grated eggs and caviar. All the other committee members were there, as well as the Doyles, Bertram Fennell and a few close friends of the Harringtons' to whom they wished to show off. In addition, Harrington had invited the reporter Simpson, not wanting to miss out on any possibility for press. Bess stared momentarily at the big-busted ladies in their salacious chiffons and varicolored jewels. She noticed the discordant and eclectic design of the room, miniature rusticated obelisks and wrought-iron grilles dating back to some historical French period of a Louis.

Two identically liveried footmen in black satin waistcoats, trousers and coats silver-buttoned served everyone various recondite shrubs and bounces to drink. The scent of cinnamon and Bordeaux filled the yellow room. Bess noticed that nearly every last detail in the rotunda-shaped eclectic Moresque room, from the out-of-place gilt cherubs, onyx tiles and silk tassels to the needlework panels, was yellow. The chatter of guests somehow defused the glare.

"Houdini, wonderful!" Harrington shouted across the room. "You must have brought the weather."

The publisher and his committee had seen some inexplicable phenomena, but they were not evenly divided in their opinion and nothing that had occurred was sufficient to weigh them in favor of an affirmative judgment thus far. Houdini betrayed no setback, even if he had been privately shaken, his mother's Yiddish rumbling in his gut.

Doyle, who stood beside his wife in her summer drape of cool satin, felt differently. Massy, to his way of thinking, had hit a crucial and sensitive spot in Houdini. He'd seen it in Houdini's eyes, the way he seated himself, catching his breath with the papyruslike message in his just-trembling hands.

Doyle watched the agile trickster saunter down the two steps into the slightly sunken room while thunder serenaded his advance. The two men connected for an instant. Houdini dressed sparingly, in night-blue ribbed rayon and a tie of plain white lawn. Doyle stood his own double-worsted ground, with the exception of the cuffed trousers, which did not quite work. There was more mud in Sussex, of course. He sported a little flare, too, figured brocade and dark butterflies here and there in his tie.

"Well, well, you made it through," Doyle said.

"Excuse me?"

"You looked disoriented this afternoon. I sense that the medium struck a profound truth."

"No. You're wrong. The guy struck out. The message was total nonsense!" Houdini seethed inside.

"You speak of it with an obvious personal anger," Doyle replied. He knew how to harass a point politely.

"Frauds disgust me."

"You're quite sure he was a fraud?"

"Sir Arthur, maybe they buy that horse manure in England. New York knows crime when it sees it."

"With the highest crime rate of any city in the world, I'm sure you're correct about that, Mr. Houdini."

"And most of them are spiritualists like yourself," Houdini asserted.

"Gentlemen," Harrington broke in, a Kentucky mint julep in one hand and a conciliatory arm around Houdini.

Doyle, not in the least daunted by his early run-in with Houdini, soon captured the attention of all those present. Glancing at his apparent adversary, he ranged across the moment, intent upon the fixing in time of a significant argument.

"I define a skeptic as someone who feels that he must count the legs of a centipede."

Bess laughed. She got it. Houdini did not.

"So what's that supposed to mean?" he said reproachfully.

Doyle looked to those with knowing smiles for encouragement.

"Spiritualism begins where science has become vulnerable and impotent," he stated with resolving power, his intense and paternalistic posturing singly devoted to the cause of winning over the recalcitrant magician.

Harrington grinned. The other committee members drew near.

"I thought you *were* a scientist," said Houdini sharply.

"I was. In a sense I still am. But in between, I saw the light."

"What light is that, Sir Arthur?" Harrington inquired.

He drew in his breath and tightened his belt. Lady Doyle leaned away. She knew an anecdote was coming and looked to Bess, who stood near her, for female commiseration. Both wives were already talking the same language.

"Gentlemen, I am a Scot, as you know. In Scotland our highest summit is Ben Nevis, an icy, stormy peak which years ago attracted my fellow countryman, a chap named Wilson. The strange lighting effects common to Ben Nevis inspired Wilson to embark upon a major photographic study of minutiae—raindrops, dust, and particles in clouds. Wilson's goal was to photograph the unknown. There was a physicist named Thomson who at the time was investigating electrons and so he asked Wilson to try his hand at photographing one." Doyle drank from his glass and looked around the room for any corroborative signs from the guests. None seemed to know the story, so he went on. "Now by definition an electron, as I understand it, is negatively charged, a void, that which isn't. But Wilson had faith—not in his apparatus, but in his *idea*. He created a fog chamber and—lo and behold!—was able to capture the mysterious trail of electrons through the microscopic ether. He got a Nobel Prize for that and yet it was only the beginning. Wilson then developed these peculiar fog-track pictures of helium, of helium atoms which he'd managed to catapult at colossal speeds through gaseous nitrogen. And there, seen recorded on the photographic plate, was something even smaller than an electron, a particle that was essentially invisible, eternal; something that could deflect a tidal wave of electrons traveling at seventeen thousand miles per second. What was it?"

"Hydrogen," the Lubbockian physicist Timothy Crowded countered with a suggested ennui. "The most common element in the universe."

Crowded's cleverness was intended to carry the authority of the mundane.

"Correct. But do not overlook the broader point," Doyle proffered. "Science struggles to weigh an electron. But in the end, on the edge of the invisible, emerges unexpected substance, reality, traces of a new world. The founding father of your very discipline, Sir Isaac Newton, intelligently grasped what I am saying to you now. *Optiks*, if an old man's memory serves him correctly. Query number 30: 'Are not gross Bodies and Light convertible into one another?' " Doyle toasted with his glass.

In Houdini's mind, the gesture resembled a toast to arrogance, to the suffocating pomposity of British air in the room.

Houdini's nervous energy bounded with ridicule. He was out of his collegiate league and didn't care. He plowed through the hors d'oeuvres instead.

Ever the sportsman, Doyle recognized the yards he'd acquired and the defensive positions that his peers had been forced to take up.

"What's your point, Doyle?" Houdini blurted derisively.

"God has always spoken through faith, belief, miracle. Microscopes, cameras, test tubes and chemistry labs are merely the humble tools of an impulse, of a human *instinct* that far outweighs the technology; spiritual revelation which cares nothing for sulphates of sodium or airplanes. I quote *Romans* and *Corinthians*, 'Through mighty signs and wonders and miraculous deeds, comes the power of the Spirit.' "

Lady Doyle lowered her eyes. Bess squinted after her in a grin. God if I had to put up with *that*, she thought, her heart going out to the dutiful British wife.

Amy, meanwhile, juggled her own inner directives, from the mentor of her dreams to Thomas.

Houdini swayed impatiently. Harrington gave his wife a look.

"On that note, ladies and gentlemen . . ." and Dalores proceeded to ring a little pewter server bell a footman had just provided her.

The crowd headed for the blue room to dine. Everything, or nearly everything, save the food, was in blue, from gardenias to a Persian rug. Houdini led the troupe. The table was a modern, well-bred and expedient spread. There were chafing dishes with lit lamps underneath for the oysters, chicken gumbo simmering inside a sterling tureen, three enormous platters of roast duck in currant sauce with wild rice sauté, croutards of sweetbreads and potato croquettes, a minimalist alligator pear salad to round it off and pumpkin pie with

American cheese, followed by demitasse and liqueurs from Canada.

The Doyles consumed their meal prongs down, while Bess and Houdini were zigzag eaters, employing their forks and spoons with haphazard, free-for-all efficiency. Throughout the meal, Houdini kept hammering on Doyle, skewed and driven by the deceit that had somehow been perpetrated over the grave of his beloved mother earlier in the day. Houdini would brook no overture to his mother. Wounds caused by previous quacks, regarding her state of being in so-called "Summerland," had not healed. Doyle fought back, confidently launching, upon questioning from the pressman Simpson, into an intimate portrait of the afterlife, exactly as it had been communicated to him by various spirits and mediums.

In and out of these heated exchanges, Amy and Thomas Weckstin, who'd been seated together, shared more than a few looks. When Amy passed him the salt, he took her hand rather than the shaker, and commented on the lovely lines of her fingers. Her own pleasure amazed her.

"And what about sex in the afterlife?" Thomas said, picking up from the Scotsman's unabashed admission that cigar smoking and whiskey were not forbidden to souls upstairs.

Amy and Dalores seemed to hang on the prospect, while Lady Doyle tended to shrink. As for Bess, like her husband, she found such badinage to be utterly absurd.

"Everything I've learned indicates that lust is no longer an impediment up there," he began.

"Excuse me, Sir Arthur. When was lust *ever* an impediment?" Simpson egged.

"In Summerland, there are more important matters," Doyle informed him.

"And what of the beautiful, the sensuous, all that is female in the world?" Thomas added.

"Her beauty is not interrupted," Doyle offered for the benefit of ladies present. "Woman is woman, every muscle, bone, soft beam and elliptical curve. Her grace and charm are only amplified in Heaven!"

"The young man asked about sex," Simpson repeated.

"No," Doyle said with finality.

"In that case," Dr. Grundranvodst said, singularly mired until this time in his own illegal beverage, and contemplating a Heaven with no sex, "I must fall in behind Professor Huxley, who once remarked that 'the only good thing I can see in demonstrating the truth of spiritualism is to furnish an additional argument against suicide.' "

Doyle, who had suffered every share of rebuttal and scorn over the years was not about to be outdone. He enlarged upon the Icelandic professor's quip by citing the poet— Oscar Wilde, he thought—who'd alleged that 'Being dead is the most boring experience in life, that is if one excepts dining with a schoolmaster."

"Touché!" Harrington seconded.

Everybody laughed.

"You really believe there's life after death?" Houdini asked Doyle point-blank.

"Yes," replied Doyle. "You will too, someday. If you ever let down your defenses. In fact, Houdini, you are living proof."

"Oh really? Be specific."

"In London, I saw you pull needles from your mouth. It was no trick."

"It *was* a trick," declared Houdini.

"And I suppose your emergence from the river in Pittsburgh, after being submerged under ice for over ten minutes, was also a trick? For God's sakes man, the press had pronounced you dead! How can you continue to deny the obvious? You are a world leader. We need you. Confess!"

Bess withheld her jocosity. "You don't know my husband, Sir Arthur. He's not the type to give confession."

"I can see that," Doyle deferred warmly.

"Hell, I've stayed under for ninety minutes. Also a trick," Houdini went on.

"As a medical doctor I can assure you that the *trick* was on *you*! You can fool the multitudes, perhaps, but you can't fool me, Harry. And you can't fool this committee. Your powers speak for themselves. What you call a stunt, an escape, a sleight-of-hand, I call being in touch with the divine."

"I know. And I pity you for your gullibility."

"Why don't we all move back out into the yellow room?" Dalores suggested.

"Good idea, dear!" Harrington said, getting up from the table with a hearty grunt.

Houdini asked everyone to gather near. "Let me prove my point as graphically as I can," he began. "Thomas, my bag."

Thomas went to the cloakroom and retrieved the small carrying case.

"Now everyone watch very, very carefully," Houdini started.

He took out a small piece of smooth slate in which had been bored two small holes. He produced from the bag two wires, four small cork balls, a bottle of white ink and a spoon.

"I'd like a volunteer to cut open one of the balls for me, anyone . . ."

Doyle himself stepped forward, seized a random ball, took out his penknife and sliced it in two. He handed the pieces back to Houdini with a quizzical look. "All right?"

"As you can see, there's nothing in the cork balls. The other three are the same. Now, Sir Arthur, if you please, dip the three balls in the ink."

Doyle did so. Houdini asked for a newspaper and laid the balls on top of it on the floor. He then went to the chandelier and hung the slate from it by the two wires, which he configured and tied through the holes on either end of the stone. It hung at eye level with Doyle.

"Now, Sir Arthur, I'd like you to take the elevator down to the ground floor, secretly write out a message, a word, anything, on a slip of paper—your own paper, with your own pen—then stuff that slip of paper in your vest pocket and come on back up here."

Doyle did so. Five minutes later he returned. The paper, with a message written upon it, was in Doyle's shoe, though he didn't tell Houdini that.

Houdini now asked Doyle to select one of the three inked cork balls. Houdini then held the ball in the spoon and pressed its spherical upper surface against the flat bottom portion of the hanging slate.

"Now behold!"

Houdini carefully rolled the ball along the bottom of the slate, and as he did so, magically, a set of incomprehensible words appeared, which all could easily decipher: Mene, mene, tekel, upharsin.

Doyle looked at his wife, then sat down.

"What does it mean?" Amy asked Houdini.

Houdini turned to Doyle for the answer.

Astounded, Doyle reached into his shoe, brought out the slip of paper and opened it for everyone present. *Mene, mene, tekel, upharsin.*

A dull, painful caesura engulfed the entire living room.

"I don't believe this," someone said with a swoon.

Doyle uttered a flabbergasted expletive.

"I never saw that one," Bess remarked offhandedly to Thomas. "What's it mean?" Her hand just slightly quavered.

Thomas shook his head.

"It is a twenty-five-hundred-year-old Babylonian alchemical cipher, a formula for turning excrement into gold."

"Really?" Houdini said, feigning fascination.

"How did you know it?" Doyle demanded.

Houdini stood silently with a deceptive look on his face, a trickster's trademark of a visage.

Doyle tried to see through Houdini's slyness, for surely if there were ever the proof that Doyle had insisted upon, it was here, now, out in the open for all to see. A profound opportunity.

"Hidden mirrors," Houdini remarked.

"Show us, then!" Doyle insisted.

"Actually, it was mind control," Houdini added.

"You would still deny your miraculous powers?" Doyle said. He was frustrated. The opportunity was slipping by.

"It was no miracle, Doyle. Genius, perhaps!"

"I'll ask you one more time: how did you do it?"

"Be a sport, Harry. It will never leave this room. All agreed?" Harrington pressed.

"No," said Houdini resolutely. "I just wanted to prove a point: it is easy to be tricked by so-called spiritual mysteries. If the ladies will pardon me, you might think you're seeing shit turned into gold. But in actual fact, the words also come from the Book of Daniel," Houdini reminded them all. "They mean, 'You have been weighed in the balance and found wanting.' "

"You must admit it was one hell of a trick," Shleihauffen said.

"Damn right," Houdini puffed. "One of the best. And if it had been my calling to claim divine powers, I'm sure I could pull it off and you'd all fall for it. I'd be hailed the new King of Jerusalem. It's really funny! No, it's actually pathetic. It makes me sick. Wake up, people! You're so deep in this malarkey, you can't see straight!"

"Harry, stop it!" Bess shouted.

"The committee decided," Harry said to Doyle, coming down off his temper as quickly as he had risen. "And they simply don't believe you. You will be demolished in the next round. You ought to quit while you still have your dignity."

"You baffle me," Doyle said, unaffected by a little pugnacity.

"I baffle me," Houdini crowed. "But if I were really the King of Jerusalem . . ." and he considered his words. "There'd be sparks, real sparks. None of this childish paper-and-ink chicanery."

Everyone in the room turned. There was a draft. The window swung open. Doyle looked at his wife. There was something—undefinable—static . . . suction . . .

"Ohhh dear. . . .," a voice called out.

"Pheneas?" Lady Doyle inquired hesitantly.

Houdini dove to the floor. And at that moment a mighty burst of lightning broke over Manhattan. The ladies caterwauled.

The flash came in horizontally, thick and jagged, miles long, illuminating the sides of every building from midtown to Harlem. Houdini saw it squarely in a mirror from the floor.

Bad luck, he thought, as the concussion of thunder accompanied the light.

"My God, it hit the park!" someone cried.

The guests all hesitated, frozen silly.

"Don't go near the windows!" Dalores howled emphatically.

"Jesus. . .," Harrington hooted.

The suction ceased.

Now everyone contravened logic, flocking to the window to see the blaze. A rustic wooden dwelling far below, one of several sylvan blights, had burst into flames.

"It's about time that was taken down," Harrington said, toasting to the shanty's demise. It didn't occur to him that there was a family living in there.

The sound of fire trucks could soon be heard arriving in the rain.

"He said, 'real sparks'! Houdini said the King of Jerusalem would show us *real sparks!* Now please, Houdini, be reasonable, man. *What is going on!*" Doyle importuned.

Lady Doyle sat silent and isolated. She hadn't counted on anything like this. By second sight her husband felt it too. In Lady Doyle's mind, entangled in the skein and overlap of her hearing mechanism, the voice of Pheneas quivered and sighed . . . *It's him . . . He's the one, all right!*

Houdini was caught in a moment of rare abandon. The fire and brimstone had perfectly articulated his anger. The fury was his own. Just then, he could believe his own publicity. He hated everything that Doyle stood for.

He wanted them to see that he was—for all of his spectacular artistry—merely a man. And being so, so terribly ordinary, made him even more amazing. And someday he would
be buried beside his mother, and Bess too, the three of them
in humble, earth-renewing soil. He wanted no part of
Heaven, no group therapy of the beyond. He wanted to get
the hell out of New York. *Let them see the truth,* he raged inside.

"I will stop the rain," he boldly announced.

"Huh?" Bess muttered.

Doyle grinned appreciatively. Houdini was coming
through, he thought; he must be ready to admit everything.

Houdini walked to the window, opened it to the wind and
rain and danger of destruction. Everyone gathered around
him, bracing for the unknown.

"Now listen up, rain. I command you to stop. And I give
you thirty seconds to heed my warning, or else!" he shouted.

Bess couldn't believe her husband was blowing it like
this. Doyle's mouth remained open, tentative. Scientific eye-
brows were uniformly suspicious.

Then, one of the most peculiar and misappropriated events in Houdini's life occurred . . .

The rain miraculously ceased, just like that, not ten seconds after Houdini's command. The rain and the wind, as
well as the last dying rumble of thunder, vanished. The sun-
set just managed to poke through a layer of otherwise impen-
etrable electric storm, as the fire raged below. Seconds
passed. The clouds swirled centrifugally. A sunspot grew
larger in the sky. The weather quickly dissipated above Central Park, after hours of downpour.

"My God!" Lady Doyle said out loud.

Expressions blanched. Sir Arthur, pale, credulous,
squirming with excitement, made for Houdini and embraced
him with the ferocity of old reunion.

"I knew it! By jove I *knew* it!"

Houdini gave him the cold shoulder.

Harrington, tipsy enough for the miracle to have been diluted, put down his glass. He confronted Houdini. "That's a good trick, old boy. But I wouldn't call it religious, unless of course you were also able to make it start raining all over again."

Doyle studied Houdini. The magician stepped again to the window, a figure of immutable force unto itself, arms, fingers, stretched to the limit, like Joshua commanding the sun to stand still, above the park where the fire burned and the trees glistened in the damp stillness. Clouds churned above.

Houdini heard his blood coursing through his forearms.

Doyle heard the same pounding, felt a union and started to rise up on his toes. Lady Doyle also felt something—the whimsy, the improbability of the moment as Houdini delayed, longer and longer.

No one stirred. A brief spell passed, the clouds continued to race overhead outside, throwing shadows across a decorative panel by Vuillard, two rearing Chinese horses in jade and an icon from Kiev, all along the Harringtons' rear wall.

Houdini closed his eyes, and spoke: "The Great Houdini now demands rain, *rain*!"

There was an instant of nothingness. Harrington reached for his glass.

The light—burnt, blitzing, too sudden.

Then—*crrraaaackkkk!*

The ladies and men all shrieked; some fell down, overwhelmed. The lightning smashed somewhere in the skies with a compliant ferocity that threw Houdini back away from the window. The shutters convulsed, then slammed shut with the menacing force of atmospheric suction in the room. Just as suddenly a downpour raged, adamantine, wrathful, all at once. The sky had closed in on cue.

"It's hail!" Shleihauffen called out in a weak voice.

The golf-ball-sized stones broke windows, pummeled car hoods.

"How is it possible?" Harrington said, wriggling for cover below the couch. *I'm finished,* he thought. *Ruined!* And ironically it was because of the *one* man whom he'd counted on to utterly devastate all claims to psychic experience.

Bess walked up to her husband, scared to death. "Harry?" she motioned, probing the faraway eyes.

Once on a bridge, a week after they'd met, still teenagers, he'd insisted that she never expose his one terrible secret. "What secret?" she'd asked timidly, frightened, ready to run away from this strange Jewish kid on the block. Seeing her shy, fleet-footed discomfiture, he had opted then not to say. Now that moment on the bridge returned. Bess repeated her husband's name. "Harry?" She wasn't sure what to believe.

There was great perplexity in the room. The committee members marshaled a host of pressing ratiocinations, none of which actually explained Houdini's phenomenon.

Harrington took Houdini into his bedroom.

"We've got to talk . . . this King of Jerusalem business was not part of the deal. Are you trying to ruin me, or what?"

"Your money's safe, Ralph," Houdini said, more becalmed now. "I'm no rainmaker, trust me. Hell, I can't even get the goddamned plumbing to work in the master bedroom at home. Tomorrow that Nina Rafaella has her turn. You mark my word: she's dead. *Fini!* Like all the others. In the meantime, enjoy the publicity. That's what you asked for, isn't it!"

Houdini paused, shot up with a sudden brainstorm. "I got an idea."

"Now what?"

"How would you like another twenty-five thousand dollars to up the ante?"

"You're not serious?"

"You don't have to mention it's from me since I gather that would come under the category of conflict of interest. You just go out there and tell them that the day's results were so disturbing . . . so . . . unsatisfactory that the stakes are being greatly escalated in hopes of bringing a real spirit out of the woodworks. Something like that. They'll love you, Ralph. That's how much you can count on me. Okay?"

They went back out to the yellow room. Guests were taking their leave. Simpson was just heading out the door. Harrington grabbed him with the added piece of information. The Doyles were delighted.

By morning, Houdini's "miracle" would be front-page news. And according to Simpson's article, if there was anyone who deserved that thirty thousand, it was probably Houdini.

11

The Destruction of Nina

In which a Neapolitan psychic comes to town and has the last laugh . . .

Nina Rafaella struck a forlorn countenance that was accented by her etheric beauty. Some had speculated that the source of this melancholy was her unhappiness at being "inspired." And they were right. What Nina really wanted was a little villa, not fame, a small place, in the Neapolitan quarter of Piedigrotta, beneath the cool forested flanks of the Posilipo, say a smaller version of the Nazionale, a prominent neighborhood manor that had always given over starlight and fantasy to her otherwise impoverished childhood. A few embroidered rooms, a tranquil courtyard in pozzolana stucco, a generous swath of warm soil given to roses, a couple of faithful servants, a manly lover and a sinecured husband—perhaps a successful spaghetti manufacturer or farsighted chief magistrate. This imagined life was more appealing to Nina than the occasional levitation up the slopes of Vesuvius, or making the ancient marble faces of the Farnese collection to weep, both of which she had accomplished according to some, though not according to others. The ambiguity of her alleged psychic powers had fueled both sides of an ongoing scientific debate in Italy.

After leaving home, Nina had remained alone, tormented, branded by the Italian authorities as possessed, caught up in a perpetual road show of blandishments from her disciples in other countries. They came to her to be healed, reconnected with their recently parted. When she wasn't taken ill herself, Nina tended to capitulate. She was weak, needing solace. It wasn't easy being a medium. Imprisoned by this inner turmoil, Nina suffered from an acute nervous disorder, easily triggered by the slightest aggravation, like not getting any mail, the sight of a cooked lobster, losing her earplugs, or having to wait in line. Such neuralgia impeded her psychic gifts and manifested a physical descent into pustular hell. The otherwise beautiful thirty-two-year-old with her fox-gray eyes, dewy, Belleek skin and hayrick-colored hair, became a hideous thing of swollen glands, burning eczema and poison boils. At such times she would become desperate, wearing a mask of the Venetian carnival and resorting to trickery, if need be, to compensate for her diminished psychic abilities.

"No one's forcing you to go through with this," her lawyer advised, sensitive to Nina's painful dilemma. He had before him the paper, with its announcement of a revised thirty-thousand-dollar cash prize from *Scientifica Americana*.

"The spirits *make* me do it," Nina cried resignedly, affixing a black carapace of tough resin and hard papier-mâché to her throat and face. Her eyes peered out at her lawyer.

The phone rang. The lawyer picked up. It was one of her assistants.

"Nina, it's time."

She'd waited two whole days, Sunday having been a day off for the committee and contestants.

She and her lawyer left the hotel suite. It was a sterling clear Monday morning in New York, swept clean by the night's storm. They passed across the lobby, where one of the phone booths was now covered with towels, exited from the hotel and crossed the busy avenue to enter the Masonic Hall. Byron was there standing guard.

"You're one of Houdini's boys, aren't you?" Nina said.

"That's right, ma'am," Byron replied, taking off his hat.

"Good for you," Nina said. She took his hand and shook it, then she put her own hand to her breast as she continued walking.

Byron was impressed by her scintillating getup and intimidating Venetian mask. He noticed the killer diamond on her right hand, easily ten karats. Byron couldn't earn enough money in five lifetimes to buy a broad like Nina.

Inside the Masonic Hall, the committee, Harrington, the Doyles and Houdinis, Amy and Thomas, as well as a horde of reporters, were all gathered and ready to receive the final contestant.

Nina walked onto the floor, dressed in a white garment of tarlatan gauze, hands painted phosphorescent. She removed her shoes.

"Search her," Houdini ordered, deferring to Lady Doyle and Bess. They were authorized by the committee to check for hidden articles. In this, the Houdinis and Doyles were working together as a team, having survived the acrimonious exchanges of the dinner party on Saturday.

"Spare no orifice," Houdini added with relish.

"Please excuse us," Lady Doyle began, as she escorted Nina to a back room. Nina then uncovered her face.

Lady Doyle stepped a pace backward. "Oh, you poor darling. Perhaps my husband could prescribe something?"

"It takes a day or two for the pus to evaporate," Nina replied.

Lady Doyle searched her very quickly and haphazardly.

"Both my husband and I have heard wonderful things about you," the Englishwoman went on.

"And I about you," Nina replied.

"You have all our confidence, my dear . . ."

Meanwhile Houdini and Thomas made a thorough search of Nina's special cabinet, from which she proposed to call forth the spirits. Houdini announced that it gave them no reason for suspicion.

"She's fine," Lady Doyle said in conclusion for everyone present as she brought the Italian medium back out onto the stage.

Houdini and Thomas now tied Nina up in her cabinet, using wet hemp and padlocks.

"No need to break my arms," she said.

Houdini gave some slack. Fishing wire was connected to her limbs and pulled taut, then tied to sensing devices on the outside. Her slightest movement would be duly noted.

Thomas returned to his seat, beside Amy. He knew Nina hadn't a prayer. Nina's two assistants sat down near the committee members, who activated their myriad analytical instruments and assumed their seats beside their respective apparatuses.

Nina then called out, "Okay, I'm on," and asked for the hall to be blackened.

There was silence for three minutes. Suddenly the sounds of "Sambo" could be heard, as done on a harmonica. Scientific needles started shaking in a flurry of response.

Houdini, seated beside his wife, could hardly control himself, while Doyle just smiled.

"I'm picking up a synchronized electrodynamic pulse," Shleihauffen said.

Suddenly, half of the cabinet lit up in the same phosphorescent green as Nina's hands. And now that same half began to rise off the floor.

Houdini stood up, infuriated though perplexed.

"Sit down!" Doyle whispered emphatically.

The cabinet continued to rise, a foot, two feet, until it hovered three feet off the stage, severed in two, leaving a dark identical half on the floor. It was impossible to tell from which half Nina was speaking.

"Initial magnetic interference," Shannon O'Nearly said.

"The same," Timothy Crowded added.

"Dr. Abraham, any oscilloclasms?" Doyle pressed.

"Yes, yes . . . I'm definitely picking up a few ohms of resistance . . . Incredible!"

"Incredible," Doyle repeated.

Now the invisible harmonica played "Little Bright Eyes."

A rash of electronic reactions continued to prick the incredulity of the committee.

"Someone's coming through!" Nina called out excitedly. "He's going to speak in rapping sounds."

Houdini got up and made for the first row of reporters, mumbling something in Simpson's ear. ". . . got it? And pass the word. Quickly!"

A chain reaction of murmurs rippled through the crowded hall of reporters. The one radio commentator covering the event this day informed the untold numbers of listeners that a remarkable levitation was taking place and that Houdini and the press were abuzz with excitement.

"Who's coming through?" asked Doyle.

"Wait . . . wait a minute . . . the name is Sard . . . No, Sardee . . . Sardeen! That's it, Sardeen. He must be a very close friend of Houdini! And he wants to say hello from . . . wait a minute . . . it's coming . . . from a boat on the Amstel River in Amsterdam. That's it. He's on the boat!"

Bess looked at her husband, and both of them cracked up. Hardeen—not Sardeen—was the moniker adopted by Houdini's brother Dash for his own stage routine. At present, he was touring Europe. But he was in Germany, not Holland. He was supposed to have finished his tour of Holland nearly three weeks earlier.

"Ask Sardeen if there's a phone number where Houdini might reach him in the next few minutes," Doyle said, trying to preempt the obvious point of contention on Houdini's part.

"He says he'll be staying at the Imperial Hotel in Berlin as of the fourtee . . . Wait a minute . . . uh . . . Just a second . . . no . . . He says he'll be out in the country for many days. Unreachable. But he wants to say hello. Are you ready, Houdini?"

"Ready!" Houdini shouted. "I love sardeens!"

"He's coming now. Do you hear the telepathic rapping?"

There was a knock.

"No," Houdini said.

"Well I heard it," Doyle admitted.

"As did I," pledged Lady Doyle.

No committee member spoke.

More rapping came, louder this time.

"Do you hear it now?"

"No," cried the audience of reporters.

"But surely that rapping is audible by now?" Nina called out.

"No, *no!*" the audience persisted, though the committee members nodded in the affirmative.

There was a sense of urgency now to the rapping.

"Now see if you can hear it," Nina cried, determined.

"Nothing!" the audience screamed.

"But that's impossible," the frenzied medium hollered. "Are you all deaf?"

Now it sounded like a sledgehammer.

"Still nothing!" the two-hundred-odd reporters howled, many suppressing tears of hilarity. The radio commentator found he too couldn't keep it together.

"This is outrageous!" Doyle upbraided the crowd of conspirators.

"Now!" Houdini called out, grabbing his bag and lunging from his chair.

In the darkness, he and Thomas rushed the cabinet. There was screaming. Someone hit the floor. Clanging could be heard and then—"Houdini, you son of a bitch!"

"Someone get the lights!" Harrington screamed.

A switch was struck and floodlight poured over the whole scene. Houdini was wrestling Nina to the floor.

"My God, man, get off her!" Doyle shouted, flustered.

The whole miracle of levitation had vanished like a candle, snuffed out. In the garish light, the cabinet now sat sprawled open for all to see.

Nina lay on the floor kicking and squirming, a penlight in her hand. Houdini was on top of her.

There had been no levitating half of a cabinet. The effect had been achieved by a one-way mirror not previously detected, which formed the outer wall of the structure.

Houdini confiscated the penlight, then turned to Lady Doyle.

"Did you check her vagina?" Houdini demanded to know.

"I certainly did not!" she declared.

He held up the flashlight for all to see. "Well you should have!"

Emboldened, Houdini ripped Nina's dress off. She struck him in the face. Houdini threatened with his own fist.

"No, Harry!" Bess screamed.

Nina's lawyer ran forward. "Excuse me, I say *excuse me*! Mr. Houdini, unless you want rape and assault charges brought against you . . ."

"Hold your horses, mister. . .," Houdini said, as he continued to hold Nina down, exposing not flesh, but an intricate series of concealed undergarments, each containing devices.

The reporters flashed their cameras in an orgy of exposure.

"And look at this . . . and this . . . and this!"

He struggled to get the paper from Nina's hand.

"Give me that!" he growled.

"Get him off me!" Nina pleaded, holding firmly.

Their tug-of-war resulted in the paper ripping in half. Now Houdini yanked off Nina's mask, exposing a mass of chancres.

Suddenly, he felt a rush of air coming from those running

sores. Her body started to rumble. Houdini froze, crouched over her like a wrestler. The rumble exploded.

"Goddamn you!" she roared, throwing Houdini off with a ferocity that totally broke his own power.

He flew a good ten feet or more through the air, crashing into the huddle of scientists across the stage.

"Huh?" he cried out, astonished.

He started to stand, then fell over, dizzy with what had happened. Bess ran to him.

Nina stood up. Her eyes were on fire. She pointed her finger at Houdini. The finger shook. Her lips drew forward, her chin curled up and her eyes just got more and more fiery red.

"Today you made a big mistake, Mr. Houdini! *Ma va fa in culo!*" she decreed, spitting.

Her paroxysm died down. She put her mask back on her face, half a piece of paper crumpled up in her hand, and walked off the stage. Her lawyer, and two assistants, followed behind.

Houdini stood up. No one else seemed to understand what had really happened. Houdini was speechless. He looked down at the portion of paper in his hand. It was a previously unopened letter from his brother in Europe. Someone had gotten into his study and copped it.

Houdini spent the next ten minutes detailing the Italian medium's carefully plotted deception. There were blades sewn into her clothing, he pointed out, a minute harmonica under her arm, pieces of wire, a flat vial of alcohol, a wire cutter and electrically controlled dice up her drawers. Lady Doyle, he said, had deliberately assisted this fraud in her act to bolster her husband's fast-waning possibilities. But all through his exposé, Houdini trembled in his heart.

She threw me ten fucking feet through the air . . .

The cabinet was seen to possess needles and pistons, he said, a lead hammer, cork, piston guides, threads and hooks and a steel body belt.

"If my wife is guilty of anything," Doyle retorted loudly,

"it is of maintaining decency. Whereas you, sir, are an insult to everyone in this hall."

Houdini grumbled, then appealed gauchely, "It won't work, Doyle. Why don't you go back to looking for fairies under toadstools!"

"I understand," Sir Arthur said, calming down with benign vigor, gentlemanly undeterred. He stepped up to Houdini's open bag. "Now perhaps you'd like to tell us what was in the bag?"

"Well, Houdini?" Harrington asked, unable to avoid the clear suspicion.

Houdini held up a set of keys. "Keys. I thought I'd let the poor bitch out of her padlocks. But it seems she did it for me."

"You needed a bag to hold two keys? Come on, Houdini," Lady Doyle protested.

"Well it also contained this!" Houdini said. He lifted a heavy electrical battery pack. "To test her tomfoolery. I figured there'd be some charged wires and such." He touched two of the hidden wires obtained from the cabinet and they sparked. "You see?"

Doubts were cast.

"You and your assistant checked the cabinet. You gave it a clean slate. We trusted you. I think you've lied, Houdini," Doyle vociferated. "You put those things in there to frame an innocent woman! A woman of renowned powers."

"The hell I did!"

"Gentlemen, gentlemen!" Harrington appealed. "What is this? Come on."

"But the piece de résistance is this," Houdini said, accenting his flourish of French. "A letter. Somebody stole it. From my brother. She got it and she read it and you were all expected to believe that it was a floating spirit that just happened to be in the neighborhood! Right!" Houdini turned away from Doyle in disgust, relishing his victory.

Cameras continued to flash wildly. Harrington grinned. The committee members turned off their equipment.

"Wait a minute," O'Nearly stated for the record, as three pressman shoved themselves in close. "I've got a lingering magnetic interference here." He pointed to one of his devices and scratched his chin.

"I believe it must be Houdini's battery," Crowded said.

"Maybe, maybe not," Grundranvodst added.

Houdini ignored them. "Come to California, boys. That's where I'm headed. To Los Angeles, and Yosemite Valley. That's where the *real* action's going to be!"

"What's in California?" they shouted.

"The most dangerous work of art in my entire career, and, I assure you, it will be a hell of a lot more compelling than these pathetic mountebanks and impersonators you've been eyeing for the last two days."

"Now hold on," Harrington shouted. "This contest is by no means over. Houdini and Doyle are in it all the way to home plate. We're not there, yet. In the hours since the cash prize has been raised, we've gotten hundreds of calls. The phones rang all night at the magazine. Doyle and Houdini will both be appearing in Denver in less than a month. That's where this contest shall be concluded. In the meantime, there are plenty more mediums to screen. *Scientifica Americana* will continue to report any and all progress in the selection process. Daily reports will be given to the papers. You can count on that. And mark my word: there *will be* a final showdown in Denver. The greatest spiritual battle since the Crusaders rode into Turkey, since Galileo battled the Pope."

Harrington continued hyping the coming event three weeks away. Thomas brought Amy over to a quiet corner out of the way of the commotion.

"What are you doing for the rest of the day?" he said, breathless.

Amy was convinced that Nina was no fraud. She knew that Thomas had his own obvious affiliation with Houdini, but that did not stem her budding interest in him. Not in the least. In fact, the tension excited her, gave the prospect a certain spin.

"Whatever you're doing," she said with a winning smile.

Byron drove the Houdinis home, where they spent the afternoon packing for their trip. While he bided time in his usual quarters, a sort of guard cabin adjoining the driveway, Joe and Royale assembled all the gear and took it down to the train station. There was a new addition to the usual tonnage: a wire mesh cage and a thick rope braided with a long dynamite fuse.

Bess prepared an elegant eggplant casserole, which she and Houdini ate by candlelight. Houdini drank water. Bess had some classic Chianti. Then they made love. Houdini's agility always lent such intimate moments a degree of unexpected exertion, or position, or finale, which Bess looked forward to throughout her life. She knew—not just in her head—that she was sexually blessed and often wondered what women saw in any other man.

They lay curled around each other at the far end of the bed. Bess noticed a new bruise on Houdini's elbow.

"Harry," she said.

"Huh?"

"You flew through the air on the stage. Did you happen to notice that?"

Houdini didn't say anything.

"Well I found it rather peculiar myself." Bess was trying to downplay the event without ignoring what was so remarkably obvious. "How'd you fly ten feet, Harry?"

He still didn't speak, looking toward the bathroom with an angry assault on the empty air.

"Harry?" she repeated, not wishing to be a nag, but not about to ignore the obvious discrepancy in reality that she knew he too had experienced.

He smashed his fist against the headboard. "How do I know how I flew ten—or was it fifteen—goddamn feet . . . Goddammit! She catapulted me, she pushed me, I don't know, that's how!"

Bess turned away, closed her eyes and took a gulp of nerves. "Jesus, Harry."

After a few minutes Harry turned over. "There was something. . .," he muttered.

"What?"

"I don't know."

"What something?"

"I don't know! There was something, all right?"

Bess didn't say anything.

Harry's voice got dreamy and unconnected. He lay propped up on three pillows, staring up at the white ceiling with the gold Viennese trimming.

"I've always wanted to be able to fly like that . . . ten feet, hell, five feet would have done it for me. I mean to break free. But you can't. You can't break free. The harder my escapes, the more I understand that. If I could, then I would: I'd break free forever. I held onto that possibility once. Now I know better."

She took his hand and looked at him. "We're going to California and you're going to finish a wonderful movie," she said. "It *is* wonderful, you know?" He'd worried about it and she had tried, as was usual between them, to bolster his confidence.

"You haven't even seen it."

"I've seen enough of it."

"I'm forty-nine years old, Bess."

"That's young."

He paused, contemplating. "Forty years ago I got a job in a circus. There was a monkey screeching his head off. The organ grinder had the leather straps too tight around its head, I think. I wanted to free that monkey but I was afraid that the terrible man would hit me. You know I was only nine and this guy he was huge and grizzled. And I was also afraid the monkey might blame me and bite off my fingers. It screeched unrelentingly. It was horrible and a month or two passed and the poor thing died. He poured kerosene all over it and burned it to a crisp, then tossed it in the local river. I think he truly hated that monkey because people liked the animal more than they liked him. It was the monkey that passed the hat around and got the money."

Bess lay there holding her man, stroking the back of his neck.

"I should have saved it."

"You were nine years old."

"I still hear it, Bess. And the calliope and the meandering crowds, mostly bored, from act to act, fat lady to he-man. Pickpockets, fire swallowers, human sewing machines, one guy who could drive a nail through two-inch planks of hardwood with his teeth. They were all wonderful, desperate nobodies. I knew it even then."

"What did you do?"

"I was bait for the lions."

"No."

"Yes. Tigers too. They're weirder. You can't really trust them. Later, I did rope tricks. I got a nickel a night. I remember seeing lovers strolling. Summer evening after evening. Little squirts, my age, making mischief. Throwing things at me. Fireflies and crickets. And cleaning up at one in the morning, then tiptoeing into my room so as not to wake Mom and Dad. Those summers are one summer. All those nights one night. And you know what, Bess?"

"What?"

"Nothing ever happened worth remembering. For three years. Then I ran away. New crowds, new lovers strolling, new crickets. It's all a blur. Remember me, then? Fresh and green. Nothing in my head. A few tricks and slippery cotter pins and jerry-rigged padlocks to my credit. Like I'd been born the day we met. Thirty years ago."

"I thought you knew the world, then. You were so mature. You were a big city boy. Smart. Handsome. You had twenty dollars. You were rich."

"You were pretty dumb."

"I was not. I was in love. I still am." She rested her head on his stomach.

She had other visions of their past, less self-damaging.

She could never quite reach the center of his darkness. She cleaned off the blood, but did not bleed; she rubbed the tiger balm into damaged muscle, but caught only the odor, none of the agony. Bess took home the glory. She remembered Paris most of all. That was always her favorite. Harry became so mild in Paris, confirming every romantic cliché known to the city.

She recalled a château of gray sandstone out in the country, beyond the blossoming almond and jacaranda trees, the slate roofs, the pagodas overlooking the parterres, the ingenious jets and granite cupids peeing into reflecting ponds. There were two little girls, preschoolers, in white petticoats, prancing and tumbling over the wild marsh grass that bordered a rippling lake. A refreshing west wind dusted the bonnets of the women who'd come to the sprawling estate for an intimate picnic with the famous Americans. Houdini was the rave of Paris. Bess remembered the women's thin arms, tied in expensive lace, their delicate hands raised into the moisture-laden air. Pastel skies. Walls inside the château painted by Delacroix. That's how Bess took home the experience, whereas her husband returned to New York focused on a damaged kidney, a cracked rib, a broken tooth and water in his lungs.

"What is it, Harry? What's wrong?"

He looked at her. She used to be such a freshly plucked virgin. "I look backwards and there's nothing there."

"You're being dramatic." She didn't know what to say.

"I mean it . . . What do I have?"

"What do you have? What don't you have? You want me to scratch your back?"

"I'm destitute."

"Why is it every time we make love you say you're destitute and start talking like a corpse?"

"I never said destitute before."

"No? Well then it was some other word. Depressed, maybe. Or forlorn. You're always depressed after we make love."

"It has nothing to do with that."

"Well what does it have to do with?"

"Bess, why do you love me?. . . I mean it, tell me. What will anyone remember about me?"

Bess reflected. "They'll remember you as the freest of men, Harry. And that's what I love about you, about our life."

"I'm not free."

"Nobody can hold you, my dear. Not even me."

Houdini held his wife rigidly before him. She was pliant. "Look at me. I'm not free . . ." He paused, downcast, introspective. "Because I have hope."

"What is that supposed to mean?" she said, a loving query forming between her lips.

"Deep down, I hope to God that Doyle's right. I don't believe it. I can't believe it. I'll never believe, but oh God if only he were right!"

Bess puzzled. "Right about what?"

"How the hell did Nina get out of her constraints, throw me across the stage, and what about that rush of air? I *did* feel it, Bess!"

"I'll never tell," Bess said, as she started goosing her man. Whether Doyle spoke to the dead or not, whether psychic experiences were real, Bess didn't give a hoot. Or certainly not tonight. She wasn't tired yet. And it was the living that interested her.

12

The Body Electric

On their journey west, the Doyles encounter a force greater than their own . . .

Houdini arrived to much fanfare in Los Angeles, with his entourage, which now included Amy Beckwell. Harrington had sent her along at the last minute to report back regularly, by wire and by phone, on Houdini's activities. A fair number of reporters, Simpson among them, also joined the Houdinis. His tour of the West was considered big news.

The evening before her departure with the Houdinis by train, Amy had visited the Doyles at the Ambassador Hotel in New York, where they too were preparing to check out. She confided in them her disappointment over the insensitive handling of the mediums by the committee during the first two days of the contest and concurred with Sir Arthur that one true spiritual experience out of a hundred failed attempts was sufficient to prove the existence of life after death.

Doyle, nodding in compliance, reminded both her and his wife that God spared the world, in Biblical times, for one honest person.

Because of these shared beliefs, and her own imminent departure with Houdini, Doyle solicited Amy's trust. She was already won over herself, of course—eager to speak with her deceased brother, and eager to please Doyle. Lady Doyle could see that the young woman idolized her husband.

"We would ask that you tell us everything of importance," Doyle requested.

"Everything," Amy assented.

"Houdini's state of mind during his travels. His fits of rage, sagging confidence, his boasts, his tricks, his physical feats, his mental well-being, the influence of Bess. It could all help us to help him."

"I will do everything I can," she assured them.

"It is for his own good, dear," Lady Doyle threw in. "Houdini is struggling within himself. I think that's clear. He wants to believe. He undoubtedly has the power to believe. It isn't easy. I know." She grinned in a motherly manner. "I've had to talk myself into it on occasion. These things are not obvious. Overcoming doubts is work. It takes courage."

"You two are so wonderful!" Amy gushed. "Sometime I'd really like my mother to meet you."

"We would be ever so honored," Doyle said in conclusion, hastily writing out for her the names of the hotels where they'd be staying on their way to Denver, and the dates. Then the couple left. They had much to do.

That last day at the Masonic Hall Sir Arthur had sensed that Houdini's impermeable shell was breaking down. There was the sign of stress in his eyes, about his diction, even in his erratic, unsure movements. He had resorted to aggression, probably subterfuge, Doyle believed, and managed to damage the reputation of a notable mystic, Nina Rafaella.

Two members of the committee—Barkwaithe and O'Nearly—had expressed lingering confidence in the medium's powers, but they were outnumbered. While a certain spiritual aura was palpable in the Hall, the scientists, according to Doyle, were not sufficiently susceptible to understand it. Their array of instruments were dumb, unfeeling, and mere atmospheric or magnetic registration was not sensitive to finer lines of experience.

"The soul speaks when it is spoken to," Doyle had stated to Nina, commiserating with her over the awful experience she'd undergone. He meant to let her know that both he and Lady Doyle appreciated her greatness, which they assured her was too rarified and exquisite for these meddling men of insensate logic to appreciate.

Lady Doyle had picked up on the "gusher of air" that came from Nina's head, while examining her, and Sir Arthur had felt the paralyzing burst of energy that catapulted Houdini across the stage. They knew that the Neapolitan medium was genuine. She had had a bad day, to be sure, thanks to Houdini, and thanks to the fact she had had to wait forty-eight hours for her turn at bat.

But in spite of these grievances, the Doyles were elated at the prospects and very sorry to see Nina leave the United States under such an unjust shadow.

In the meantime, Pheneas had begun to leave little hints for Lady Doyle, presentiments of a coming collision course. Her dialogues with Pheneas took up increasing hours, down to choosing garments at the department stores. Pheneas, like Lady Doyle, found the shopping in New York to be exceptional.

It was already abundantly clear to both Sir Arthur and his wife that however positive the results with Nina, it was Houdini himself who truly possessed the key to that door of the beyond, harbinger of eternal life—and they were intent upon canonizing him accordingly. It was not going to be easy.

But then Doyle had what he thought to be an ace up his

sleeve. Quite by accident, he'd fallen into a stream of presumed predestination.

One quiet night over dinner at the Medford Hotel in Toledo, ten days into the Doyles' trip to Denver, Lady Doyle received a remarkable spiritual communication from one thin-voiced "Cecelia." Pheneas had provided the introduction. Lady Doyle was studying the dessert menu when the old woman came across bearing good tidings and two words that she told Lady Doyle her son was sure to recognize: *"Apfelkuchen"* and *"Torten."* Neither were on the menu, which led Doyle to believe that the message was authentic.

A flurry of kinetic jabber ensued, translated by Pheneas.

"What language?" Lady Doyle asked.

"Yiddish, madam," Pheneas replied.

Within minutes Lady Doyle understood that the woman's son had tampered with his first locks as a child, while trying to get at the sweets Cecelia had kept padlocked in the cupboard.

"He was addicted to my pastries," the old woman reminisced.

Lady Doyle repeated the old woman's statement, as translated by Pheneas, for the benefit of Sir Arthur.

"And who is her son?" Doyle asked.

"It is Houdini," Pheneas stated with condescending resolve. He did not particularly care for Doyle, but he was also not unaware of the importance of this encounter.

"She says Houdini!" Lady Doyle repeated, devastated by the possibilities.

"You're telling me the woman is Cecelia Weiss?" Doyle blathered, nearly falling out of his chair.

"That is what she calls herself," Pheneas said, hearing Doyle's response and speaking through Doyle's wife. "Though I have no way of knowing for certain."

"Why doesn't this Cecelia go directly to her son, then?" Doyle asked, brushing away the waiter.

Moments later, Lady Doyle conveyed Pheneas's interpretation. "She says her son is a mule. He won't listen. She hopes that I will help her reach him."

Eureka! This was the answer. If Lady Doyle could get a sitting with Houdini, Sir Arthur was certain that history would be rewritten. In six months' time, Doyle would be going to Paris for the International Spiritualist Convention. He hoped to bring Houdini with him, and prove to the world once and for all that immortality—as practiced knowingly or unknowingly, willingly or unwillingly by Houdini himself— was a fact of life. Doyle knew that the one way to guarantee Houdini's conversion—which was in fact tantamount to a confession—was to overwhelm him with incontestable proof in Denver.

"My dear," pulsed Sir Arthur. "We must now submit you to Harrington's committee as a contestant."

"I'm ready." Lady Doyle nodded.

"Ask her if she'll meet us in Denver in three weeks," Doyle pressed.

Lady Doyle's face jerked and contorted as the repartee shot up and down her every nerve and follicle.

"Well?" asked Doyle impatiently.

"She's checking her calendar," Pheneas snapped back.

Lady Doyle waited to translate. "Well?" she reiterated impatiently.

"Got it! The answer is affirmative. Tell your husband he doesn't deserve her . . ."

The whole arrangement made for awkward entertainment, or would have, had the event not been so utterly, wonderfully significant. The waiter, who had exhibited a servile attentiveness throughout the strange goings-on, bringing multiple creams, sugars, replenishing water, could not but have overheard portions of the table conversation. He offered his congratulations to the couple. At the time, Doyle dismissed him without a thought, and gave him a favorable tip.

The Doyles then headed upstairs to their suite, called Betcham back in Crowborough for a household status report, and got Doodles on the phone. It was her ninth birthday and she had decided to be a girl after all. The rugby season had gone badly and she was returning to her dolls.

The following morning Doyle telegrammed Harrington, submitted his wife as a candidate, referred to the miraculous encounter with Houdini's mother and asked him to keep it a secret until Denver.

Harrington was enthralled with the prospect. Barkwaithe, meanwhile was already working out all the travel arrangements for the scientific committee.

That afternoon in Toledo, Doyle, still buoyed by the remarkable incident concerning Houdini's mother, showed five minutes of footage from his film-in-progress, *The Lost World*, astounding the local spiritualists with psycho-telepathic celluloid depicting the authentic battles and copulations of South American dinosaurs. The studio technician, Willis O'Brien, had spent two years painting and animating the film cells. Doyle sincerely believed that the resulting effect transcended the technology and somehow stemmed from the spirits of the dinosaurs themselves, growling across many millennia to the meek anthropoids who had inherited the earth, for better or for worse.

Upon returning to their room, the Doyles found a message slipped under their door, written in an unknown, unsigned hand. It referred specifically to "H.R.H. Princess Anne's" request that the Doyles meet her at midnight at a certain location along the waterfront in order that she might convey additional information from Cecelia. This was an injunction of the highest priority, the message alleged. The Doyles looked at each other in astonishment. Moreover, the name Princess Anne rang a bell, but they couldn't place it.

"Astounding!" Sir Arthur kept repeating.

Captain Pushcart hired a taxi to take them to their destination and wait there for them. The city slept silently beneath a pall of mist typical of this time of year. The taxi wandered through the seedy industrial part of town at the entrance to Lake Erie, where foghorns could be heard from all quarters.

The Doyles' taxi stopped before an unlikely-looking place to meet a Princess. It was an abandoned warehouse, run-down and vandalized. By the glare of the headlights, the Doyles could make out exposed steel girders dangling from the roof. Garbage, broken glass and old trolley cables lay strewn on the ground around the entrance. Fog concealed the back of the building.

The taxi driver put his vehicle into reverse and moved slowly backward down the street to the previous building. He drove over the curb, aiming his headlights at a storefront in order to read the number, shook his head, then crawled forward again to the apparent destination. This was the place, all right, though no other vehicle could be seen.

Pushcart accompanied the Doyles to the entrance.

"This whole business is mighty peculiar, if you ask me," the Captain said, looking around.

"It will be fine," Sir Arthur rejoined, ever the optimist. "There must be a good reason for this."

They stepped over the cables, which were wet from the mist, as well as the abandoned debris of other sundry metal-work. In her evening shoes and gown, Lady Doyle had a difficult time of it, though she said nothing. Two bouncer types emerged from the sordid dark, nodded at the Doyles, then led them to a lit area inside.

In a cold bare room there was a table, ceremonial in appearance, wall shadows quavering with candlelight. A thin strand of wire tightly encircled the legs of the table. Behind it was a formidable cabinet. In the two rear corners of the room, Doyle at once detected identical apparatuses, not easily described, like old-world standing ovens.

Suddenly, out of the cabinet appeared the Princess, dressed in a single draping piece of black, like a misshapen sack.

"Good evening," she said.

Doyle extended his hand, felt the manly grasp and realized that he was looking at the largest woman in his experience. Her hair was hidden by a hood attached to the sack.

Her face was a baby face, like a gauze mannequin or thin rubber form. Lady Doyle offered her own hand with utmost trepidation.

"Please be seated," Princess Anne said.

Doyle happened to sniff his hand as he sat. In the ill-lit enclosure he knew at once that his fingers were coated with a residue of seven percent metallic copper, found only in the droppings of the rare white-crested touraco from South Africa. It was just one of those things he happened to know, having once lent the uncanny but important detail to his much-loved character of Mycroft.

South Africa? There was something about it, and the name Princess Anne, but he couldn't quite . . . and he noticed the same metallic dust coating the table and chairs.

"Now," she said. "Let me begin by explaining the nature of my business, and a word or two about my past."

"That would be splendid," Doyle said. He saw that the Princess's two assistants had taken up positions at the entrance to the room.

Captain Pushcart kept his left hand under the table, close to a small jackknife that he carried on the inside of his thigh. He didn't trust these proceedings one jot.

"I am a medium," she started. "Unknown in this country, but famed throughout Africa. My powers were patiently sharpened by my experience of the South African jungle, and I began to attract some notice. A Professor Jeelai and the Baron von Nozy tested me. You must know of their work? *Phenomena of De-Materialization*, etc.?"

"Naturally. I wrote the preface to one of Nozy's early texts."

"That's right. Well they in turn submitted their findings to none other than Ricardo, who of course received the Nobel Prize five years ago in physics. He came to see me—"

"Where?"

"In Venice, where I was living at the time. Soon, he also subscribed to my abilities. Like yourselves, I have had my share of abusive skeptics. I had to flee South Africa, if the

truth be known. But enough of this. I invited you here tonight in order to conduct a séance of equal importance to all
of us." She paused, gauging the feeling in the room.

Doyle had numerous questions on his mind, including the
veracity of her supposed "royalty." Having been knighted
himself, he had quite a few international connections in that
realm and could easily determine who she knew, and if she
really knew them. But he opted to suppress such queries for
the time being, not wishing to seem rude. "Go on," he said
politely.

"About a week ago I received a direct communication
from Cecelia Weiss, Harry Houdini's deceased mother. At
the time, I was in New York, having just arrived from London, where I had addressed the All Africa Council of Nations on the issue of postwar partitions and visited the
Hogarths at the Tate. You see, I also take an active interest in
matters other than spirit. I believe we all are as much in this
world as in the next."

Doyle liked that and nodded in agreement. He smiled at
his wife. His wife, however, smelled a rat.

"We both know that Houdini poses a delicate problem to
the world of the spiritualists."

"Indeed he does!" Doyle readily conceded. It was now
obvious to him that the Princess knew exactly what she was
talking about.

"When his mother came to me, it was as if by divine intervention . . . You see, for years I have sensed that Houdini
was himself a medium . . ."

"But that's *extraordinary*!" Doyle boomed. "Why my
wife and I have firmly held such a belief all along!"

Lady Doyle kicked her husband under the table.

"I *knew* it," the Princess exclaimed. "Oh, Sir Arthur, I felt
certain that you and Lady Doyle would grasp this complex,
psychological situation. You once wrote, and please allow
me to quote from treasured memory, 'I have been compelled
to endure horrors baffling description, for no other offense
than trying to convince the multitude that they were not

beasts that perish and leave no sign, but rather, are immortal, grave-surviving souls.' "

"That's marvelous," Doyle proclaimed, all puffed up with himself.

"Such words and sentiments rightly describe my own life, Sir Arthur." The Princess smiled with an embarrassed, down-gazing femininity that further ingratiated her to Doyle.

"Leave at once . . . You're in danger!" Pheneas whispered to Lady Doyle.

Lady Doyle nudged her husband. He ignored her. She nudged him a second time and began to rise, but Sir Arthur pressed her hand. He would not be disturbed at this important moment. Obediently, she stayed seated.

"When Mrs. Weiss spoke to me, it was for the purpose of reaching her son," the Princess continued. "She mentioned pastries, lox, and, I think, bagels, ways to Harry's heart, if you can picture it. More importantly, she emphasized that it was imperative that I should take part in this science contest of which I have heard mention. She said you would be able to see to it."

"Well, yes!" Doyle began. "Of course I can. I *do* exert some clout in that matter."

"No . . . I tell you NO!" Pheneas throbbed.

"Dear, may I speak with you for a moment, in private?" Lady Doyle urged. Her tone was all flummoxed and grave.

Sir Arthur leaned over and in an angered whisper said, "What *is it*, my pet?"

"Pheneas is getting bad vibrations here. I think we should leave at once!"

"Yes, yes. But let's give it a few more minutes."

"At once!" she reiterated, nonplussed.

"Excuse us," he said to the Princess. Then in lowered tone, chin to jowl, "Sweetheart, there could be no more significant coincidence, wouldn't you agree?"

"That's not the point."

"No?"

Lady Doyle steadied her hands. "Then at least test her, see what she can do . . . I tell you I don't like this, Arthur!"

"Fine, fine." Sir Arthur smiled, turning back to the Princess with remedied composure. "Perhaps you wouldn't mind displaying some of your powers? As chief judge of the contest, along with Houdini, I am responsible for screening applicants, and while you refer to Cecelia Weiss—a most remarkable piece of timing and serendipity, I assure you—it is still my duty to—"

"A séance it will be," she declared, standing up. "You needn't apologize. But please, just the two of you. I must ask that your associate wait in the taxi, away from the building."

"But he's with us . . ."

"Where such intimacies are concerned . . . even the slightest antagonism or distrust . . ."

Doyle could easily appreciate her concerns. "All right, then. Captain, would you please be so kind?"

Captain Pushcart gestured his displeasure but did as he was told. As he left, the two shadow figures relocked the door behind him. Doyle saw them walk to the oven-like contraptions against the far wall.

"What about them?" asked Doyle.

"Spirit controllers," the Princess replied gently.

"Of course," Doyle said.

The Princess withdrew from her smock a little wooden ball attached to a foot-long strand of catgut, wrapped the strand around her finger and let it dangle over the middle of the table. The ball turned a full circle, with no apparent prompting.

"The spirit approaching us is male," she said. She sat back down—a precarious maneuver given the enormity of her buttocks and the relative diminutiveness of the chair— repeated the word "Donnez" three times, then went quickly into a trance.

Pheneas began to cough and gasp for air. Lady Doyle put her hands to her throat. "Arthur," she struggled to say.

"Now what is it?" He dispensed with further courtesies. She was really getting to him.

"It's Pheneas! He's in serious trouble. Medical trouble!"

Suddenly, the Princess said the word *"Floreat."*

"Floreat Etona!" Doyle exclaimed, completely forgetting his wife's obscure dilemma. "Marvelous!" He knew it was the motto of his late son Kingsley's college, Eton of course.

"That's all the proof I need," Doyle said elatedly.

"Don't be an idiot. She's read all about you!" Pheneas cried, choking for air.

"Why must you be so rude, Pheneas!" the Princess said.

Lady Doyle froze.

"You heard me!" the Princess continued. "Now come here, I want to show you something . . ."

And with that, the Princess's face began literally to come apart, as if a gas burner had been applied to a wax doll. The features seemed to coalesce into a liquid jelly. The frontal bone softened, while the eyes melted into their sockets and the nose began to come unglued.

"Ohhh stop!" Lady Doyle groaned, as the spirit of Pheneas clawed and writhed inside her.

The Princess's upper torso under the black cape started to light up phosphorescently. The limbs gave way, while the hair on her head burned, throwing off a scent that Doyle at once recognized as chloride of sodium and phosphate of calcium.

The whole figure rose up, smoking, as ectoplasm poured from the disfigured mouth.

"Have faith!" the Princess clamored from some twisted mouthlike pile of lips and throat.

"Arthur, help me!" Lady Doyle screamed.

"Jean? Are you all right?" Sir Arthur pushed himself away, stricken with the light show that spun and toppled from unknown quadrants of the room.

And with that Lady Doyle rose and walked unsteadily toward the brilliantly illuminated slab of flesh that was the Princess. Doyle was unable to check his wife's movement.

Lightning sparks hissed, splattered and smacked the floor, thick dabs of color careening through the air from no apparent source. The whole room glowed.

One small explosion after another ripped between walls, major electrical shorts, and all at once the dark night, carried by the streak of fire, came alive. The mist turned gold, as if the whole of Lake Erie had just emerged from an eclipse into burning sunlight.

"Holy Toledo!" the taxicab driver yelled outside. The building appeared to be on fire.

Captain Pushcart pulled out his knife and ran for it.

The waterfall of ectoplasm was also the color of gold, and as it continued to stream from the electrical vortex of what was the Princess's mouth, it gathered additional hues until it looked like a peacock's tail stretching through the window, around the side of the building and down the block. Hundreds of liters of gushing ectoplasm, tons of it—animated in midair by the quicksilver, slinky fizzle of something like mercury. Metallic and blinding. The whole warehouse was transfigured.

Doyle couldn't move. Everything he touched was also touched by the ectoplasm, by halos burning into the table, conducted by the bird's copper resin he had initially detected.

Outside, Pushcart narrowly escaped the enormous snake of scintillating fluid that cinctured the building and continued down Front Street. He lunged for the door. The moment he touched it, he was thrown backward by the electrical shock. He came to, then rushed at the steel door again, kicking furiously with his rubber-soled boots.

"Sir Arthur!" he screamed frantically. The noise coming from inside was horrific.

But it was no use. Doyle was somewhere else, mesmerized. His wife had just been forcefully brought into perverse but magnificent communion with the dazzling pyre of standing spirit. The Princess had clasped Lady Doyle's hands ecstatically.

"No . . . ," Pheneas pleaded, drowning in the deafening epiphany.

Lady Doyle shook violently as the electrical energy passed into her, Sir Arthur helplessly watching.

Far away, across the continent, Harry Houdini had just minutes before closed his eyes against his pillow, digesting his nightcap of milktoast.

Suddenly he spasmed, jolting upward in bed.

"What is it?" Bess cried out. She'd already been in dreamland.

"I don't know," Houdini said. His face was burning with sweat. He was breathing hard.

"Bad dream?" Bess asked, laying her cool hand over her husband's chest.

"No."

"You're scared about tomorrow?"

"I don't know."

"I have a bad feeling about it," she admitted.

She knew how superstitious Harry was. "You don't have to go through with it, you know. The director told me that himself."

"It was something else, Bess . . ."

He stared up at the ceiling in the dark, then looked at his watch. The sensation had come from far away. And now it was gone.

"Go back to sleep," she whispered.

13

By a Wing and a Prayer

Fulfilling prior engagements on his way to the Denver showdown, Houdini's western tour skirts unexpected peril . . .

Houdini was in Los Angeles for the first time in fifteen years, under contract with a film company. In addition, he was doing two benefit performances. After that, he and Bess were headed to the famed Yosemite Valley for one stunt, and then some rest.

But this morning his mind was troubled, calculating. He'd learned from Harrington that one Princess Anne had become a contestant—along with Lady Doyle—for the Denver showdown. Frank had reminded Houdini that Princess Anne was that fat monster, Holstein, from New York. She'd apparently worked her way into the Doyles' hearts. Houdini saw his opportunity. He just hadn't exactly worked out the fatal blow.

He turned on the radio that sat upon a wooden shelf between the two adjoining beds. The newsman predicted a hot, windless stretch of several days. Perfect for what Houdini had in mind.

The announcer went on to describe the top news-breaking events. A Finnish runner, Paavo Nurmi, had just set a new world record for covering the mile in four minutes, ten and a half seconds. Houdini figured he better give running a shot when he got back to New York. Surely he could do better than that. A mile wasn't that far, after all. In Paris, news had come of the sculptor Rodin's death, from neglect and exposure to cold. A scandal. Closer to home, Aimee Semple McPherson, the flamboyant evangelist, had preached to a record-breaking 130,000 fans at her Angelus Temple downtown the previous evening.

Houdini looked up from the side of the bed where he was putting on his socks. Bess had just reached over and flipped off the radio.

"I can't listen to that," she muttered, leaning on one elbow. He knew that she was not thrilled about the final scene Houdini had resolved to shoot this day, especially considering the schedule Dexter had worked out for him over the coming three days: a burial, an immolation and then an arduous journey by coach along the dirt road to Yosemite, through Indian country.

Houdini, on the other hand, had been too excited to sleep all night. Whatever unexpected jitters he may have felt had quickly vanished. The fact remained, he *loved* airplanes!

This was Houdini's day to outperform the likes of Douglas Fairbanks and his double, Richard Talmadge, in one. The movie was called *The Grim Game*. Houdini had already shot fifty-seven scenes intermittently over the last four months, in what was his third feature film. So far in the process he'd received seven black eyes, and cracked his wrist, as well as nearly drowning when he tried to rescue four damsels stranded on a boat during the tail end of a hurricane. It made for great footage, but Bess was losing patience with the risks her husband was needlessly taking.

"It doesn't matter in the movies!" she'd argued. And she was right. Because of the editing process, audiences were wise to the fact that any schlemiel could perform amazing feats, like those actually accomplished by Harold Lloyd, hanging off high clock towers, or leaping across a Grand Canyon or two. There was no reason for Houdini to do dangerous stunt work.

"Make them simple, Harry," she'd said, echoing the director's own concerns. "Let the editor turn it into something scary." But he was stubborn, thinking action was all he had to offer.

Three Handley Page 400 twin-engined bomber planes had been hired. The wing span, camber, corrugated Duralumin and steel struts offered the safest combination for a stunt. Frank and two mechanics had exhaustively searched the aircraft for any problems or hidden explosives, even for loose or missing shear pins. A wing could come off in a loop if such pins had been tampered with. The biggest problem, in Frank's mind, was the three pilots, who'd been hired from a different field. But he had interviewed them, and they checked out.

At six o'clock, Houdini arrived at the airstrip. Three trucks were already there. Several men were fitting the two cameras onto the wings, coating the lenses, preparing the metal riggings. The scene called for Houdini to leap from the wings of one plane to another, at an altitude of four thousand feet and a speed of one hundred ten miles an hour.

Standing beside the whole Houdini crew, thirty-seven in all, Bess was in a state. Houdini had never gone anywhere near so high, nor had he practiced the stunt. The wind shear, the unknown forces at work, the lesser amounts of oxygen— these were all unknowns which Houdini preferred to laugh off.

Even that laugh bothered her. Houdini never trivialized

anything. His career was in part fortified by his demeanor and she had only known him to be a real heavy.

"You're nervous," she nudged, concerned by his gaiety.

"A little."

"There's still time to reconsider."

"Don't make a big deal out of this. You and Amy go get some breakfast. Order me an omelette."

Amy had stayed close to Bess all the way from New York, partly on account of her desire to be with Thomas, and partly as a result of her pact with the Doyles. Bess greatly appreciated Amy's candor when it came to her husband's risk-taking. It was her only source of support for her own views, which had been largely suppressed for years.

"I wouldn't do that," Amy would say, loud enough for everyone to hear. It certainly annoyed Houdini. If Bess said it, he'd simply ignore her.

Thomas or Frank would invariably soothe the friction, but Bess was frustrated. The ongoing engagements had taken their toll on her easygoing style. Moreover, she didn't like this contest business. It gave her husband too much power to destroy others. So she took refuge in Amy, and had started telling her more than she should have about their marriage.

The three planes took off in formation. Harry sat behind one pilot, the director and cameraman behind another, and a second cameraman and the villain behind the third. Both the villain and Houdini would appear to be flying their own planes. The trick required Houdini to seemingly abandon his own craft, jump onto the wings of the bad guy's plane, punch him out and retrieve a precious satchel, then get back to his own plane before it crashed.

Within five minutes the three aircraft were positioned for the scene. The Handley Page 400 had retractable landing gear, slats and flaps, an exhaust-driven turbo-supercharger and variable-pitch propellers that allowed the pilots to slow down to a near grinding halt in midair following dive-bombing, then continue to dive once again.

Houdini did not know enough about the advanced

technology—and its delicacy—to be in the least frightened. He breathed easily, for now.

The planes separated. At one hundred feet apart, in parallel, Merv waved at Houdini. The two cameramen took this as a sign to begin rolling their hand-cranked Pathe movie boxes. There would be no sound of air growling over the wings, no roar of the propellers. Despite some high hopes down on the ground, in the studio backlots, synchronized sound was still years away.

The man piloting Houdini slumped down in his seat and disappeared so that Houdini appeared to be the sole occupant of his bomber plane. The crouched pilot was still in total control of the aircraft, of course. Houdini scowled like a samurai at the bad guy, playing excessively to the camera, gesticulating wildly. His plane veered toward the other plane, leveled off, and then he made an even more threatening show of force.

"Give it back to me!" he screamed, shaking his fist, his lips registering an accented rage.

"Go go go!" Merv screamed from behind, over the din of the engines. Houdini crawled out onto the wing, clinging to the first strut. The wind was terrific, stretching his face, tousling his hair. But the altitude meant nothing to him. He guided himself to the second strut, then to the third, giving full vent to the wrathful expressions called for in the script. He silently uttered the Hebraic *Shema Yisrael Adonai . . .* took a deep breath and jumped!

It was perfect. The forces actually slowed him down, if anything, making it physically easier to accomplish the aerial acrobatic. He reversed the process, pulling himself strut by strut against the wind pressure, as up a ladder, toward the villain. Houdini rapped him a few times on the head and screamed, *"Die!"* with exaggerated enunciation. He then yanked the satchel free of the open cockpit and proceeded back to his plane. At the third strut, Houdini realized he had a problem. He heard the other actor screaming behind him— "Harry, Jesus Christ—your pilot!"

Houdini looked out over his shoulder and saw Merv flailing with disparaging signals, but he could hear nothing at the distance separating the planes. He figured he had to do the scene over again, which was OK except that his plane had drifted too far away for him to get back.

Clinging to the outermost strut at one hundred ten miles an hour, he started shouting above the infernal roar of the wind and the engines. "Hey, bring the plane in closer!"

"Harry!" the villain screamed again.

Houdini looked back at him and shouted, "The plane's drifting!"

"I know! Your goddam pilot parachuted!"

"What?"

"Parachuted! Your pilot. He jumped!"

The cameraman in this plane kept filming the whole event.

Just then, Houdini's abandoned aircraft seemed to rise, out of control, and smashed into the tail of the other plane. Houdini hung on. There was fire, a horrible lurching, then both planes seemed to collapse in mid-flight, the air knocked out of them, and fell downward in a tailspin.

Houdini's heart sputtered. And yet he was feverishly excited too. How many times did one get a chance to partake in such dogfights? And maybe it was part of the script. Maybe they just didn't tell him. His thoughts froze, shifted, dive-bombed, gathered confidence, as his legs were thrown out from under him and the satchel disappeared from his hand into the buzzing ether.

Bess saw the smoking planes. "Something's wrong," she cried. "Thomas? Frank? Do you see that? What is it?"

Clinging to the bending strut like a weather vane, Houdini was pinioned horizontally in the air, as flames shot out all around him.

"Ohhhhh, myyyy Goddd!" he mumbled toward eternity, holding on with raw verve.

They had precious few seconds before the engine blew up. The pilot was howling as they stared at the fast-approaching orange groves of the San Fernando Valley. The cameraman remained silent, doing his job, continuing to crank his Pathe. As the plane got close, the pilot managed by brute force to pull it out of its dive. They were engulfed now in black smoke, roaring at thirty degrees or so toward nowhere. At the last moment, a lake came into view, surrounded by marshlands, just over the crest of a rocky hillside.

"We can make it!" the pilot shouted.

Just below, the abandoned aircraft whistled in a higher and higher whine—then smashed into the rocks and instantly exploded.

Bess fell to the ground. Amy screamed. There was pandemonium now.

Houdini's plane kept going, with all three members aboard, topped the crest, then hit the water, barreling over the surface at a fantastic speed. Houdini let go. Seconds later, a wing dipped, throwing the plane into a high somersault. It came down again, then sank to an elegiac chorus of slimy gurglings and steam. There was no explosion, only a few eviscerated carp that floated peacefully to the surface.

The crew back at the field had watched the horrifying ordeal. It took them ten minutes to reach the fire on the cactus- and boulder-strewn hillside. They did not know who was in the demolished plane. There was no fire department in this part of the Valley, no town, and the aircraft just continued to billow smoke while those all around it took futile jabs at getting in close, for survivors, and for pictures.

But there was no way to tell anything. Nor had they been able to see what happened to the other plane. Bess was silent, stoic. Thomas held her.

Suddenly the third plane, the one carrying director Merv Letofsky and the second cameraman, flew low overhead at a creeping sixty miles per hour, the occupants pointing frantically beyond the hill. The plane disappeared and all those on the ground starting running after it.

"Hey!" Frank shouted, the first to reach the summit.

The second plane was down below, intact, floating atop mud.

Frank, Thomas and the aircraft mechanics reached the water and dove in. The pilot, the villain and the cameraman were all lying on the mangled wings. They were hurt, one of them groaning in serious pain with a broken hip, another having passed out, but they were alive.

Houdini was nowhere to be found.

Bess waited with Amy. Reporters ran around the lake, covering the incident with predatory zeal while the field crew and other movie people waded through the mud or converged around the survivors.

Suddenly, when the coast was clear and Bess was at her lowest, a cold hand covered in mud appeared from behind and smeared her cheek. She breathed in with a fright, turned and beheld the *Thing*.

Amy jumped away with a yelp.

Bess collapsed against him. Houdini, laughing with nervous, hysterical energy, was completely drenched in marsh, mud and oozy duckweed. He was Stone Age New Guinea. Monstrous. Adorable. The two lovers kissed frantically. Bess continued to weep.

Later, a search for the pilot who'd parachuted proved fruitless. Frank learned that he was a stand-in at the last minute for the regular ace, who'd been there for years but had called in sick. Whoever that pilot was, he had it in for Houdini. The local Los Angeles police would make every effort to investigate. In the meantime, the lawyers would fight it out over which insurance company had to pay for the two Handley Page 400s.

Houdini had two more days in Southern California, and though his shoulders and back ached from having hung on to that dive-bombing plane, he had no intention of letting down a delegation of Camp Fire Girls or a troop of Santa Ana Boy Scouts.

The press was out in force. The morning newspapers were

full of Houdini's miraculous escape. *The Grim Game*, they said in print, was bound to be the biggest hit of the year.

It was exactly what Houdini needed. For weeks he'd been comparing himself to Doyle, fretting that Doyle was more famous. He was running scared. Doyle's literary fame was unbearable. Houdini's only chance at attaining a similar reputation for posterity was a stunt that could never be equaled, and had never been imagined. A stunt that was philosophical, even religious. He had to be careful. He was no god, despite what some people were saying. But he knew he could get close to Doyle's fame if he played his cards right. The airplane crash—though no stunt—was being claimed a miracle. That was a good beginning.

But there was a more inspired fixation in the works. For some time Houdini had been preparing for what could well be the ultimate. He had cultivated an extraordinary lung capacity and forced expiration rate. He'd studied Waddell's translation of the *Tibetan Book of the Dead* and had experimented with cataleptic trance technique. He had figured out how to utilize a minimum of oxygen. In sealed coffins, which physicians vouched were good for fifteen breaths, Houdini had managed to survive for upward of ninety minutes. In other words, a half a breath gave him enough energy to last for three minutes—proven out in an astonishing succession of thirty such privations.

Typically, following such actual efforts, Houdini would emerge the color of the sky, his blood pressure dangerously sluggish. But he felt refreshed by such ascetic amusements, cleansed and purified. All were preparations for the mightiest stunt of all: a secretly planned first ascent—solo—of Mount Everest, without oxygen. The publicity alone would *keep* him at the top of the world.

For now, his engagement was more mundane, but it would continue the training of his lungs.

Houdini and party reached the cemetery at ten o'clock the next morning. Over one hundred eager Camp Fire Girls and their parents and paying friends were there, along with the normal mob of reporters. It was a charity thing. Houdini was big on raising war bond money, or helping out the disadvantaged. A grave, six feet deep, had been dug in preparation for a heart attack victim who, as fate would have it, pulled through surgery. Dexter worked out the details with the locally hired impresario: the hole should not go to waste, not with Houdini in town!

Houdini said a few sobering words to the pressmen and then silently meditated before the hole. It made a good showing. He knelt down and checked the consistency of the dirt that would be shoveled on top of him.

"It looks pretty deep," Houdini mumbled to Thomas.

Thomas didn't hear him, as he was busy explaining to the Camp Fire Girls that they were to knead the dirt into a fine powder, eliminating all clods or rocks.

"The hole's too—" But Houdini stopped himself, thinking what the hell.

There was applause as he climbed down inside and gave the "Ready!"

Three men standing by proceeded to shovel a huge mound of dirt into the hole. Houdini protected his face with his hands. He'd practiced this stunt a few times before, in his backyard, but never so deep. He'd gone one foot, then two feet, and finally three feet.

The local impresario, prompted by Byron, thought it would be a telling and symbolic treat for Houdini to be buried six feet under. Dexter had been informed of the hole's depth only at the last minute. He was not fazed by it. Houdini surely would have been, had the information not escaped him in the momentous rush of other details, phone calls and the general, hair-raising aftermath of the airplane crash.

Now, as the earthen darkness solidified around him and the onlookers vanished above, Houdini grasped the sickening significance of his present depth. He couldn't even squirm. He couldn't cry out. His nose was clogged with the fine silt of bacterial earth. Houdini blinked haltingly, dirt caught against his eyeballs. The claustrophobia was as enormous and unrelenting as if a galaxy had closed in on him. There was no more air.

It was over. Houdini sensed that he had a minute or two, and then his involuntary musculature, over which he had for years practiced rigorous mind control, would cave in, he'd suck for air, devouring earth instead, and his lungs and throat would explode. The fragile light would go out.

And all the while, crowds up above had been instructed to stamp upon the grave to make certain the soil was compacted. Now they waited with mirthful anticipation. No backup had been planned. That's how confident Houdini had been, just moments before.

Pain is the dawning of consciousness. . . . He'd repeated it so many times throughout his mature years.

Ferociously, Houdini awoke from the grimace of submission. In a world war of inner discharges, combining all the bayonet plunges, besieged beach landings and mustard gas, groveling with pointed fingers, he gained purchase on an upward-tilting hole, tunneled like a harried rodent as if God himself were cheerleading, his lungs holding forth, his eyes sealed implacably shut.

How far to go? Sides were caving in, dirt on his chest doubling his effort, obscuring the summit of his labors. Dumb. Mute. The desperation of a star ready to explode. He vibrated like an overheated engine, as his fingers continued to trounce the muffling tomb of solid dirt.

Suddenly, Houdini saw the same enormous snake that had slithered into his consciousness the night before. It was white, like a coral snake, though its tail had the glistening palette and shape of a peacock's. It stretched for miles, like a prehistoric phantasm, rumbling toward oblivion.

He heard screaming. The tunnel collapsed. Houdini burst into the open air.

A brandishing of shovels, the glints smashing downward . . .

He lunged . . . edges of steel missing his face by fractions of an inch.

"It's him!" the screams roared.

Air, air and sky and Bess . . .

He threw himself upward, then vomited all over the grass that creeped to the edge of his life-sucking pit.

It was over.

The Camp Fire Girls jumped up and down, shouting and clapping, grabbing hold of each other in a frenzy of fun. Cameras flashed. Frank took a napkin from one of several mourner's benches temporarily transformed into picnic tables readied for the cookout to follow, and scrubbed his brow.

Houdini stood up on weak knees, virtually a dead man. Bess pulled dirt from his mouth. Bubbles of earth belched forth, frothing from his nostrils.

"This is it!" she hissed, while restoring him to freer breathing. "Dexter, water, on the double!"

Dexter came with a bottle. Houdini guzzled from it, spit it out, coughing, then retched. Bess doused the corner of her blouse to help remove particles of dirt from Houdini's eyes.

"How long was I down there?" rasped Houdini.

"Not long enough," she stated pointedly.

"Almost half an hour," Thomas declared with astonishment.

That night at the hotel, Bess confronted her husband with an ultimatum.

"It's fiendish of you, Harry. I can't go on like this . . . Never knowing which day is going to be your last, or how your corpse will look . . . burned to a singe . . . stuffed with dirt . . . waterlogged . . . sliced into pieces, strangled, suffocated or simply riddled with gunshot . . ."

"Don't be dramatic," he applied counterpressure sweetly.

"No. I'm finished, I tell you. Either you give up this nonsense, or I'm leaving you. Do you understand?" She turned

her back on him and walked to the dresser, her hands fretting
with a bobby pin.

"Don't try to play my mother."

"Your mother, may she rest in peace, wouldn't even *look*
at you with dirt down your throat, Harry Houdini. I have to
look at you. And it *MAKES ME SICK*!"

"You're upset," he commenced calmly a futile attempt to
save the evening.

She spun around and glared at him. "You're really a dumb
bastard! You don't get it; you refuse to get it. You are going
to die not getting it! You schmuck!"

"We're all going to die," he said quietly.

"No. Not like that, not for idiotic Camp Fire Girls or a stupid movie—"

"It's not stupid—"

"*It's colossally stupid*! With young girls laughing over
your grave . . ."

She held off, took a deep breath, placed her head in her
palms, and just as he was about to speak, she stared up again.

"A straightjacket is precisely where you belong—yes—in
an asylum with all the other bozos. You need help, Harry. Serious help."

"You knew what my life was like when you married me."

"Oh, fine, fine. Throw that up to me again. No, I didn't
know. I knew of a gentle young man from Appleton who saw
bright lights in vaudeville. And loved the circus and gum
balls and exotic places. I knew a dashing young boy without
wounds all over his body who did silly little handcuff tricks
and pulled heads of lettuce out of his tuxedo. And listened to
reason! I did *not* know the psychopath that's standing before
me. I did not know about self-mutilation, the stupid goddamned destruction of everything we've worked for. I do not
plan to be around for your last hurrah, Harry Houdini."

He wiped tears from her eyes, greatly moved.

She brushed his hand away. "You go to hell!"

"What are you doing, Bess? Why are you behaving this
way!" he demanded.

"I'm not *behaving*!" She kicked at his legs.

Houdini held her back.

"Don't play the innocent with me, Harry! I read the schedule. I saw that demonic-looking cage. Those fuses. And I know damn well that you're booked for a stunt using dynamite on a cliff."

"Thomas told you?"

"Oh no. Thomas loves me too much to inflict that kind of worry. Dexter told me."

"It's not a big deal," he said, quieting down before her evidence.

But Bess was painfully wise to his weak disclaimers.

"So, all right," Houdini continued, "one little rock, one measly trick. What can it be? Thomas'll be right there—"

"Yeah, like he was right there for you this morning."

"I told him not to do anything. It wasn't his fault."

"And after the cliff?"

"After the cliff we'll go to Denver and that'll be it, the buffalo business. That'll be it, Bess. I promise. From then on it's safe ghost-busting, books, a little teaching, leisure. I've been thinking I'd like to take up hiking. Along the Hudson. Maybe visit Tibet . . . And maybe we could try again to have kids."

She halted abruptly. "You go to Tibet. I'll go to Paris." Then she managed—albeit against her will—a laugh. "Kids. That's funny. Some father you'd make."

"What do you say?"

"Leave me alone." She pushed him away with less force this time.

"Huh?" He nuzzled in closer.

She gave up. He embraced her, slobbering on her ear, mouthing her neck, cupping her breasts.

A few minutes later she asked, "How safe is the buffalo trick?"

"I don't know. You can ask the buffalos when we get there."

He was feeling better, though the dirt had left a dull, indescribable grief in his throat. The pain of earth, prematurely.

The press made much of the airplane disaster and of Houdini's amazing survival. The plane had plunged from four thousand feet. Houdini's nationwide publicity was running into four columns, what with his spectacular victories over Doyle and all the mediums, the "miracles" of Pittsburgh, as well as the rainstorm at the Harringtons' party in New York. Adding to the spring's triumphs were his controversial testimony before Congress, the escape from the Federal Prison in D.C., the so-called sludge routine at the Hippodrome, etc. etc. There was much to celebrate. Not to mention surviving the Camp Fire Girls picnic. New offers were coming in by telegram at a rate of half a dozen a day. And he intended to turn them all down.

In the morning they drove out to Santa Ana. There were gusts of wind whipping in from the deserts of Twentynine Palms, dust twisters nobody had anticipated.

Houdini pulled up at a local baseball field where several hundred Boy Scouts had prepared a large pyramid of logs atop kindling in the sandy training pit.

"Hi, boys, how you all doing?" Houdini shouted. More than three thousand spectators who had donated money to the scouts were seated in the bleachers.

"Fine, Houdini!" they shouted, many flocking around him for autographs.

This time, in addition to the press, a live radio announcer was on hand. Houdini found it a trifle overkill and whispered to the guy that this was hardly a trick at all, just a few knots and a handcuff or two, and that he should play it up real big, or it would seem silly. After all, he explained, he was simply doing this for a good cause and it would be over in less than five minutes.

The boys in their freshly pressed knee breeches and long argyle socks converged upon the amused Houdini, tying him up with their best knots, handcuffing him, then carrying him to the top of the pyre, where they tied him again.

The normally poker-faced Houdini was ticklish and found himself laughing uncontrollably as the boys held him aloft. Amy too found it delicious and would remark upon Houdini's one apparent weakness to both the Doyles and Harrington.

Frank and Byron and Thomas had checked the place out amidst the boyish merriment. They were all on twenty-four-hour overdrive, given the aircraft fiasco. The police had also cordoned off the ballpark and were keeping close lookout for any suspicious types.

Houdini figured he'd be out in sixty, maybe seventy seconds, at the worst. It would take the fire much longer than that to get going big, even with the wind.

Three torches were tossed by those older scouts with seniority. There was a silence, a hiatus during which nothing happened. The fire was thinking—Houdini had counted on the fire to think for several minutes—when suddenly the whole pyre literally detonated!

People cried out, ran back away from the heat. Houdini disappeared beneath smoke and flame. Thomas ran for buckets of water. Bess ran toward the wood. Frank held her back. She kicked, screamed, threw herself toward her husband. Dexter and Byron struggled to keep her from immolating herself.

"Water! Help me get water!" Thomas shouted. The police converged in a panic.

But there was no time. Houdini's clothes were already on fire as he threw out his joints in a massive paroxysm to gain slack. His hair caught. The first lick of flame scorched his eyelids.

He dove forward, clawing to get out. His ankle caught. He dragged himself in spite of it, pulling behind him a burning stake.

It all happened so unbelievably fast. From complacent confidence and pranksterism to desperation, within seconds.

Houdini had hardly come down off his ticklish high. Smoke covered everything. Excited, unknowing screams from the bleachers rained down as if goading the man at bat, while Houdini struggled for his life. Bess was furious. The third time in as many days.

Suddenly, Houdini crawled out of the gusting conflagration. Thomas had just run back with the first bucket of water, which he poured over the charbroiled magician. Smoke rose from his head and back.

Thomas got him down on the sand, rolled him over like a carpet, beating at him with his own shirt. Frank arrived with more water and splashed it atop him. Bess kneeled beside him, trying with her own overcoat to put out the hot spots that remained on his clothing.

"Someone poured kerosene!" Thomas concluded, smelling it now.

"Frank! Did you hear what Thomas just said?" Bess shouted insanely.

There was no love in her voice, not now. She could hardly speak. And Houdini said nothing, busy ripping off his smoldering clothes.

As the fire burned out in a massive blaze, Frank rounded up the scoutmasters and explained the situation. They in turn horded all the boys and their parents together.

Bess saw Houdini into the car and spoke without sentiment. "I'm taking you to the hospital. Your neck and your ankle are burned."

"Wait," he said.

A Los Angeles city detective had some words with Frank, and then spoke to the scoutmaster.

"This here fella's a detective," the scoutmaster shouted. "Now which one a you fool-assed kids poured kerosene on those logs, huh?"

No one moved.

"I'll give you ten seconds," the scoutmaster shouted, furious with his charges. Cops were controlling the crowds off in the bleachers. There was some confusion now.

A fat freckled boy in uniform pushed the un-uniformed kid next to him forward. "I bet he did it!" the fat boy said.

"I saw him do it," another boy shouted.

"Me too," hollered a third.

A radio announcer wondered whether the near disaster was deliberate on Houdini's part, part of the box-office draw, and offered the conjecture to his listeners.

The scoutmaster grabbed the teenager by his collar and delivered him to Frank, saying, "He's no scout. I've never seen him before."

Frank and the L.A. detective withdrew their guns. "Who are you?" Frank demanded.

"There's no need for any weapons here!" a father called out.

"I said who are you, kid?" Frank repeated.

The boy turned toward Byron and said, "That man paid me to do it! He said he worked for Houdini and it's what Houdini wanted. That it was all part of the act."

It all made sense to Frank, now.

He whirled around, targeting his longtime partner with his semiautomatic. "Don't move, Byron!"

That's exactly what Byron did. He didn't move.

Houdini stepped out of the car. "Put down your gun, Frank."

"Didn't you hear what the kid just said?" Frank implored.

"Yeah. I heard."

Houdini looked at Byron with a morose glint, but didn't say a word for what seemed to everyone like an eternity. He was waiting for Byron to look down, which he finally did. Then Houdini turned back and faced Frank. "It's okay. I asked Byron to get that kerosene."

Frank and the other detective lowered their weapons. But Frank didn't believe it. He'd had his doubts about Byron ever since the affair with Massy.

Frank was rankled. "Harry, let's get the hell out of this town," he said.

14

Explosion on El Capitan

Houdini's visit to Yosemite is clouded by the arrival of an unexpected guest . . .

"*I most definitely did not* ask Byron to pour kerosene on the kindling," Houdini informed Frank after dinner. Bess had gone up to her room while the two men remained seated in the dark smokey corner of a Beverly Hills hotel lounge.

"Then *why* didn't you let the police take him away? That was a cold and murderous act, Harry."

"I don't want the press to know. Plain and simple."

"It's that important to you?"

"Think about it."

"So now what? You just say, good-bye, Byron. It was nice while it lasted?"

"Hardly. Figure it out, Frank. He can be useful to us."

234

Houdini had already worked it out in his mind. He knew he was taking a gamble, having publicly gotten Byron off the hook of any crime.

"That slime has one redeeming quality. Do you know what that is, Frank?"

Frank shook his head.

"That's why I can trust you. I'll tell you what it is. It's greed."

"What are you saying?"

"I'm saying that Byron was bought. He can be bought again."

"But—" Frank was indignant. "We had him. Why deal with him—"

Houdini threw up a hand to still Frank's justifiable impatience. "You'll see. Go to his room and bring him here."

Frank left Houdini and returned with Byron.

Byron approached his former boss with an air of penance about him. Frank didn't trust it for a minute.

Almost as an afterthought, Houdini asked him, "So why'd you do it, Byron?"

Byron nervously strained his neck and loosened his tie, averting both Frank's and Houdini's eyes. "To be honest?"

"Right. To be honest, Byron."

"Yeah. Uh-huh. Well, sir, how many times did I ask you for a raise in the last three years?"

"A raise?" Houdini was boggled. "Never, that I know of."

"Try a dozen times. You're an uncaring bastard, if you'll pardon me. Making all those thousands of dollars, living high off the hog, and what do I see out of it? Trouble. No girl. No savings. Could hardly live on what you paid me. What's more, you're mean. Hurting the careers of honest mediums like that."

"Well, Byron. I had no idea!" Houdini looked downcast. Frank couldn't believe the inanity of it. "You should have said something."

"I did. That's what I'm telling you."

"I would have given you a raise. I guess I had other things on my mind."

"Maybe you did."

"What you did is unpardonable, Byron. But that's water over the dam." Houdini was exploding inside. So was Frank. This was the most pathetic excuse for attempted murder they'd ever heard.

Byron appeared prepared for whatever was going to happen. He had no gun. Frank had already seen to that.

"So you snuck into my bedroom, secretly copied a page of my diary for Massy, as well as for Holstein, and stole a letter from my brother for Nina Rafaella. And then you tried to kill me in a manner that no one could possibly detect. You're lucky I didn't throw you in that pyre," Houdini chillingly declared.

"I'm very disappointed in you, Byron," Frank added. "You're a disgrace to the Pinkertons."

Byron said nothing.

Suddenly, Houdini grabbed the man's hair and yanked his head back, speaking up close, nice and intimate.

"It isn't over yet, Byron." Houdini uttered each word with a calculated elocution guaranteed to put the fear of God in him. "I think Holstein already offered you money to have me killed." He waited for an answer.

Byron denied it.

"Then what compelled you to wait around today?"

"I wanted to make amends."

"You did, eh?" Houdini didn't doubt what Byron had said. "Well here's how you're going to make those amends, as well as stay out of the penitentiary. No deals, no backing out, no options. Just this: you will continue in your job, as if nothing has happened. Frank, and the three new Pinkertons, will be watching you. We'll all be watching you. You will tell this Holstein that Houdini miraculously escaped the fire, which all the newspapers have already reported. But you will explain how there is another opportunity to beat him, and that's in Denver. From her point of view, it should be better than merely killing me off. I will provide you diary information of a seemingly incriminating character that Holstein will believe can easily be used against me in the Denver showdown. Whatever Holstein pays you for this purloined information, you can keep, in lieu of a raise. That should put us on an even footing. And once your old buddy Frank and the police have nailed Holstein, you can consider our association forever concluded."

Byron thanked Houdini for the second chance.

"It's no second chance," Houdini finished by saying. "Be sure you stay out of my sight, forever, after Denver. You got that?"

It was a momentous time in Yosemite. The first director of national parks, Stephen Mather, had declared the valley safe for democracy and for America's more than one hundred million restless inhabitants. He wanted to assure everybody that this incomparable shrine could be visited in the luxurious style to which some of the multitudes were accustomed. A few million automobiles piled in, as the last resident Miwok Indian couple, and grizzly bear, were rudely eliminated.

The Houdini entourage entered the big groves of the Sierra mother lode with that burgeoning stream of vacationers, eventually passing through the monumental hole in a sequoia tree. Houdini had managed to borrow a four-seater, three-liter Bentley for the occasion. Thomas and Amy sat together in the back.

"You two are pretty nauseating," Houdini told them, skirting the perimeter of Ribbon Falls. The cataracts rumbled off the unimaginably high rims. They were the highest things Houdini had ever seen. Higher, even, than Woolworth's in New York. He stopped frequently to try out his movie camera and feed salami sandwiches to the deer and coyote that cleverly blocked traffic for soliciting purposes every fifty yards along the dirt road. After the dusty congestion and repeated traumas of Los Angeles, Yosemite was everything Bess and Houdini had hoped it might be, except for the car fumes, which didn't quite go with Yosemite, she said. And she suffered from a foreboding. The idyll of syrup-smothered flapjacks, tame deer, games of horseshoes and the sheer aesthetics of the place, lasted all of one day for Bess. Then Houdini had his stunt to do.

Houdini and Thomas went directly to the monolith of El Capitan in order to check it out from the clearing at the expansive base of the rock.

"It's one of the biggest skyscrapers I've ever seen," Houdini said somberly.

Thomas pointed to an aquiline spot on the prow beneath the summit. There was a large mineral-stained chunk of cliff, square-shaped, which suggested an overhang. That was more or less the region of rock wall Thomas had in mind for the stunt.

In fact, Houdini had no sense of the vertical distance before him. The scale swallowed his internal altimeter.

Bess and Amy cooked everyone trout the first night in camp, while the men put up a dozen pre-ordered tents in the ant-infested grass. The next morning, Houdini, Thomas, Joe and Royale prepared the equipment. Early that afternoon they drove three vehicles up to Tuolumne and headed south along a lumber road toward the summit of El Capitan, lugging the necessary gear. For the last thousand feet, the men had to drag the cage they'd brought through the snow-laden woods. Their trail would serve the gaggle of reporters expected for the event. At least a dozen of those reporters had caravanned with the Houdinis from Los Angeles.

Houdini sat near the smooth, sloping edge, studying the drop-off down which he'd be lowered the following morning. He didn't say a word now.

"I think the height of it has sunk in," Thomas reported to Frank.

Next day, at least ten thousand tourists, many gawking through binoculars, relaxed in the El Cap meadow awaiting Houdini's show while ticket men collected half-dollars.

"No pay, no watch!" the advertisers shouted through megaphones. It wasn't strictly kosher, of course, this being a national park. But any regulations were impossible to enforce, and enough did pay to make it highly lucrative. Houdini expected a minimum of three thousand dollars for a morning's workout. In addition, salesmen who'd arranged to pay twenty percent of their take to Houdini made their own rounds, trafficking in everything from fishing poles to popcorn.

Up top, a good fifty people, mostly reporters, were present for the send-off. Their pants were all wet from the snow conditions. Houdini calculated the worth of his stunts according to the columns or newspaper lines of free publicity he received. A stunt like this, once syndicated across the country, was worth tens of thousands of dollars based on the cost of taking out equivalent-sized ads for himself. He kept telling himself that now, as the moment neared.

Houdini was scared.

It was a windy summer morning. Rain clouds were already billowing above Half Dome at the opposite end of the Valley. Most had come from Nevada, Houdini figured. No problem. If they'd come from the west, it would have meant a real storm.

The apparatus was ready. Houdini ran through the stunt, looking over the quickly sketched theatrical gymnastics involved. Houdini and Thomas had never actually detonated the device.

"It's a small enough charge," Thomas reassured him. The wind, gusting around twenty knots, made Houdini shaky as hell up there, near the edge.

His associates confined him to a straightjacket and handcuffed him. Houdini posed for a battery of photographs. He was then chained with leg irons to the inside of the cage. It was a circus coop gotten from Houdini's friend Barnum, and it still reeked of tiger urine.

Bess kissed her husband good-bye through the bars of the hanging jail and gave the hearty press elite plenty of her own nervous looks about which to speculate. They snapped more photographs, making lame jokes.

Using a power winch, Thomas, Joe and Royale lowered Houdini one hundred feet off the overhang. The cage scraped and got stuck repeatedly. Joe climbed down a spare rope, hand over hand, to free several hanks of cable that had jammed and collected on an upper ledge.

"Jesus!" Joe kept saying. Neither he nor Royale—nor anyone for that matter—could quite believe the awesome depth of the valley below. It staggered the reasoning faculties and made their hands shake.

When the cage dropped eight feet Houdini screamed, "*Hey!*" and everyone else screamed as well. The cage lurched away from an obstruction on the rock and then continued to fall in slow jerks.

The enclosure swung free of the wall once it was lowered past the overhang. Houdini's breath was sucked up as he rocked back and forth, staring down thirty-two hundred feet to the soft blur of forest. This was much rougher on the system than stunt flying. His knees started to shake.

Once the countdown began, Houdini would have to free himself from the constraints, finesse the locks on the cage, get out, bodily swing the two-hundred-pound prison, which hung from a burning rope, back and forth until he was able to grab hold of the cliff and there attach himself to a fissure using homemade suction devices. Several safety ropes were tossed over the sides, but they hung out too far from the rock to be of any use.

On paper, this stunt had seemed remarkably clever. Houdini had heard about the great El Capitan and figured it would make headlines. What he hadn't figured on was the horrifying reality of the largest granite monolith in North America.

Once Houdini was connected to the rock via his suction cups, he would have the unpleasant task of climbing hand over hand up, and out, around the overhangs to the summit. He had used the suction devices on buildings and had gone out over brick and wooden cornices, hanging by a special hook attached to his waist harness. This was different.

To the spectators below, it would appear as if Houdini were climbing without the aid of any artificial implements.

The stunt had one final source of jeopardy: Houdini would need to distance himself as far from the cage as possible before the explosion. Otherwise he might receive pieces of shrapnel, or be shaken off the rock, as the cage detonated and plunged toward earth. The overhangs had been chosen to limit the possibility of falling rock from above. Had the wall been even vertical, Houdini would have been a sitting duck for any loose scree or avalanches that poured off the summit. Still, the whole thing was mad. Houdini knew that, but he also sustained the most prominent sense of immunity from nature of any man in America.

The pendulous cage of steel hung fifteen feet from the wall. Thomas couldn't see anything, as he continued lowering it with the winch. Bess walked two hundred feet along the edge, where many reporters stood, and there had a perfect view of her incarcerated husband in stunning, ridiculous profile. Everybody could see that he was already struggling.

There was a countdown, the press adding their own flurry of voices to the 10,9,8,7 . . . Thomas had locked off the winch, and now ceremoniously set fire to the rope. He and Houdini had worked out the timing down to the second, based on one hundred feet of rope. They didn't count on any wind accelerating the rate of the flame, however. As far as Houdini was concerned, he had three minutes to get onto the rock. Three minutes exactly.

By this time Houdini had more or less relieved himself of the straightjacket and shackles, the cage bobbing back and forth with his prodigious effort. The jacket had been fitted with enough slack to insure an easy extrication. Houdini was not about to risk any dislocations, not with an unpredictable climb staring at him. The leather halter and padded coverlets were down around his ankles, leaving him clad only in a bathing suit.

Rock swallows swarmed at the cage, gliding in the upper thermals at high speed. There were hundreds of the little charcoal birds whose bawdy manner of hooting resembled laughter. Their boisterous goings-on echoed in the vertiginous hollow where Houdini stood, dangling free. He could see no descending sparks, as yet.

Then something happened. As Houdini prepared to carefully swing back and forth, he suddenly heard a voice, stuttering oddly.

"Thomas?" Houdini said. Then he shouted, "What?" This was annoying to him. *"What did you say?"*

Bess could see her husband reacting to a voice from above. Except that no one from above had said anything.

"What is it, Harry?" Bess called out.

"Nnnnot thththththreee mmminutes! Nnnniiininety sssseccccconds!"

Houdini cocked his head. A wave of new panic drenched him in sweat.

"Who are you? Where are you? Thomas???" he cried out.

Once again the stuttering specter called to Houdini. But the sound came from inside the cage, from inside Houdini's ears, which rang like a telephone receiver.

"Gggggeeett out, nnnnow!" the stranger's voice—a youngish timbre—pleaded.

Houdini went nuts, not about to question the veracity or source of this phenomenon, not just now. The stuttering intervention had broken his own train of thought—his countdown. He had lost track. Now he didn't know where he was.

He swung like a madman, gaining speed, rocking harder and harder and harder.

The spark appeared over the lip of the roof, much, much sooner than Houdini expected.

Oh fuck! He squirmed.

Houdini lunged for the wall. His feet slipped, leaving him lodged by a jammed fist in a slimy crack—an impossible situation. He slapped a suction device onto the arching gold granite. It clung. He hung part of his weight on it and slapped a second one just above it. It also held. The spark fizzled past him, seconds away . . .

Don't look down. My God . . . His blood and guts gawked.

He was afraid to move up. He ducked, curling as much as possible against the face, squishing his bare feet into the crack and forcing more weight onto them. The cage was still swinging back and forth. And back . . . and forth!

When *WHAMMMM!* With a horrible burst it exploded, not twenty-five feet away from Houdini. Dozens of small chunks smashed into the cliff, some penetrating his back, his leg. He felt the singeing arrows of metal clanging all around his head. Something hit his hand, his waist. He didn't look. The noise was deafening . . . then rumbling, as the fractionated hulk of debris sprayed into the void.

The rumbles continued, up, across, echoing diagonally over every overhang. The entire cliff—over a mile across, hundreds of acres of rock—was like a radio receiver of ululations and frantic birds that massed in circling flocks, screeching. The wall seemed to shiver, like a vertical lake gripped by ripples.

The crowds gyrated with wonder, as the black mushroom of smoke and the display of shrapnel dissipated out into oblivion. Down below, in hidden parts of moss-covered boulder fields, juniper and manzanita, burning steel smashed into earth.

The force of the explosion jolted Thomas. He could tell the burst had exceeded predictions. He untied from his anchor, got out his own rope and hooks and raced downward.

Blood coated Houdini's back and legs, as he clung to the wet, freezing, shadowed crack thirty-one hundred feet above the Valley floor. The water dripping from the melting snow covered large parts of the rock face. It was imperative that Houdini attach his suction devices to dry rock. He jammed his feet into a second crack that was about three inches wide, running uniform all the way to the top. With his hands attached to the suction on either side, he began working his way up.

Thomas rappeled over the edge. He reached the lip of the row of overhangs, beyond which he was not prepared to go. He didn't know how. He could see Houdini, a sickening twenty feet below him. Thomas was overwhelmed with dizziness. He squeezed shut his eyes and forced his muscles to obey the instincts of the summit. Slowly, he started back up, silenced by the horror of the heights. "Don't move," he shouted to Houdini. "I'll be back."

The rock was completely saturated with water and mealy ice. Houdini had a big problem. The suction devices would go no farther. His legs were shaking uncontrollably. A frog looked out at him from the crack and started to croak.

Thomas re-ascended hand over hand up the ropes. He reached the slope, tied heavy rocks to the ends of three secured ropes, took a deep breath and rappeled back down again, holding onto all three lines. He reattained the lip and fed the three ropes down to Houdini's level. They hung fifteen feet out from him.

"I'm going to swing them back and forth. The rocks at the ends should help get them to you!" Thomas called out.

"Do it!" Houdini ordered, his voice as dry as starch and groping. He was hurting inside. His hands were the washed-out color of soap.

The wind was against them. The gusts impeded Thomas's efforts to force the ropes into the wall. Houdini leaned out, but he was not particularly tall. He could not grab hold.

"I'm losing strength, Thomas!" Houdini cried. It was the first time in his life he'd ever admitted it.

Thomas had no choice. He closed his eyes and continued down, into the blind, unknowing zone of forces. His rappel system was a Swiss-styled *dulfersitz*. Two ropes tied at the summit went between his legs, around his waist and over his back, down his chest and into his controlling hand. It was an unstable system and rarely used for overhangs. Thomas didn't know that. He knew hardly anything about mountain climbing.

He dropped half a foot and took in a huge volume of air,

opening his eyes. His feet did not want to let go of the rock. Finally they gave in, as he sat in midair, the equivalent of three hundred and twenty stories above the Valley floor.

The frog continued to commune with the first primate in geological history to attain the summit overhangs of El Capitan.

Thomas lowered himself in a sitting position, relying almost entirely on his biceps for control. He reached Houdini. The two men were two body lengths apart. Thomas managed to get the three suspended ropes in his mouth and started swinging toward Houdini. With each exertion, he was carried that much farther away, then back again. Houdini would not be able to let go of the rock to pull him in. Thomas would have to somehow get his own purchase in the crack, while swinging like a pendulum.

Ten tries later, desperate, Thomas finagled himself onto a foothold, twisting his ankle to the breaking point in a dark fissure. Now he was trapped at a slant, his body wanting to swing back out in a straight line with the rappel rope, his foot unwilling to let go. Thomas's guide hand held the ropes at his crotch, and with his other hand he reached out. Houdini could not resist. He reached for Thomas.

Houdini's suction cups came unglued, but his foot, like Thomas's, remained caught in the crack. They looked as ridiculous to that frog as any two men ever would.

Houdini lunged for the three ropes that Thomas held in his teeth.

"Let go!" Houdini rasped.

Thomas got confused, letting go of his rappel lines rather than the lines between his teeth.

Houdini pulled. Thomas fell over backward. Only Thomas's sturdy, Wisconsin buck teeth could have countered such forces as were at work against them.

Now Houdini was additionally pulled by the weight of Thomas, who clung to his leg.

"God, hold me!" he cried.

Houdini pulled the two of them into the wall. The rappel ropes dangled tantalizingly close but beyond reach.

Houdini held three lines in his hands, each approximately an inch in diameter, made of hemp that was still relatively dry. He righted Thomas, whose mouth was drooling blood, and stabilized the both of them. "Pull!" he bellowed, his entire body quaking, his thoughts fighting off the expanse of space all around him.

Houdini held on, making sure Thomas held on as well. The two of them muscled their way to the lip. Five minutes of total hell.

Then they were there, muscles pumped, the air ready to rush out of them. Both men squinted and groaned, wracked with the violence of their effort.

And then Houdini slipped, at the least expected instant. Thomas was there, his foot having found the flat, one-foot-wide square of ledge for anchor atop the roof. He caught Houdini's arm and with the last of his iron will held firm. Houdini hung free. The blood on both of their hands, slimy and partially dried, seemed to coagulate according to strange laws of weather and physiology that made for friction. The hands stuck. The muscles endured. Houdini dug in, pulled on Thomas's damp pants leg, groveled upward until he stood on that ledge, grabbing with the free hand for the ropes . . . *Shem U'Malchus . . . shehecheyanu . . .* a prayer, his father's, from infancy. Lost. Now recovered.

Both men knew that Thomas had just saved Houdini's life, that Houdini would have plunged at the breakneck velocity of a bullet from a silencer.

Toe to toe, they shared the minute ledge. It was over. From here the sheer wall gave way to a forty-five-degree summit slab.

Together, they climbed up the wall to safety and to the cheering and camera flashing that awaited them. Down in the Valley, fireworks were set off to mark the achievement. People whooped and clapped.

Houdini's stomach was a knot. His veins felt frozen. He

was shaken as never in his life, not by the nightmarish sequence of physical events, which he was already exorcising from his being, but by that *voice*!

A hallucination. It had to be.

But as he reached the actual summit, the echo of that voice returned, rising eternally from his bowels. It whispered, covered in the static of far away, a sinister, blithering stutter, dark and horror-filled, pleading, that let him know it—*He*—was real.

Houdini's own inner convictions were obliterated. The impossible intruder had understood his situation down to the second.

Thomas rolled onto the granite rim. Houdini sat down beside him. There was a rush of spectators toward the two men.

"That was the worst," Thomas groaned. "I mean *the worst*!" He was spent. He was broken. He was gone. It was the first time he'd ever experienced one of Houdini's myriad perils in the flesh.

Joe and Royale were sweating for all four of them.

"Welcome," Houdini croaked.

Bess embraced her husband, furious, choking on dual emotions.

That night the Houdini entourage, along with thousands of other visitors, watched as some Indians brought in by the park service, former residents who now lived in shacks outside the Valley, performed one of their rites from the top of another cliff, the Fire Fall Wall. Burning logs were tossed over the lip. The wall was twenty-five hundred feet high. The slowly turning logs, draped in a ribbon of flame and spark, required nearly half a minute to hit a lower cliff and then disintegrate into the talus slopes at the bottom. That was it. From where the enthralled visitors stood, in the parking lot at Camp Curry, there was no sense of ritual particularly. They did not see that well-seasoned buckeye had been used, or a drill called *kayana*. Or the torch of pine needles known as *haku*.

There weren't many around who could make much sense of Indian ritual, but the burning logs made for quite a sight, definitely worth rehashing over roasted marshmallows later that night, which is exactly what Amy and Thomas did, cuddling beside a camp fire in their own corner of half-darkness, a woolen blanket draped over their fast-burgeoning tryst.

Amy had been routinely sending word to Harrington and Doyle of Houdini's escapades. Three near misses in seventy-two hours in Los Angeles. No one who was there could fail to grasp the odd sense of contagion involved. Something strange or terrible was finally catching up with Houdini. To Harrington and the others at the magazine, it was the same old Houdini—brilliant, aloof, untouchable. To Doyle, the incoming news presaged of more and more miracles, greater affirmation of first principles, fodder for his own inevitable victory.

Houdini and Bess returned to their tent. Houdini wore the duncolored Holland jacket his mother had given him, years ago, to keep warm in rugged places.

Both were sullen, but Bess was the one to register Houdini's coming fit. "Why don't you lie down," she said unemotionally.

Outside their tent, Amy, who had temporarily left Thomas on the pretext of a beckoning Mother Nature, stood and eavesdropped. She had seen the two of them earlier and knew something major was in the wind.

Houdini was standing at the portable mirror that had been hung at one end of the tent. A large pole, man-size, stood in the center of the canvas housing. Two metal cots, side by side, lay opposite the mirror and the movable basin in which the Houdinis could wash if they wanted. It was an army tent, with one large flap that opened to the outside.

Dr. Mayer Samuel Weiss, Cecelia Steiner . . . I pronounce you man and wife . . . The words came back to him for no reason, words he'd never heard, of course. Outside, night noises, campers, cars, fire crackling, girls giggling, upset the delicate balance. Dust blew in through the flap.

"Harry? Why don't you——"

"Why don't you shut *up! Leave me alone!*" he screamed viciously, turning around, lifting the mirror from its strings. He looked at himself, then smashed his fist into the glass, holding the wooden backing for support. The mirror quietly crumpled inside its frame. Houdini's knuckles, calloused by the years, shed no blood. He let the glass fall to the dirt underfoot.

"All right," she said. Bess pretended it hadn't happened. She undid her blouse, removed her saddle oxfords, folded her corduroy trousers on a steel chair and propped herself more or less comfortably on her cot.

"I'm sorry," he sighed.

Houdini played the stuttering voice back in his mind. It had saved his life and he could not begin to account for it. It was no hallucination. His inner world was in jeopardy now.

"I can't cope with this," he finally said in a boy's defenseless voice. His animosity toward Doyle had turned on that cliff into a grudging question mark that even now began to rewrite his own history, his relationship to his parents, his wife, the children they had never had. His future hung totally in the balance of the moment.

Bess saw a pain as full and ripe as any rosebush in season blossom, all over her husband's face, which was flushed with the red of antipathy turned inward.

"Don't take your insanity out on the one person who loves you. Never a good rule of thumb," Bess finally stated with calm reserve. She would ordinarily have let her silence weigh upon Harry until he begged for some kind of mercy, or came around to her side and apologized like a man. But events had escalated.

"Bess, Doyle's right."

Outside, Amy's eyes widened to receive the full brunt of moonlight up above. Her blue eyes stared all alone at the perplexing shadow play inside the Houdini's canvas tent.

"Oh that's brilliant. Doyle's right," she repeated glibly. "Right about what?"

"About . . . about the future."

"You're mumbling."

"Life after death."

"Just because you pulled another fast one on the grim reaper is no cause to get all religious, Harry. I heard enough of that rancid church bunk growing up at home. Don't you start siding with them."

"I'm not siding. Something happened on the cliff."

"Harry, you need a vacation."

"Bess, a voice spoke to me in the cage. It warned me how much time I had to get out. The voice stuttered. A voice I've never heard before. It knew, Bess. It knew everything, down to the second. How do you explain that?"

"You imagined it."

"No. It was there, all right. And he followed me to the top."

"Oh, so it was a he?" she carped cynically.

"A young man. In pain. Wanting to help me."

"You're crazy." She closed her book. "I'm going to sleep."

Houdini held her tightly. "Bess, listen to me. I can't go on with the contest. First that damned Italian broad throws me across a stage. Now this. Doyle's in touch. I've been out of touch."

Bess stared at him. "You're a pitiful sight. You resign from the contest and you might as well write off your whole career."

"How can you say that?" It wasn't the response he'd wanted. "Bess, there was a voice. A spirit of some kind. I can't keep up the pretense in the face of such evidence. I just can't do it."

"What do you want me to say? Maybe lunacy is your just reward for putting me through so much . . . Ahh, Harry! My mother was right." She shook her head. "What am I to do with you?"

"Love me." He never talked that way. Bess leaned into him.

"Are you hungry?" she said in plain English.

"We just ate."

"I mean for dessert?"

She put her arms around him.

Amy hastened back to Thomas, who was busy keeping the fire alive.

In the morning, Houdini got up early, walked around outside, through the slanted Sierra blues of smoke and early morning motes that penetrated the high-standing cedars. Houdini looked and felt bad. His body evidenced all the places where he'd been hit by the flying pieces of steel. One of his eyes was swollen, black and blue. He looked at it in his car mirror. Walking back to the tent barefoot over the forest duff, he stepped on a sharp pine needle and danced in pain. The inscrutable spike had gone deep, puncturing an enormous blood blister on his right foot, which he'd jammed into the crack on the cliff. The foot remained twisted-looking. The toes might have been broken. He sat down on the ground, resolved. He would announce his decision at a press conference. It was the end. He decided to wake the others.

"Don't do it, Harry," Bess said. She was flustered by doubts, troubles, questions about her husband's uncanny powers that had never been resolved in her own mind. "Finish out the contest for Christ's sake. What does it matter?"

"It matters!" And with that he stormed out of the tent, his temperature up again.

"Hey, everybody . . ." And soon there were Thomas and Amy, their tents side-by-side, Frank, Dexter, Joe, Royale, Byron and a few reporters standing, putting their boots on, sipping mugs of coffee.

"Harry, it just doesn't make any sense," Bess said, trying to stop him. There was no doubting the emotional strain, the profound turnarounds, or the reminiscences of his parents, which always set him back some. But Harry was no medium, and Bess was certain that his confession would set them both in a tailspin.

"I'm quitting the *Scientifica Americana* contest," he announced.

"Why!" Simpson and the others shouted. This was big stuff. The biggest.

But Houdini would not say. This was his concession to Bess.

"There's got to be a reason," the press pounded.

Finally, Houdini said that he felt badly about his vigilantism. "Who am I to shut down another man's dreams" is how he politely put it.

What neither Bess nor Houdini knew, of course, was that Amy had overheard the previous night's soul-searching. She had caught enough to understand that a mystical experience involving a stuttering boy had saved Houdini's life on the cliff. It was the immortal truth she'd been secretly praying for, the great hope of the beyond which Doyle had first inspired in her many weeks before at Carnegie Hall. When Houdini announced that the contest was off, her wildest hopes were confirmed. Her brother's soul had not perished after all. There was continuation on earth. The spirit lived. Death meant nothing.

Amy was ablaze with the news and made for the nearest telephone, while Simpson and the others were writing out their respective stories for various newspapers.

In New York it was the middle of a workday. Harrington was at his desk when Amy called to tell him the news.

"That bastard can't do this to me! We have a contract!" he shouted.

A few minutes later, after examining their westward itinerary, Amy placed a call to Illinois and reached Lady Doyle at her hotel in Chicago.

"A voice which stuttered and saved Houdini's life! He's quitting . . ." Lady Doyle repeated the words to her husband later that afternoon, over tea in the hotel restaurant, where Sir Arthur had just returned from lecturing at the university.

Before even stopping to consider the mixed company of reporters, Doyle burst out with the glorious news.

"Kingsley! Did you hear!" he shouted to all those present. "Our son has saved Houdini's life!"

And within two days it was in nearly every newspaper in the United States and England.

15

Buffalo Stampede

Houdini and Doyle approach each other, as the lines of battle draw nearer.

It seemed to Harrington that every street corner heralded his downfall. "Extra! Extra! Houdini loses. Read all about it!" He grabbed a copy on his way to Penn Station. The headline was terrible: "DOYLE'S DEAD SON SAVES THE GREAT HOUDINI ON CLIFF IN YOSEMITE!"

The night before he'd reached Doyle by telephone, and talked things over. It was imperative, both agreed, that Houdini be induced to come back into the contest for the final go-around in Denver. According to Harrington's train routing, he and the committee would be passing through Chicago in three days, where the Doyles would meet them, and they'd all continue to the Mile High City together.

"I do sympathize with your concerns," Doyle said. "But you must know that what happened in Yosemite was a miracle that should take its place beside Golgotha, Bernadette of Lourdes or the Bo Tree in India." It was under such a tree that Buddha once discerned his past lives amid a downward flurry of ten thousand red blossoms.

"Perhaps, perhaps not," Harrington decreed, his gut churning. "But with no contest, who the hell's going to know about it?"

"You are sworn to objectivity. We are both men of science. Yet whatever you say or do from this point on will never alter this great irrevocable moment. This is the dawning of a new age."

"I hope so." Harrington wanted Doyle, at least, on his side. He had one goal in mind: conciliation.

Doyle felt the sweet rush of conquest. "I have every expectation," he said, grinning over the phone while the maid freshened up their room and puffed up the pillows, "that my wife, together with our new friend, Princess Anne, is going to win that thirty thousand dollars. More importantly, Ralph, they are going to secure the long-overdue triumph which spiritualism deserves. You *do* understand?"

"We'll see," Harrington replied. He fervently hoped that the Doyles might soon be released from their madness. *Denver, may it be Denver*! resonated through him.

Releasing Houdini from his agreement, however, was a mule of a different stubbornness. Harrington had spoken briefly with Houdini after the latter's press conference in Yosemite. They'd quarreled over the phone, as could have been expected. Harrington was choleric, accusatory, and tried to make Houdini look ridiculous and pathetic. Houdini stumbled slightly; his newfound reticence had not had time to dig in. Harrington still avidly sensed hope.

As for Doyle, he knew exactly what to do to coax Houdini back into the contest. From Amy's interpretation of events, and the perplexed and hesitant comments attributed to Houdini atop El Capitan, as well as the sparing press conference the magician had given on the Valley floor, Doyle divined that Houdini was running scared. Doyle knew that he—or rather, his son Kingsley—had hooked the grandest, most stubborn trout of all. But the fish could get away if the event was not handled properly. Houdini was still no believer. The Sherlock in Doyle was a good reader of human nature. And he knew that Houdini was as taciturn as any criminal mind.

So was Doyle's late son, Kingsley. Often, the two of them had argued.

"This is sheer lunacy," the lad had said of his father's inordinately large donation to one of many spiritualist charities in London. "Don't you see how they're using you; how unbecoming. Why, it's embarrassing to the whole family!"

But death had changed the boy's temperament. One of the first things Pheneas uttered, coming from Kingsley, was "Forgive me, father."

And since Houdini was also known to change his mind, Doyle had every reason to expect that Houdini would reverse himself within a few days and come out punching once again. In Doyle's mind, Houdini was as vulnerable to suggestion as a street fighter. He'd have to be thoroughly beaten, broken, black and blue, before he could see the true light once and for all.

Sir Arthur spoke about it with his wife. "I think, as in any battle, he's simply retreating to size up his troops, recollect energies and weigh strategy."

"And I think you're reading too much into it. We've won, Arthur," Lady Doyle affirmed. She was riding high on the communion of Toledo. Her soul murmured constantly now, possessed as it was by the Princess. Pheneas too seemed to have made the dark, interior adjustment and found apparent solace.

"There has been no judgment by the committee, my dear. Until there is, we've won nothing."

It was now up to Doyle to feign extreme weakness, show his own vulnerable side, rebolster Houdini's moment of pause, seduce his adversary into certain defeat. Doyle knew his Clausewitz. He had the gaming spirit. And even though "adversary" was not right, since both men were headed in the same direction, like it or not, Doyle would reel Houdini in all the same, with the suave and cunning of a Scotch fly fisherman.

If it had been up to Ralph, he'd have kept the contest going for a whole year. Subscriptions to the magazine were pouring in. Readers seemed frantic to get the "inside story" on spooks and goblins, mediums and other extrasensory phenomena, to analyze for themselves the committee and Houdini's ghost-busting techniques and determine whether they had really been sufficient. Even "Daddy" looked approvingly on his wayward son-in-law's sudden turn of fortune.

Harrington was gambling. The committee had not yet been tempted to cite any verifiable after-death experience. Harrington could call it quits and consider his magazine the victor.

On the other hand, Houdini *had* given the press cause for rampant speculation in favor of something spiritual. Why had he quit? Had Doyle convinced him? The new subscriptions would not continue for long in such a climate, and there was certainly not enough new revenue to secure the magazine's future. Harrington had to play it out. Yet were Houdini to come back into the contest, and then lose . . . that would be disastrous. The magazine would never recover. Not only that, but the very basis, the rational, American *way* that was *Scientifica Americana*, would be ruined. Harrington himself would be the laughing stock. These thoughts had him shaking inside.

His editors calmed his fears. Fennell assured him that everything would be all right. Committee members had already shown their scientific bias. It would take more than a mere miracle to change their minds.

● ● ●

A few days later, as planned, Harrington and crew met up with the Doyles at the busiest passenger station in the world, that of the Chicago and North Western railroads.

Captain Pushcart continued to travel with the Doyles, arranging their affairs en route. Eighteen porters were required to move the committee's crates of delicate scientific equipment from their incoming trunk line to the outgoing. As the expedition boarded the train, a woman appeared before Sir Arthur carrying a copy of his latest nonfiction work, *The New Revelation*, a blueprint for life beyond. It was obvious what she wanted. Doyle generously took out his pen and leaned down to autograph the book.

"Make it out to my son, Bobby," the woman said. "He died in the war."

"I'm sorry," commiserated Doyle. "I lost a boy as well."

He wrote something very moving and personal for the woman.

"I believe in the spirit world just like you," she went on. "What you said at your lecture—about eating chocolates with our loved ones in the afterlife . . . You were wonderful!" She began to mutter something . . . "reunited" . . . spirited away by her own convictions. Captain Pushcart saw that the lady was coming unhinged, clearly on a crazy roll.

"Train's leaving," Pushcart yelled.

Sir Arthur tried to excuse himself. Lady Doyle saw it coming—a knife pulled out from the woman's cape—but it was too late.

"Arthur!" Lady Doyle screamed.

Pushcart lunged for the woman as Sir Arthur threw himself out of the way.

But the woman was no murderess: her knife raised, she then resolutely drew the dagger into her own heart.

"I'm coming, Bobby!" she cried, collapsing against Pushcart. The Captain let her sink gracefully to the concrete floor and backed away, horrified. A space opened up all around her. Her bonnet fell from her head. Its bright tanager feathers were covered by the spreading pool of blood.

A blue-uniformed policeman ran up and knelt over the expiring woman. "You best be on your way," the officer advised. "There's nothing you can do for her."

"I'm a doctor, you fool!" Doyle shouted, rummaging through his traveling kit for something that might help stop her bleeding.

"If you're a doctor then you should know a dead woman when you see one," the presiding officer stated authoritatively. "I see them all the time."

"We're going to miss the train!" Pushcart informed the party.

Doyle had circled the woman's face with his hands. "Death, leave this woman be!" he whispered, to no avail.

The officer leaned down and closed the woman's eyes. Doyle stood up. With his back tall, and his hat fixed in tribute against his heart, he and his wife boarded the train.

"What did she say before she killed herself?" the local reporters shouted at Doyle, running alongside of the train. But he and Lady Doyle had removed themselves to the interior.

Several hours later, passing mile after mile of sun-drenched corn, alone in their compartment, Lady Doyle took her husband's hand. He was feeling inconsolable.

"It happened so fast!" he ruminated out loud. "Could I have stopped her?"

"Her mind was already made up. She knew where she wanted to go," Lady Doyle assured him.

"Jean, have I failed my public?"

She shook her head. "No. You've given this whole generation enormous inspiration to go on."

"Then why?"

"She was obviously unstable, Arthur."

"Or she took my inspiration to heart."

"No. She took it too far. That is not the way and you've never once said that it was."

"Do you see that!"

There was blood from the woman on Doyle's right shoe.

He removed it with incredulity and examined the remains. "Oh, God, I feel so bad."

"Dear, dear . . ."

Lady Doyle comforted him, whispering, crying. They both needed to hold onto loved ones who had departed and were stricken with a desperate fear of releasing the familiar. Yet, she held out all kinds of poignant hope, as did Sir Arthur. Hope in the corporeal reality of spirit, the continuity of souls, hope that was, in the end, merely Christian and good.

"You gave her a reason to live on, in the next world," Lady Doyle concluded, renouncing all pessimism or angst. And she continued to reflect on all that had happened to them in America thus far.

On a second, eastbound train, the Denver and Rio Grande Western, Houdini was working out on the caboose, using his own improvised gymnasium of bars to do pull-ups, and climbing all over the sides of the train. Chugging across the narrow gauge of the twelve-hundred-foot Royal Gorge, Houdini made bold his unwillingness to be intimidated by death, traversing along the outside of passenger windows, clinging with fingertips that had been honed on El Capitan. He was preparing for what he'd promised Bess would be his final stunt—ever—at Denver.

The whole Houdini entourage was expectant. Simpson and the other reporters traveling along were perplexed by Houdini's change of heart. The great showman wasn't talking, either, not since the press conference in Yosemite. Something had happened. The press had missed it, though Simpson was not going to give up on the strange conversation that Houdini appeared to have conducted—alone.

Simpson kept pressing for ways to get at that conversation.

"What do you *think* it was?" he bugged Thomas.

Thomas denied that anything out of the ordinary had taken place. He knew that Simpson was looking for an angle, and he was not about to give it to him. But Thomas also feared the visible change in Houdini.

"What's going on?" he asked Bess.

"Harry's upset."

"I know he's upset. Things haven't gone so good lately. But why drop out of the contest?"

"Three near deaths. He's getting old."

"Come on!"

At that moment, Houdini returned along the outside of the train, hanging with adroit imperviousness. "You call that old!"

"I don't know, Tom. He's scared. Maybe Doyle is getting to him."

"That's nuts. Doyle's just an old fart if you ask me. Maybe the guy can write—I haven't read any—but . . ." He stumbled. "You saw him, he's a fruitcake."

Bess looked at her husband as he finished his unabashedly arrogant workout. It was true that his body worked like a young machine. But he looked wrinkled, worn out. And the changes had occurred in so short a time. She didn't know what was best for the two of them.

"I wouldn't talk about it, Tom," she said. "He's got a lot on his mind. He'll have to work it out. I'm done trying to persuade him one way or the other."

Thomas had his own future to work out. He knew Houdini's years at the top were numbered, and he harbored no illusions: there could only be one Houdini. Houdini's brother—that 'can of sardeens' as he was now alluded to— had tried to duplicate some of the magic, but without much success. Thomas knew all the tricks, of course, all the machinery and technique. But he was no self-abuser, no athlete. Sooner or later he'd have to strike out on his own. Whatever he did—engineering automobiles, perhaps, or airplanes—he wanted a wife to journey down that road with him. Maybe a few kids, as well.

Frank's situation was made difficult as a result of

Houdini's declaration in Yosemite. Byron's "deal" appeared to be off.

"You're really dropping out?" Frank had asked Houdini the next day, once the party had departed from Yosemite.

"I don't know, Frank."

"But the press—"

"Forget the press."

"I don't get it."

"I don't either, exactly."

Frank shook his head. For the first time since he'd come to work for Houdini, he was baffled by his boss's behavior. "Well what about Holstein? And what about Byron?"

"The contest is going to continue, with or without me. The deal with Byron is still on."

Frank went and chatted quietly with Bess. "I don't believe it. It's just not like him to give up."

"We'll see," she said. "There's still time for him to change his mind."

She was waiting for her husband's fury to resume, certain that it would. Bess gave no quarter to spiritualism and now felt more than a tinge of embarrassment for her husband's having conceded the prize, as the press made more and more of his alleged defeat.

That night, several hours after a dinner of smoked perch, sautéed carrots and ox-bone soup served up regimental style in the diner car, Thomas visited Amy in her berth. It was late, the moon was a mere sliver, and they were both feeling lulled by the rhythmic clappady-clappady-clap. Around midnight their train moved from the pitch darkness of snowbound mountain walls into the garish town lights of Leadville, where they stopped, picked up a few passengers and continued on. Amy reflected on the heroic Baby Doe Tabor, a celebrated rags-to-riches beauty queen who—though now in her late sixties, and living in an impoverished cabin—still clung to the dream of her late silver mining husband, Horace. His mine, the Matchless, had gone bankrupt in the panic of 1893 but Baby Doe had never forgotten his rather universal final words. "Hang on to the Matchless. It will make millions." Amy peered out the dark window of her berth. Somewhere just out there, beyond the train tracks, in the Rocky Mountains, was Baby Doe Tabor. Amy sighed, affected by the altitude, though she didn't know it.

"Do you feel a little . . . weird?" Amy asked Thomas.

Thomas had his own interpretation of her query and now felt empowered. He stroked her hair.

"Yeah . . . I do," he said cajolingly.

"I'm so sleepy," Amy continued.

"Do you want me to leave?"

"You can stay," she said.

Thomas thought about what to talk about. He grew slightly self-conscious.

"What's wrong?" Amy inquired.

"Do you know that Lady Doyle speaks to ghosts?"

"Whoever told you that?"

"It's common knowledge. She's supposedly in touch with a spirit called Pheneas."

"I didn't know," she said.

"I think Houdini's really spooked by those two."

"The Doyles are incredible," she attested.

"You think so?"

"They're bringing a whole new life to people."

"What's wrong with the life we've got?"

She grew indignant. "Nothing's *wrong*. They're just . . . they're adding to it. Showing what's possible. I think it's important. Far more important than risking one's life for—" She stopped herself, not wanting to insult Thomas's guru.

"You can say it. I know. Bess certainly knows."

"We've talked about it. I like Bess a lot."

Thomas nodded. "She likes you."

"They've really been parents to you, haven't they?"

"Yeah."

"You never told me about your real parents."

"You never asked. They died when I was a kid. I lived

down the street from the Houdinis. They more or less adopted me. Not officially or anything."

"No brothers or sisters?"

"Nah. I always wanted a sister, though."

"Really? Why?"

"I don't know. Maybe she'd look like you."

She melted, and waited.

He'd kissed her on the cheek the last night in Yosemite, which Amy found annoyingly frugal of him. After a year in New York she was not the small-town girl anymore. She was no flapper, either, but "proper" was boring. Amy was restless, wondering, waiting. Thomas, however, was still rural Wisconsin to the core, despite his worldly travels with the Houdinis. He'd never had time to cultivate a liaison, having had to spend his late nights monkeying with contraptions for the next day's act. Houdini's life frequently depended upon him. They were perfectly matched: neither Thomas nor Amy knew what to do next.

"You must know a lot of Houdini's rope tricks," Amy said, adjusting her nightgown.

"You kidding? Sure I do. Make up some of them myself."

"You got any rope?"

"Down in the baggage compartment. You really want to see a trick?"

"Why not!"

Thomas hurried after a coil of hemp. Amy gussied herself up in a mirror, applying a touch of eye shadow and lipstick, as well as a dab of Siamese Musk beneath her right ear.

Thomas returned to the berth, having avoided waking up the guys in baggage.

"Better lock the door," Amy said.

"Oh, right."

"What do I do?" Amy began, as Thomas started to tie a knot in midair with the intention of then sliding his fingers over it to magically make the knot disappear from the rope.

"What do you mean?"

"I mean should I lie flat or sit up?"

"You want me to tie you?"

"Well of course!"

"Lie down."

She lay like an Egyptian mummy, her head touching the steel bedboard, her hip against the wooden trim of the window, her bare toes just missing the steel filigree against the far wall.

"Does Houdini ever tie Bess up?"

"Heck, I don't think so," Thomas said, applying the rope to her ankles. "Tell me if it's too tight," he went on.

Amy cocked her lips, staring up at the ceiling. "Aren't you going to tie my arms, too?" she asked.

Thomas wondered aloud, then awkwardly acquiesced. "Of course I am."

He stretched the rope in a figure eight that crossed between her breasts.

"What trick are you going to show me?" she cajoled, still looking up with an exasperating innocence, he thought. She knew if her eyes met Thomas's she'd start giggling. The rope felt good atop her nightgown.

"I don't know yet," he said, tightening the bowline-on-bites knot around her wrists and cross-tying the figure eight so that her whole body was now in a fix. "Too tight?" he asked.

"Better make it tighter," she said. "I might get away!"

He tautened every slipknot, bow tie and Windsor; doubled, tripled each interlacement, until Amy was solidly plastered to her bed, her arms extended above her head.

She tested her latitude. Her head, hips and bosom were still maneuverable, but not her appendages. "That's better," Amy stated. "Why don't you turn off the light? Houdini always does his tricks in the dark."

"No he doesn't," Thomas corrected her.

"Not even sometimes?"

His hands were trembling. He switched off the light.

"I give you until dawn to untie me," she whispered.

Thomas sat next to her on the bed. "You're so beautiful," he murmured, leaning over to kiss her on the mouth.

"What's beautiful?" she replied.

Thomas touched his finger to her lips. She opened them. He inserted his tongue. Amy had stored up years' worth of moaning.

Then, after some minutes of unsuppressible groans and the free exchange of saliva, Thomas drew a line with his right index finger from her delicious lips down to her chest. His mouth followed. Amy's nipples were firmer than gold nuggets, as hard and presaging as his own member.

Hours later, at the first crepuscular intimation of dawn, Thomas tossed the slightly bloodstained sheet out the train window and, lacking the requisite goods, plucked a single long hair from his head and deftly tied it into a slipknot around her engagement finger.

"Will you marry me, Amy Beckwell?" Thomas said with monumental politeness. He was lying naked beside her under the daffodil-patterned covers.

"What do you think?" She blushed, and started to weep.

The train whistled. They were passing out of the mountains, alongside the famous Red Rocks, where the tin roofs of a silver mine shimmered to first light, and the rocks turned golden, as the enormous orb of morning rose like God with a hangover, beyond the vast expanse of prairie.

Everything turned golden. They were even passing through Golden, the town on the Denver outskirts, that is. And from before them, light filled with two hundred miles of pulsating grasslands, from Nebraska to Wyoming, light colliding with the everlasting Rockies, spilled into the berth, touching Amy's lips, lips wet and wanting more, and more and more.

Thomas put on his pants, kissed her again, took all the rope and slipped out of her berth. He stopped in at the urinal, then ducked back to the baggage compartment, where he silently recoiled the rope and started checking out the gear. Thomas was the happiest man alive.

By nine o'clock that Saturday morning, Dexter had taken care of checking the whole clan in at the super-luxurious Brown Palace Hotel in downtown Denver. Then they all headed up in waiting Packards and Buicks to the foothills, an hour away from the big stunt.

Bess sat in the thick grass of a mountain meadow several miles across, still largely covered with snow, applying balms and taping her husband's knee, which he'd injured in his Yosemite exploit. On one side of them, two hundred yards away, were bleachers; on the other side, fifty yards away, a forest of beautiful silver spruce. Thomas was in the trees, double-checking everything. Amy was by his side, teasing him.

A few miles away, on Lookout Mountain, Buffalo Bill had been buried six years before in a tomb blasted from the mountainside. Cody had once killed 4,280 buffaloes in seventeen months, using a 50-calibre breech-loading Springfield rifle. He bragged about his carnage in sufficient degree to lend him his nickname, and give his Wild West show a theatrical send-off.

Plenty of the buffalo had survived, however. Two miles away, at the far end of the field, Houdini saw them grazing on the wild grasses that jutted out from frozen soil, a huddled mass, slightly distorted by the mirage of cold mist. Summer had come late to the Rockies this year.

There were several hundred of the huge bison, with their humps, enormous limbs, convex heads and fourteen sets of ribs, worthy of animal worship, not slaughter. Houdini planned to lie down before them.

Houdini went over the trick with Thomas one last time. Stationed in the forest—not hidden from spectators, but discreet in his movements—Thomas needed merely to activate the trick cable that ran through a few deadeyes, just under the meadow grass and remaining spring snow, completely covered. That simple gesture of the thumb would release all of the lanyards, which in turn released the locks. The system had been tested dozens of times in hotel rooms, though not actually in the wild. Thomas reminded Harry of that. But Houdini was confident. He trusted the boys, and knew that they had tested the system under a foot of soil in the baggage compartment of the train, and it had worked flawlessly.

The cable ran to a perverse-looking apparatus, low to the ground, surrounded by sharp iron stakes sunk deep in the earth.

The gatekeepers walked out onto the field and felt the steel mechanisms as Houdini lay sprawled out and trapped. The Spanish Inquisition, or the Klan, could not have situated him in a more vulnerable-looking position. Before the gigantic crowd, the officials assured themselves and the spectators that Houdini was probably a goner.

They took their hats off to him, shook their heads and paid their audible respects to the Missus—Bess—who waited visibly at the edge of the forest, fifty yards on the other side from Houdini.

These bison loved to run. Houdini knew these beasts from hearing about them as a kid during his circus days. He understood from eyewitness accounts of Buffalo Bill's show that they were benign, boasted of loving eyes, and he was relaxed with the idea that they'd never step on him as long as he remained within the undeviating narrow margin of stakes that Joe and Royale had hammered into the ground.

From the bleachers two hundred yards away, where all the thousands of arriving spectators were being seated—after paying a dollar for their tickets—it would look as if Houdini were doing the impossible. The bison were to be stampeded by men on horseback directly into Houdini's path. His only apparent chance of escape—once he extricated himself from the complex of shackles—was to roll back and forth with quick and precise dexterity, avoiding hundreds of down-crushing hooves.

The effect would be foreshortened the way a camera lens could be altered to blur foreground or background. Assuming the animals stayed together, Houdini would remain free of the coming avalanche. A margin of inches, perhaps, but free. Even if the animals divided around Houdini's little island, the river of hooves—according to Houdini's "behavioral intelligence"—would stay clear of him by sheer reflex. The audience could only be enthralled. This was the last. He'd promised Bess. With the several thousand dollars for a morning's work, he'd buy her whatever she wanted. Houdini was a new man. He was making up, making peace.

All that aside, it was presently imperative that Houdini concentrate on freeing himself from those constraints with enough advance time. If he were not able to flail visibly, the bison wouldn't see him, as his incarcerated position kept him absolutely low to the ground, spread-eagled, flat on his stomach, face to the stampede, concealed by the higher grass. He'd be a dead man.

They poured in. The grandstands overflowed. A thousand additional onlookers stood behind and to the sides. Total gate—eight thousand. Frank and his assistants, as well as two local sheriffs, scoured the many rows.

Bess had implored Harry to put it off a few days. She knew that he was still "spooked" by the events surrounding that mysterious voice in Yosemite. He was exhausted and emotionally ragged. But Houdini insisted he was just getting his second wind and not to worry about a thing. She knew enough not to argue with him on the day of a stunt. It was bad luck.

The hawkers finished selling their goods. They had the normal percentage deal with Houdini's local impresario.

The bison were readied at the far end of the field by the three men on horseback. The animals were snorting, avoiding the horses, churned up. A man sitting at the top of the bleachers with a megaphone started a countdown.

Then the men raised their guns and fired into the air, triggering the stampede.

The crowd roared.

From Houdini's ground-level perspective, the charging mass of furry monsters made a marvelous sound. The ground rumbled like an acoustical imprint from Pompei during its final seconds. Their hooves biting into the snow and mud, the snorting behemoths exploded toward him like cannon fire, bearing down on the bare-backed Houdini.

Bess stood beside Amy and Thomas just inside the perimeter of forest, her fingernails digging into the bark of a silver spruce. She could see Harry staring directly into the oncoming mob. They were a mile away now.

Harry turned his head and calmly smiled at Thomas. It was the sign.

"Now!" Bess cried.

Thomas backed away from the clearing and gave an extra hard yank on the concealed wire that led into his palm.

Houdini tried to get out of the locks. His repeated attempts were futile. He turned again calmly to Thomas and echoed his wife's injunction.

"Now, Thomas, do it now!"

Thomas struggled, yanking again and again.

"Jesus, the thing's stuck!" Thomas shouted.

"Fix it," Houdini said, still cool, a good minute left before the animals would crash down on him.

Thomas, with the help of Amy, yanked again, and again. "It's no good!" Thomas's speech was slurred. "Harry, nothing!"

He ran out into the field and looked toward the bison charging his way, then began to fumble in terror.

Thomas frantically pulled up cable from the frozen soil, like a dead fuse, to the point where it had jammed. Still it wouldn't release. Bess was now screaming.

Houdini struggled to free himself without the help of the system.

"Stand in front of me!" he said to Thomas. "Divert them. That's all you need to do."

But Thomas was intent on helping Houdini get out. He couldn't stand in front. The idea was appalling.

Spectators were rising now.

Houdini's every muscle bulged. Wriggling insanely, he

ripped one arm out of the device, blood soaking the lacerated skin; his toes squirmed, his throat burned, his eyes were bursting forward, and his fingers seemed incandescent, touched by lightning. The whole body was transformed, convulsing like a wing of a hummingbird, like fire. Bess had never seen the phenomenon. It was a slow-motion eruption, not human. The body transmogrified, bolted upward, like a flying fish seized with the idea of the sky.

In a matter of seconds all of the locks snapped open, and Houdini got every appendage out at once and screamed at Thomas, *"Get over here!"* as he waved his arms wildly, then curled back down into a ball between the stakes, leaving room for his assistant.

"Thomas, do it!" Amy pleaded.

But Thomas hesitated too long, caught in a purgatory of fear and indecision—whether to dive into Houdini's island or run toward Amy's open arms, into the forest. He went for Amy.

It was too late. The bison poured in on either side of Houdini's island. Like an avalanche down the Matterhorn, lava spewing from Vesuvius, the Nile flooding its delta— whatever analogous horror one might seize, nothing could match the indomitable force of killing hooves at thirty miles an hour. Thomas did not disappear beneath. Instead, he was hit, dozens of times, thrown like a stuffed doll, gored and trampled and trampled and gored, his chest and brain ex- ploding, his stomach sack and veins collapsing to little pops, spurting fluids that were instantly erased in the dust and up- roar of spewn mud and snow, until the pulverized source lay emptied and hard to find.

All the while Houdini jerked, screamed, rolled.

Then all was silent as the storm of passing animals contin- ued to the far end of the field. The animals stopped, and be- gan grazing once again, a seemingly docile mass.

The crowds ran toward the scene of bloodshed. Amy had collapsed out in the open. She was unconscious.

Houdini jumped up and searched for Thomas. Incredibly,

his recognizable body had virtually vanished. Mangled chunks remained. Houdini sat down and wept.

He had brought this boy up, right out of grade school, an itinerant inventor hankering after adventure. Houdini had been his dream come true. Now, Houdini was his obliteration.

The reporters were there getting photographs. One of them said that it was the stupidest, most useless stunt he'd ever seen. Bess chased them away. A waiting ambulance sped across the snowy path toward the scene of devastation.

Hundreds of people patted Houdini on the back and said they were sorry, that it was an amazing trick and accidents do happen. That it wasn't his fault.

Houdini remained seated in the grass, convulsed with shock, guilt, sorrow. Bess was unable to keep the hordes from encircling him.

But after a while, the reporters felt they'd gotten their story, and the field cleared out.

That night and the next morning Houdini hardly said a word, pent up in their hotel suite, frenzied, silent, despairing. He shivered, crunched up on a sofa in one of the hotel bathrobes.

Thomas's funeral took place the following afternoon. It was a small gathering in an open area of uninhabited southeast Denver that permitted a wild vantage over distant Mount Evans. Wind was blowing through the fresh bloom of pussy willow, aspen, iris and columbines that surrounded the grave site.

Three Indians stood off to one side. They were the grave diggers. Amy was as pallid and gray as a T.S. Eliot poem, disheveled, a flood of tears. As the minister conducted the service—". . . morituri te salutamus . . ."—Houdini heard, then saw, a wild peacock at the edge of the woods. It stood watching the ceremony. The Indians spoke quietly among themselves in native Ute. Their gestures and the tone of their voices indicated something strange about the peacock's presence, Houdini thought.

The magician said some words after the casket had been lowered, four feet. He'd stipulated the depth.

"I felt about him as I would my own son. He was brave. He was dedicated . . . I now understand that his gentleness was, well, his greatness. He came from a farm, loved the soil." Houdini reached down, grabbed a handful of earth and tossed it onto the casket in the hole, then continued eulogizing: "We will always think of you, Tom. Amy, Bess and I. Your good friends Joe and Royale and Frank. We all love you."

Houdini wiped tears from his eyes and stood away as the Indians set to work with their shovels. Frank, Joe and Royale each tossed their own handful of soil.

Bess placed a wreath of roses at the foot of the hole.

"He was the best," Joe mourned.

Royale nodded, and wiped a hankie across his face.

Amy couldn't get up from the wooden folding chair brought on her behalf. Bess assisted her to her feet and got her into the back of the Buick. Dexter drove them to the hotel.

As they drove away, Houdini saw the peacock standing in the dirt road behind them, pecking at the ground.

Frank had brought along an additional contingent of policemen. The night before, at the Denver train station, in spite of the tragedy earlier that day, and the convulsion of events since Yosemite, he'd gone on with his duties and the plan to snare Holstein. Frank had his own score to settle.

At the train station he had watched Byron exchange envelopes with one of Holstein's ghouls, who'd just stepped off the Burlington line, followed by the shuffling monster herself. Byron had handed over the falsified pages in return for only part of the five thousand dollars. The ghoul reminded him that they had no way of knowing that the information from Houdini's diary was bona fide, but if the Princess won the contest, the remaining money was in the bag. Byron's stupidity was poetic justice, Frank reckoned, secretly viewing the exchange from a nearby phone booth, concealed in the steam of the Princess's train.

All went according to plan, though it made for a slight pickle. Houdini's resignation from the contest had not sapped his will to go after Eunice Holstein, but now he needed a face-saving way to do it. Frank was to take complete charge of the operation.

Lucky for Frank, since he'd run up quite a phone bill in nightly "progress reports" to his new lady love, Ginger Riddles. He did not want to let her down. She wanted vengeance against that "pig" almost as badly as she wanted Frank. While still in Los Angeles, Houdini had called Harrington about the Princess and learned that the Doyles had already told him about this "remarkable medium" following their "miracle of Toledo," and that Harrington had welcomed the new contestant, who would work in company with Lady Doyle. Together they would try and persuade the committee.

In this climate, Houdini had gone ahead, following his near death by fire in Santa Ana, and legibly scribbled for Byron a few pages of misinformation, tellingly altered from the original diary notes.

Following his Yosemite revelation, Houdini had loaned Frank that original, with his blessing. He knew that Frank would need it as proof of the deception. Proof that Holstein was the worst sort of fraud.

"Do what you can," Houdini had offered. "Nail the bitch. But please keep me out of it."

Houdini stewed over his dilemma. On the one hand, he'd come to suspect a whole heaven of possibilities, revealed by the pathetic, yet monumental, stuttering of a stranger. How could he continue to rail against mediums in the face of such compelling evidence? To declare Holstein a fraud was to impugn Lady Doyle as well. And now he wondered: was she? For the first time, Houdini had come to empathize with Sir Arthur. The literary giant had doubtless taken his own professional curves, started out a skeptic and by increment come to believe. A reflective Houdini was now in a better position to grasp how such mid-life 180-degree turns were possible. Changing one's mind need not be construed as a sign of weakness.

But Houdini also worried about his public image, which he'd probably blown in Yosemite. It was one of the reasons he stubbornly finished up his tour in the Rockies: the stunts were his soul, his sanity. The public watched him, every day. There were thousands of youths who modeled their self-images after Houdini. Mothers had named their babies after him. In England, his movies were the rage, his onstage sobriety likened to that of an Edmund Kean, the great Shakespearean actor, and his heroism compared with Lord Nelson's. He was still considered the most famous showman in the world. And there was a new dictionary that had enshrined his name: "Houdin," something mysterious, elusive, wonderful.

Houdini reasoned that he must not now waver from his decision to quit the contest, just for the sake of putting one woman behind bars. That would totally destroy an already damaged credibility. And yet he *had* become inconsistent. And the press was merciless.

He did not see it himself, but Bess surely did: Houdini was vacillating, talking to himself, voicing an inner crisis from a raft that bashed against clashing rocks.

Bess knew her husband would come around. He always did.

"All you need is a little time to think, time to figure it all out," Bess said to him.

She needed her own time to come up for air. Her heart was numb. Thomas was gone. Houdini's destiny had killed him. Yet Houdini was all that she had, all that she had ever known. She could only forgive him. Her own crisis—a middle-aged realization that she was increasingly lonely, empty—had given her some perspective. She realized that she could no longer watch over her husband's adolescent mood swings. She had to protect herself. Prudently, she felt that the safest emotional course was compromise, resolution. She did not want to fight anymore. She would go back to New York, with or without him. She harbored an unfulfilled yearning to settle down at long last, have a child, to be ordinary, to have a white picket fence. And to look up at night and see a familiar ceiling.

Later that evening, Amy Beckwell opened the window of her room at the hotel and looked out at the darkness. She'd surrounded her bed with candles and an enormous heap of fresh rose petals, the same color of roses as the wreath Bess had placed before her loved one's final resting spot.

Amy wore the same nightgown in which she'd earlier ascended to carnal heaven. Wind blew in from outside. The Denver night was cold.

She studied the vial in her hand, unscrewed the cap and without hesitation gulped down all of the liquid. She burped, then tossed the bottle out the window into the street.

She then sat down at the dressing table and stared at herself. Her face was streaked.

"I'm coming, Thomas," she whispered plainly.

She got into bed, covered herself with sheets, rolled over and closed her lovely eyes.

Early the next morning, Harrington, the committee members and the Doyles arrived at the Denver train station from Chicago. Lady Doyle had arranged to introduce Harrington to Princess Anne that afternoon. The Princess had arrived the evening before.

There was a swarm of reporters at the station to meet the arriving ensemble. They immediately conveyed the news of Thomas Weckstin's death, hoarding any and all responses from the various personalities.

Doyle was stunned. The shattered Harrington begged off any formal statements, but intimated that the contest would continue.

As the Doyles stepped into a waiting car, Lady Doyle

looked anxiously in the rearview mirror, then inquired of the driver how far to the hotel.

"What is it, dear?" Sir Arthur said, noticing the grave color that had come over her.

"Amy," she replied. "Amy's in trouble. Driver, please hurry!"

Meanwhile, the Houdinis were in their suite. Houdini sat up in bed staring out the window, utterly abject, ready to get the hell out of town. Bess fixed coffee.

Downstairs in the lobby the press converged upon the Brown Palace. Harrington, the Doyles and all the committee members arrived at the same time. In the commotion of checking in ten people and nearly fifty pieces of baggage, Doyle found out which room Amy was in and raced up the stairs, carrying his old leather medical bag.

He reached her room. "Amy, open up! It's Arthur," he shouted. He too felt that there was something wrong. Her door was locked. He pounded on it, frantically solicited the chambermaid on the floor, who rushed up with the key, only to discover that the keyhole had been jammed. Doyle kicked down the door.

There was Amy Beckwell, sound asleep, submerged in a cumulus of heaven-scented petals on her bed. The open window, the burned-out candles, a scene of tranquility. Was she all right? Doyle paused, reflecting on the ambiguity that confronted him.

He walked to the bed and gently shook Amy. Her motionless plight sunk in at once. The deadweight of her shoulders, a certain odor.

Immediately, Doyle lifted her up to a sitting position against the headboard. Lady Doyle burst in after her husband.

"She's still breathing!" Sir Arthur said.

His wife took over, while the chambermaid ran for the house doctor. Meanwhile, the Sherlock Holmes in Doyle quickly assessed the situation and was propelled into action.

He smelled Amy's hairbrush, opened her eyelids, examined her tongue, took out a fine silk kerchief and made a print of a lipstick dab on the mirror. Doyle then applied some rubbing alcohol from his carrying bag to the kerchief, sniffed the lipstick and at once stated the answer: "Laudanum. She's taken opium, coal-tar derivative!"

He immediately concocted and applied a known antidote from his bag of tricks, a milky derivative of Gelseminum, which he himself had experimented with.

Almost at once Amy jerked. Her body convulsed. She spit up, coughed and gasped for air.

"Ohhh God!" she groaned. "Arthur?" And with that she retched into his hands.

Her eyes were soggy, afflicted and innocent. Doyle stared down at the precious life he had restored. His relief surpassed any lurking guilt—guilt for having been publicly associated with past suicides. Such implications were utter nonsense, of course. Doyle was the first to condemn the desperation that drove people to kill themselves.

Doyle held Amy.

Harrington entered the room with the doctor and chambermaid.

"I've saved her," Sir Arthur stated matter-of-factly, wiping off his hands and arms on the bed blankets, while Lady Doyle fed water to the grieving girl.

"Amy, my dear!" Harrington cried. "I heard . . . What happened?" he asked, looking to Sir Arthur, not knowing what to say under the circumstances.

"Thomas called to her from the other side. She took an opiate."

"That's horrible!" Harrington said, bewildered. "I'm so sorry, my dear." He knew of the romance with Thomas.

"Amy merely obeyed the first principle of love," Lady Doyle asserted, with a dignity appropriate to the moment.

But Harrington had a more opportunistic interpretation of the scene before him.

There was a persistent knocking on the Houdinis' door. Harry lurched out of bed, shouting, "Can't you read—DO NOT DISTURB!"

The knock persisted. "Harry? It's Ralph!"

Houdini swung open the door.

Ralph threw up his arms defensively and fired away. "Harry, I'm sorry about Mr. Weckstin. Now before you say anything, sit down. I've got very important things to tell you."

"You know where I stand on this," Houdini said, pained and nearly impervious.

"Listen, Harry, a woman died as we were boarding the train in Chicago. Suicide. Horrible, horrible! And it was Doyle who did it; Doyle's pernicious influence which—in the past two weeks alone—has resulted in dozens of other suicides throughout America and England. Maybe even hundreds, can you imagine!" Harrington had invented the other suicides, but figured it was a symbolically logical declaration, and he needed the authoritative weight. "And now Amy!" he cried out with a finality of indignation.

"Amy!" Bess shrieked.

"My God . . .," Houdini whispered, suddenly lackluster.

"She's going to be okay, I pray," Harrington went on. "The Doyles are down there in the room with her now, trying to make amends for the horrible things they've done to that poor girl. She took some poison last night, carried away by Doyle's insane sentiments and spiritualist gibberish. They've brainwashed her. She's on the mend. But Harry"—he leaned over man-to-man and put a hand on Houdini's collapsed shoulder—"this madness has got to stop! And you're the only one who can stop him! Now Doyle is bragging to everyone how he's going to bring back your dead mother! And you won't even be there to dispute it!"

"My mother!?!" His face swelled with a ruddy heat. Though he might have predicted such a base tactic on the part of Doyle, nothing had actually prepared him for this moment.

Bess held onto the dresser. Houdini stood up, taking in the full circumference of Harrington's galling disclosure. Integrity had forced him to drop out of the contest. Now it was integrity again that brought forth the full venom of his wrath. Screw inconsistency. Screw the press.

Houdini marched down to Amy's room, stepped through the open door, grabbed Doyle by the collar and seethed silently. Bess followed and joined Lady Doyle beside Amy.

"My dear," she said.

"What's this about my mother!" Houdini ranted.

"Your mother?" Doyle said, totally off his guard.

"You know damn well!"

"I-I'm sorry." And he meant to say more, not thinking fast enough to appreciate Harrington's trap, but Houdini cut him off.

"I will not allow my dear mother to be abused! Who in the hell do you think you are, Doyle!"

"Your life belongs to those who care about you. Stutterers, dearly beloved, those on the other side. You cannot deny it now."

"Damn you! Damn you!" he screamed, pushing Doyle in the chest.

Sir Arthur fell backward onto the floor.

"Stop it! Stop it, you two!" Bess pleaded.

"Ralph, do something!" Lady Doyle ordered. "He's crazy!"

Doyle got up. "I will not fight you in front of the women. I will fight you in the church. And you will lose, Harry. Then you will see that you have actually won. And you will thank me."

Harrington looked at Houdini. "Then you're in?"

"You bet I'm in!" Houdini growled, full of scorn and the old Houdini.

PART
THREE

16

Yiddish Overlook

In which the final showdown takes place, raising doubts, and leaving unfinished business . . .

On the dilapidated steps of the grand old Church of Golden, christened the First of God's Wayward, across a muddy river from the entrance to a wild canyon on the outskirts of Denver, Harrington announced the contest rules to the press and public at hand. Thunder boomed all around the assemblage of several hundred, as waves of static swept in from higher distances, bearing down upon the low, complaining Colorado sky, which was the color of a brooding black Angus. Out over the hot eastern monotony of prairie, clearly visible from where they all stood, nothing was happening, or ever did.

Harrington thanked the long-traveled Doyle and Houdini,

the indulgent committee members, the Mayor, aldermen, local constabulary and parishioners, all of whom had cooperated so graciously with *Scientifica Americana*. Then he introduced Lady Doyle of Sussex, and "Her Worshipful," Princess Anne of Central Africa, otherwise known as Eunice Holstein. The two women bowed, standing at the large stone entrance to the church.

Lady Doyle wore a smart suit of clipped English lamb, excessive for Denver in June, despite the occasional nip of mountain air. The Princess was got up in a diaphanous veil of silks from Persia, or New Jersey, that did not exactly recommend her hippolike physique. To add flavor to distaste, she was adorned in African amulets, including a brass ring in her left nostril. Her greased-back hair was knotted into an unconvincing headdress of bark and turdlike aiguillettes. She smelled of mundungus.

"These two remarkable women have promised to bring back Harry Houdini's mother," Harrington announced with parasitic pomp. "From the land of the dead," he emphasized. Houdini flinched. Harrington cleared his throat. "It should be the ultimate test of faith and the unknown, as against science and reason."

There was an awkward applause. None of the reporters had questioned Houdini's inconsistency. They all rather expected him to come back into the fray and figured his Yosemite press conference had been deliberately staged for the purpose of publicity and further excitement.

Harrington had been filled in about the so-called Princess Anne by Frank. The publisher intended to enjoy this final round, knowing full well that his money was safe in the bank. The Princess was a flaming fraud, soon to be exposed royally, and Lady Doyle's powers were not believed to be considerable. Furthermore, her husband's advocacy could, if it should prove necessary, easily be written off as a conflict of interest.

Inside, hundreds of tall sacramental candles had been lit around the periphery. The reporters tromped in and grappled for seats. All of the oakwood pews were filled. Censers emitted incense smoke that curled philosophically into the hallowed nave. The séance would take place on the wide altar, where fresh flowers had been laid.

"My mother never set foot in a church her whole life," Houdini whispered to Bess.

Following his father's death, Houdini had gone to the synagogue once a year, to say Kaddish. His mother never even joined him in that annual visit. She shunned organized religion, fearing nothing in life.

After her death, Houdini obsessively visited his mother's grave site at their family plot at Machpelah Cemetery, in the Cypress Hills of New York. He'd lie down on the grass covering her tomb and—in *Mame-loshen-ha-Kodesh*, his mother's sacred language—whisper to her spirit of his dreams, frustrations and future plans. He filled up his diary with lamentations, little matriarchal asides, marginalia steeped in her brand of humorous, Hungarian *Yiddishkite*, by way of Wisconsin.

Houdini thought about how odd and irreverent it was to hear a Ralph Harrington speak so candidly of his beloved mother, Cecelia, before a church in the Rockies, to hundreds of strangers.

And of all days, no less! For today was her birthday. Only Houdini and Bess knew that, and, of course, Mom herself. Houdini would see whether either medium divined the simple, yet crucial, detail. Hardly likely.

The committee members were carefully seated around a Ouija board, their voluminous scientific equipment ticking, whirring, waiting to monitor the slightest psychic agitation.

Frank and Byron, both armed, were in the rear, guarding the exits. Byron had to maintain his double identity through all of this, which he did. He had his own nest egg riding on the outcome. Frank had alerted the Denver police to the likelihood of criminal activities. They had their beady eyes on the Princess. Frank kept watch over Byron.

Houdini planned to devastate the proceedings at the perfect moment. He'd carefully planted the misinformation, altering words and numbers so as to expose the slightest error, and enshrine every blunder for the future annals of criminal fraud.

Professor Shleihauffen and Dr. Henden Grundranvodst monitored the magnetic resonance machines, while Timothy Crowded kept his fingers on the controls of a gravitation counter. Barkwaithe turned on his sound recorders, and Dr. Morris Abraham managed a ring of antennas and radio heterodynes. The slightest psychic buzz would be amplified and converted through the crazy, high-standing rubber receivers into a half-distinguishable sonance. Abraham had worked out the particulars of his psychic vibration device on sick people. Cancer sounded like angry hornets, syphilis like murmuring ocean waves.

Lady Doyle and the Princess, seated side-by-side at the head of the Ouija board, together invited Houdini's ancestors to the sacred circle. Doyle sat opposite Houdini. Bess remained down below the altar, in a pew. The Princess, by her size and temperament, came at once to dominate the psalm singing, the alchemical invocations and passing around of mystical objects. She initiated the secret palaver and rhythmically shook a tambourine.

Within minutes there was a lightning bolt. The surrounding hills reverberated with expressive thunder not three seconds after the incandescent flash.

Lady Doyle fell into an inspirational trance while the Princess served as the "controller." The large floor of the church was gripped by the Princess's animal-like vocalizations, while Lady Doyle, seized with the automatic urge to write, took a pen in hand and within a short time had scrawled fifteen pages of gobbledygook on large-sized notepaper. The writing was in more-or-less English, but its style, Doyle would observe, was Coptic, or Burmese, with Devanagari serifs and accent marks.

As darkness descended on the church, other noises of the jungle infiltrated the enclosure, without anything to account for them, other than the Princess's overworked warbler throat.

Another lightning blast lit up the church, followed by a roar of thunder a mere second away. Most of the candles went out, as a rush of wind got through the crannies in the old stone walls. A reporter in the audience noticed that water began trickling from under the door leading to the wash-room.

Now Lady Doyle started speaking, in a male's voice.

"Pheneas?" Sir Arthur asked, suddenly confused. It did not sound like the Pheneas his wife had always described.

"Earthquake!" people shouted.

The tremor shook with a single hit, then vanished. The tension in the room was at once relieved.

"It registered on the seismograph!" Shannon O'Nearly pointed out.

The tremor served to agitate Pheneas, who was definitely not himself. "Gotta hurry!" Lady Doyle said. "It's coming . . . definitely coming!"

"Yes yes yes!" the Princess rallied with.

And then, sweetly as a dulcimer, an old woman's voice descended on the séance as the Princess's eyes enlarged like avocado pits and her throat strained and writhed to produce the spirit visitation.

"Oh my darling, *thank God!* At last . . . I'm through!"

And with that Pheneas—which is to say, Lady Doyle—began to weep. "Mrs. Weiss, it's you!" Pheneas cried out.

"It is me!" the Princess continued. "My dear son, Harry darling, it's so wonderful in Heaven!" And with that the Princess made the sign of the cross.

Houdini sat motionless, like a cocked trigger. "I'm through" was the first sentence of the misinformation he had conveyed via Byron. The exposure was right on target. The end was coming.

Doyle, utterly mystified by the events, leaned forward.

Bess, who knew nothing of the business with Byron or the

misinformation to the Princess from her husband's diary, sat back, amused in her pew.

"What else does she say?" Houdini asked the Princess calmly.

"Wait, wait . . . I'm getting it: 'Bring back a pair of warm woolen house slippers, size four.' "

"You're sure about that?" Houdini pressed.

"Definitely," the Princess avowed.

Houdini's diary actually noted that his mother had requested size eight. He'd changed the number to highlight the discrepancy, and thus the fraud. The Princess was going down. Houdini had the original diary with him, which he'd taken back from Frank, and any moment was going to break it all up.

But then something happened that singularly troubled Houdini. The Princess seemed to get wise, or so Bess, from her own, differing vantage point, detected.

"Gibt's nicht, nur Mann und Frau," the Princess declared, looking at Bess, then at Houdini.

The line was one of Houdini's mother's favorites. *Nothing matters but husband and wife.* But Houdini had not included that line among the other misinformation!

Harrington at once caught Houdini's distress and his own sweat started to pour forth. Thirty thousand dollars was hanging in the balance here. And there was more: twenty-five hundred years of established scientific tradition, the future of materialism. That's how Harrington had put it in one of his interviews. "If it were determined that life continued after death, the world would come to an end."

The committee members witnessed a sustained blip on their myriad recording devices; there was a scientific heart-stop in the church.

Houdini was turned around. Whereas he'd been poised to leap forward and expose the women on the basis of the diary, he now felt devastated by the emergence of that unexpected line. How had it happened? No, it didn't sound like her. Of course it wasn't her.

"What day is it!" Houdini suddenly rebounded.

"What day is it?" the Princess asked. "Why it's Tuesday," she said, coming down momentarily.

"What special day?" Houdini demanded. "Ask the old woman!"

The Princess complied. "Is this a special day?" she called out ceremoniously.

"Every *moment* with my son is special," the disembodied voice replied.

"How old is she?" Houdini asked the Princess.

"Your son asks your age, madame," the Princess requested.

To which a shy laughter emanated from the Princess's deep throat. "A woman never admits her age, my son!"

Another tremor, this time a more severe one. People stood up, prepared to flee. A window cracked. Reporters flashed their cameras.

Lady Doyle was now in full swing. Her powers had never been so intense in her entire life. The weeping had escalated into a plangent throe of guttural exclamations. Doyle thought he saw butterflies fluttering about her lips.

But then the voice changed to some untoward subjugation, reeking, malevolent. She stood up. There was none of the soft-spoken humor of weird Pheneas; none of the modest, womanly sibilants that previously characterized her deeply felt connection with the beyond. Now, her voice was jagged, mean-spirited, howling with an unbecoming pride and directness. Together with the Princess, they made a chorus of disenchantment.

Doyle leaned over and whispered to Harrington, "Something's wrong, I can feel it."

"No kidding, Sherlock," Harrington replied.

Houdini meanwhile waited for the right moment to pounce.

Lady Doyle stood up on her high heels in the faint twilight. The Princess wobbled behind her, like an army tank, and there called upon Houdini to lock hands with the two mediums.

It was beginning to rain hard. Houdini rose to the challenge, standing between the two women, hands clasped. In tandem, the two female voices gave vent to a cacophony of intimacies, all claiming to come from Cecelia, Houdini's mother.

The Princess shook violently. Houdini, whom both women held onto, was lobbed from side to side by the force of the Princess's sweating bulk.

Precipitous, the Princess grabbed hold of Houdini's upper torso, thrust her face into his and whammed him with a hot, horrifying French kiss.

"My dear son!" exclaimed the foul-breathing beast.

"Ohhh God!" Houdini moaned, gasping for uncontaminated air. He desperately extricated himself. It was time to end this insanity.

But before he could do so, lightning struck the gothic nave of the church. The entire building lit up. People ran for the door. Sheets of crackling spark whipped across the walls. And then the real tremor hit: the building shuddered and skipped, a prelude to the disastrous collapse of the enormous stained glass window above the altar.

The Princess grasped Houdini in a stranglehold of flesh, casting the relatively little man up toward the down-rushing guillotine of crashing glass.

"*No!*" Houdini roared, and with one mighty expenditure he threw off her yoke, dodging the huge section. The razor-sharp avalanche exploded atop Princess Anne.

Lady Doyle had narrowly escaped harm.

Two committee members were not so lucky. Tons of colorful shards had rained down upon their equipment, devastating much of it. In their panic, Barkwaithe and Professor Shleihauffen were both knocked over, Shleihauffen's hand severed. Blood was spurting from his forearm in rhythm with his heart. "Hurry . . . help him!" a wan voice cried amid dust and the fluster of fleeing reporters.

Stillness returned to the church. Doyle raced over to the professor, who lay motionless, in shock. Immediately he ripped off his own jacket and tied a precision tourniquet to the hemorrhaging artery. "Somebody call an ambulance, hurry!" he shouted.

Houdini was just getting up, ten feet away from where Doyle leaned on all fours over Shleihauffen. At the same time, both Bess and Doyle screamed to Houdini. "Look out!"

The bludgeoned Princess was poised above Houdini, holding a huge, four-foot piece of glass, like an icicle outstretched above her head, ready to come down upon her adversary.

Several gun blasts in explosive succession ripped into her breast, discharged by Frank and the other policemen. Houdini lunged away as she collapsed forward, falling onto her knees, her face impaling itself upon the glass spike that had collided with the floor beneath the altar.

Two policemen ran up to the Princess. Her lifeless mass lay pinioned in hell and unbreathing. "Dead!" they declared without hesitation.

"Cover her, for God's sakes," Doyle implored them.

One of the men pulled a nearby tapestry from the wall and tossed it over her while the second officer took over for Doyle, who now could attend to his wife.

Lady Doyle had suffered minor cuts and bruises. She mumbled in her old voice, a sort of post-séance coming down, unsure what had happened.

The medics rushed in with a stretcher, and rushed out. Shleihauffen was evacuated by ambulance.

"Come back for her when you're done," a policeman shouted to the medics as they reached the door. "But there's no hurry!"

Chaos swept through the church, with hundreds of people racing about, and the scientists already shouting at one another with respect to their ambiguous findings. In the meantime, the lightning had started a fire in the fir trees adjoining the rector's house. Fire trucks arrived, adding their own supplies of water to the existing downpour. The whole town of Golden continued to receive one bolt of lightning after another.

Inside, the church administrator began surveying the damage, which he would charge to the sinister séance.

Harrington marshaled calm, and re-collected the principles down among the pews, out of the rain that was splashing in through sections of wall torn out by the destroyed stained glass.

"All right. Now tell us: Was that your mother!" began Harrington. His mind was focused not on bloodshed, but on the money.

"That was *not* my mother!" Houdini railed furiously, like a broken main. He deftly explained to the committee members present the discrepancies in the misinformation from his diary, exposing the ruse that his own gumshoes had facilitated, following the Princess's own bribe. He brought forth the diary and pointed to the truth.

And then he stated that his mother *never* entered a Christian church in her entire life, would never have made the sign of the cross and, most telling, never once uttered a single word of English!

"She overlooked a crucial detail: my mother's Yiddish. Her whole life, she spoke only Yiddish! And furthermore, today is her birthday. The late Princess didn't even have the obvious street smarts to find that out about her. Not only that, but her name is *not* Princess Anne." He called upon his detective. "Frank, why don't you summarize the dossier on this bitch you uncovered at the County Clerk in New York."

Frank was brief, describing her real name, and some of the highlights of her nefarious career.

But throughout the presentation of these sundry and alarming disclosures, a discordant doubt hung about the room.

Finally, one of the scientists gave vent to it. "Then whose mother was it!" Shannon O'Nearly asked. He had picked up definite chemical oxidation, atomic anomalies and voice registration of no earthly character.

Similarly, said Timothy Crowded, he had noted—prior to his equipment being wrecked—that there had been profound chemical imbalances in his light spectrometers that had nothing to do with the lightning.

Additional evidence suggested that the earthquake was no "natural" tremor.

"Now what the hell does *that* mean!" Harrington shouted, outraged by the unrestrained interest shown by his committee in these obviously coincidental happenings. "Mountains engender storms . . ."

The psycho-kinesiologist Grundranvodst agreed with Harrington, as did Abraham, both investigators acknowledging that the weather and earthquakes, the wind, the voices, were all matters of trickery and meteorological coincidence, nothing more. Their colleagues argued. Timothy Crowded suggested they more carefully analyze the data for a day or two before making any decisions or official statements, particularly in light of the tragic death of the medium and Shleihauffen's absence.

"*Tragic??*" Houdini cried out. "You call that monster's death tragic?"

Harrington was not prepared to stall the inevitable decision that *must* be made.

Surprisingly, Doyle agreed with Harrington. Houdini knew his own mother, Doyle argued. Obviously. And the Princess was evidently a known criminal. He himself, along with Lady Doyle, had been bamboozled in Toledo. That was now clear. He professed ignorance as to how she had managed it. But there it was, a dossier elaborating horrible deeds that recommended the severest punishment. And indeed, that punishment had already been meted out by God.

It was best that these proceedings be concluded quickly, he reemphasized, before the whole character and pure intent of the contest were tainted and dragged down by such disreputable elements. There had been mischief perpetrated here. He conceded that the séance was not convincing proof.

Doyle was also looking out for the cause of spiritualism. He felt the enormity of his, and of his wife's, ignorance. Toledo had seemed *so* convincing. Maybe it was the hour—midnight—way past Doyle's bedtime. He *was* groggy, what with all the train travel, the demanding lecture schedule, insufficient sleep. It had all *seemed* so convincing. But in retrospect, that heap of sorrowful fat, that fraud, was nothing more than a pathetic charlatan, a desperate woman. Doyle wanted out of the church. A fresh start.

With both Houdini and Doyle weighing in against the mediums, and half the scientists also negating the authenticity of events (Shleihauffen was in no condition to sway the tie), Harrington declared the contest null and void.

"Materialism is saved! You got the scoop. Go to it, boys!" he concluded on behalf of all the reporters present, gesticulating with a valiant show as if to say that something truly monumental had happened this day.

The huge crowd of reporters was in a state of journalistic fever. There had been one hell of a séance, which had occasioned lightning, fire, a leaking crypt, an earthquake, animal voices, quaking candles, death and disfigurement. That was pretty damned good! They stuck around for interviews before venturing out into the rain.

Doyle took Houdini aside, unafraid of any violence, and referred to the tears he had seen in Houdini's eyes.

"You're out of your mind, Doyle!" Houdini boomed, flying apart and ready to flatten him. He was not about to let Doyle get away with commiseration. But Doyle was tenacious in his compassion. He knew that Houdini wanted nothing more than to speak with his mother, as Doyle did.

"You and I are one," he declared quietly, his back turned to the corpse on the altar.

Houdini felt surges of disgust rising in his bowels. Doyle stood his ground without blinking.

Finally, tired of this business, anxious to go home,

Houdini said, "I feel sorry for you, Doyle. I feel sorry for your wife. And for all of those ignorant bastards who look to you for . . . for I don't know what. Certainly not Heaven. Because you're going straight to Hell." No one screwed around with Houdini when it came to his mother. He started to turn toward the door.

"And Yosemite? You know very well that my son saved your life up on that cliff. Why fight a truth that was kind to you," Doyle pressured.

"Nothing happened of importance in Yosemite," Houdini stated for the record. "I made up that business about stuttering. It was my own fear speaking. You've probably heard by now: I'm not crazy about heights. El Capitan is what you'd call heights." His vitriol had dissipated. He was tired of this.

"I understand," Doyle said lovingly.

This infuriated Houdini all the more. But he was no longer in a mood to rant or fight. "Understand this: you can't alter the way things are. Neither prayer, nor hallucinations, nor book writing, will bring back those we have loved. I tell you this out of the goodness of my heart. Because I don't think you're a bad person. I think you're simply wallowing in delusion, groping. I'm sure you've had your own sadness in life. Sir Arthur . . ." He stopped himself. There was no point in continuing in this vein. "Why don't you and your wife go back to England. Go back to writing your detective stories. You're good at that." He started to extend his hand. Doyle grabbed it and held him firmly. "I've got to go," said Houdini. "And I'm sorry I pushed you yesterday. It was not a good day for me."

Doyle was greatly moved by Houdini's capacity to reason in the face of all that had happened, particularly Thomas Weckstin's death. But Doyle was not finished. In fact, he believed that he had Houdini exactly where he wanted him. They shook hands and then Doyle spoke.

"I can accept that in the public mind you've won, Harry. But this is between you and me."

"What are you talking about?" Houdini was annoyed by this pertinacity of Doyle's.

"The contest is not over yet. I will prove everything to you once and for all," he mustered, challenging Houdini to one final endeavor.

"Why are you so intent on this . . . I don't know what to call it—this mission of yours?"

"Because I know. I know!" And he shook Houdini by the sides. "I want you to know, as well."

Houdini looked down at the floor and slowly shook his head. "You're really a very sick man," he said.

Doyle waited patiently.

Houdini, seeing an implacable foe, having survived every conceivable roller coaster of passion and upset, high pedestal and devastating trench, finally conceded. "What do you have in mind?"

Doyle smiled confidently. "Lock me in one of your own contraptions, lower me off a cliff, or into the water—it doesn't matter which—and I will get out, with the help of my dead son. Kingsley will save me from whatever fate, just as he has saved you."

"All right," said Houdini. "If you think that will solve anything, be my guest. When?"

"As you like."

"Two weeks from now. New York Harbor."

"Fine," Doyle said.

Houdini knew that the water would still be cold. It was deep, rough, unrelenting. Doyle would find out.

"No press," said Doyle. "Just you and me!"

"I have no problem with that," Houdini said, all business-like. The rumbling passions of the previous incident, a grotesque corpse lying thirty feet to his side, that pitiful excuse for mysticism and its disgusting exploitation of his dead mother's name, had left him firmly back in step with his true, vigilante self. No more crap. No more crime. No more mediocrity. If Doyle wanted to kill himself, it was fine by Houdini.

Workmen were cleaning up, amid the clearing out of commotion. The church was scarcely lit by a few remaining candles. Suddenly, there were exclamations from the workers.

The bulk of dead flesh that had been Princess Anne, alias Eunice Holstein, had somehow disappeared! In its place, the wall tapestry that had been used to cover her lay flat and deflated against the floor. Yet the face was still there, skewered right through an eye.

"Wait a minute," Frank said, utterly perplexed. "What is this?"

"Did the medics come back for her?" a policeman asked. Nobody could remember.

Frank moved swiftly to the corpse and threw back the tapestry. Nothing!

Like a golliwog of thick rubber, the punctured face was merely a mask. There was no blood. The glass had probably missed her by no more than half an inch. Her accomplices must have been waiting behind the church in a car. She escaped through the collapsed wall of stained glass.

"But the bullets? We hit her repeatedly," a sheriff whined.

"Her billowing costume, and all that excess adipose, must have absorbed them," Frank theorized.

"Check around back!" the sheriff shouted.

The area was searched but turned up no clue. In all the rain, tire tracks on the cobblestone left no trace.

Houdini and Doyle stood amazed, as did Bess and Lady Doyle. Houdini stepped over to the place where the mask remained. He picked it up and considered the situation. There was more work to be done.

Outside the church, Harrington announced to the crowd that it was the opinion of the panel of experts that the séance had been inconclusive. Houdini was the victor. Future mediums would be invited to submit their powers to the editorial staff of *Scientifica Americana*, though the contest, per se, was finished. Science had prevailed over superstition. Harrington, echoing Houdini's sentiments, hoped that this crucial judgment would send a message throughout Congress, and to lawmakers in every state. Fraud, extortion—crime—was evil, under any guise, including spirituality. And needless to say, none of the prize money would be dispensed.

Or that's what Harrington thought.

The church administrator stepped up to Harrington, having just finished tabulating the destruction, and publicly informed the publisher, before police and cordoned-off bystanders, of the extensive damage done to these premises.

"Irreplaceable window!" he said, among other things. A bill totaling twenty-six thousand dollars would be paid by Harrington, unless he wanted his prestigious magazine dragged into a Denver courtroom.

Houdini and Bess, Frank, Joe and Royale got into their cars and drove off toward downtown Denver, as a drenched, harried and steaming mad Ralph Harrington was last seen blundering. "You can't do this to me—it was an earthquake, goddammit!"

Beside him stood a row of cops. "Tell that to the judge, buddy!" one of them cracked, putting his face into the hard rain the way they do in Colorado.

17

Revelation

Amid the certainty of life and death, Houdini engages in one final combat, only to discover a true friend.

Back in New York at the Ambassador Hotel indoor gym, Doyle spent his mornings training for his final bout with Houdini. He took various strength-boosting therapies, like hydropathy, brain massage and homeopathic electrocution. The sessions were exhausting. In the afternoons, he stuck around his hotel suite, attending to a voluminous correspondence.

Captain Pushcart paid Sir Arthur over fifteen thousand dollars, which was the net profit from Doyle's lectures all over the country. Doyle, in turn, spent the good portion of that on "causes." In addition to his interest in Sacco and Vanzetti, he had assumed all court costs in London of an innocent Jewish refugee who'd been framed on charges of murder. Doyle was also setting up a fund in Rochester, New York, for the construction of a huge pyramidal monument to photography. Kodak had begun in Rochester, and Doyle believed that the invention of the snapshot was the precursor of much significant psychic endeavor.

While her husband was busy muscle building, and crusading through the mails, Lady Doyle hit the department stores with a vengeance. She could be blithe in her souvenir hunting on two counts. First, she felt not the least embarrassed by her short-lived association with Eunice Holstein, because she remembered nothing of the fiasco. Nor did Pheneas. Total amnesia. The only things she recalled were walking into the church, a lightning blast and then Arthur rousing her. Secondly, Arthur had made money on their American tour, lots of it! She'd never felt so good, free and easy.

In the evenings, the Doyles enjoyed New York, though by nightfall Sir Arthur could scarcely keep his eyes open, even for Marilyn Miller in *Sally*, or Helen Hayes starring in *Coquette*.

In the meantime, Houdini was re-ensconced at home in Brooklyn. For more than a week he had done nothing: performances were out of the question. He'd promised. Not a single workout in the laboratory. Bess even detected an ounce of new fat on his stomach. This was paradise! she thought.

But Houdini was *anything but* comfortable. He remained a wreck over Thomas's death, and deeply suspicious as a result of that stuttering voice in Yosemite. Whatever brio he had projected in Denver, whatever skeletons he'd weeded out of the closet and conclusions he had reached, the nagging reality of his salvation on El Capitan, as well as that flight fifteen feet across the Masonic Hall in New York, still seethed within him.

Houdini went out of his way, with Joe and Royale, to make certain that the cage and shackles that would incarcerate Doyle were foolproof. If anybody knew how to ensure an inextricable constraint, it was Houdini's technicians. Thomas had trained them.

Houdini would be the one, at the last possible second, to save Doyle, not some ghost. Houdini might not ever get over El Capitan, but at least he would silence the infuriating knowledge of that stuttering voice.

Frank, meanwhile, had come back from his western travels to be devastated. He called upon Ginger Riddles, having worked assiduously to capture Holstein, only to learn that Ginger was gone. Gone to Europe with another man. Frank had spoken with her almost nightly since his departure from New York weeks before. He couldn't believe how she'd two-timed him. Frank learned an important lesson from his painfully brief liaison: some people are guided by destiny, meaning that Ginger probably got whatever she deserved.

At the same time, Holstein had vanished from the face of the earth. The Denver sheriffs found no clue.

When the Doyles, accompanied by the fully recovered Amy, as well as Captain Pushcart, reached the docks on Ellis Island, there was another sort of destiny at work. Houdini could easily have chosen the quay adjoining the Battery for this final combat. He selected Ellis Island out of some sentiment, because it was the same island where his parents had first landed years before, in the last century, fresh from Budapest, and been temporarily detained.

A federal immigration law stated that any "alien" lacking proper papers, or a country willing to accept him, or not up to the medical standards, could be "detained for life" on Ellis Island, at least in theory. Proper papers might not be enough, rumor had it, when, as a refugee, you were seasick, cold, tired, hungry and scared. Houdini knew the law, as had millions of other would-be Americans who arrived by boat at the turn of the century, having been forewarned about the ins and outs of disembarkation. There were metaphysical hurdles attached to immigration. You had to be strong, healthy, mentally alert. You had to smile, smell good, look like a patriot. Old people had a tough time getting in, unless a rich American cousin was there to vouch for them. If you were young, and passed the various medical exams—eyelids checked for any indications of trachoma, scalps scrutinized for fungal infestation—it might only take three hours at the "Great Hall" immigration station. But however one pulled it off—and as many as twelve thousand a day did—you had to have nerve and tenacity. In short, it was a physical contest. You had to slip through.

Houdini considered Doyle something of an alien. The cage in which he'd be lowered offered no possibility of slipping through. None. But Ellis Island, and all of the tens of millions of spirits—living and dead—who had started on their great American odyssey here, would be the real judge.

Doyle had expected to find four people present—Houdini, Joe, Royale and their inveterate guardian angel, Frank Lattimer. Those were the terms: no press.

Instead, half a mile from the dock, the crowds were already pressing in.

A good ten thousand people had turned out, along with Movie Tone Newsreel crews, radio announcers and easily one hundred members of the New York press corps. Doyle knew most of them by name now.

Sandwich men milled through the droves, their signs boasting,

"SIR ARTHUR CONAN DOYLE

CHALLENGES THE GREAT HOUDINI.

DOYLE SAYS HE HAS MORE STRENGTH, AND IS A BETTER ESCAPE ARTIST THAN HOUDINI. HE WILL BE SECURELY HANDCUFFED AND LEG-IRONED, PLACED IN A PACKING CASE, FIRMLY NAILED, ROPED, ENCIRCLED BY METAL BANDS, THEN INSERTED INTO A STEEL, UNBREAKABLE LION CAGE AND LOWERED BENEATH SURFACE OF HARBOR. THE MOST MARVELOUS FEAT EVER ATTEMPTED IN THIS OR ANY OTHER AGE. APPROACHING THE SUPERNATURAL—OR SUICIDE!

SATURDAY, RAIN OR SHINE."

"He's impossible!" Doyle stated irritably to his wife.

Thirty feet above water, suspended by a crane and dangling alongside the pier, the cage hung a foot off the wooden dock. Houdini wore a white boxer's robe that covered his bathing suit. Doyle wore his bathing suit under his cotton trousers and jacket.

"Still the chronic publicity hound, I see," Doyle proclaimed upon reaching the roped-off combat zone.

"That's what it's all about, old man," Houdini replied unamicably.

The "old man" may have gone too far this time. That was certainly the verdict among the pressmen. It had not even been stated whether Houdini would attempt to save him once it became apparent that Doyle was not going to make it.

"I hope you've got plan B worked out. I don't even know if he can swim!" Bess quietly reminded Harry, seated near to the hanging cage.

"Down to the second," whispered Houdini. "But we'll let him sweat it out before I save him." He didn't want anyone present to know what was going to happen.

But one thing was clear: the master sleuth would need more than mere detective work to get out of these constraints. And he'd have all of about a minute, at most, to do so before he joined Kingsley.

Joe and Royale had "timed" the locks. It was a technique Houdini used on many of his easier jobs, whereby a single flick of his finger released all the locks at once. The system was known to screw up, as it had in the Rockies. But it had since been refined. Joe and Royale had done a complete overhaul of every conceivable jam.

The announcers took their cue from Houdini, who had motioned his own readiness to Doyle. Doyle was ready as well. He stepped out of his trousers, folded them and handed them to his wife, who put them on the passenger seat of their car. Amy and she remained in back, the door open.

Doyle stood now in his bathing suit and tank top.

"Let's do it," he said with a touch of the truculent that surprised Houdini. Doyle had psyched himself up. Houdini recognized the signs.

Live radio commentary recorded every gesture, each second of ritual and coming jeopardy. Doyle had some excess on his bones. He was pale but not exactly paunchy. He stood tall, proud and confident.

Are you there, son? he intoned internally.

Houdini's assistants locked Doyle in. Reporters snickered to themselves. They knew there was no way Doyle would get out. Only Houdini could get out. Some of them still remembered how, six or seven years before, Houdini had been sewn into the belly of an oarfish, a sixty-foot serpent caught in Long Island Sound, half whale, half giant squid, the scientists at the time declared. The guts stank to high heaven and Houdini nearly passed out when the creature shifted in the currents, trapping Houdini on the underside. It took him three minutes to get out of that horrible monster. Houdini was amazing that day. David inside a pelagic Goliath.

Whereas Doyle looked merely foolish. A noticeable belly, hairy, English-white legs, unexercised, complete strangers to cuffs, shackles, ropes, leg irons. Behind the metal grating, he was a forlorn looking sight. To put him underwater was criminal. They all took notes, their hearts beat extra loud, and they cheered on the coming calamity. That was news. And they trusted in Houdini's valor.

A team of two corny radio announcers speculated live as to whether Doyle was likely to meet his death by water the same way his alter ego, Sherlock Holmes, had—falling off and drowning in the waters of Reichenbach Falls, locked in a mortal embrace with Professor Moriarty.

The second announcer pointed out that Doyle contrived to bring Sherlock back to life.

The first announcer took issue with that suggestion, delighting in the belief that Doyle would be especially hard-pressed to resurrect himself this time.

The cage swung free of the pier. Doyle hung above the water, a condemned man. Before Houdini instructed the crane to lower him, he asked Doyle whether he had any last words for the human race. Doyle just smiled. He was at peace with himself, he said.

"Okay, let's get it over with," Houdini shouted.

The crowd roared with anticipation. They clapped; they laughed. Doyle looked too gullible and cockeyed for words. The cage alighted in the waves with its silly standing prisoner inside. Nautically speaking, the currents were moving up into the East and Hudson rivers. Doyle would have a devil of a time even holding his breath for sixty seconds, Houdini calculated.

The cage dipped below the whitecaps. Now it was totally submerged.

Houdini watched the clock.

Time elapsed.

"Now!" Bess said.

"Not yet," Harry replied, tensed.

Amy held Lady Doyle's hand. She couldn't watch.

"Harry, for God's sake . . . you'd never be able to live with yourself!" Bess insisted. Thirty seconds had transpired.

"What do you say, Harry!" the pressman Simpson yelled.

"You're not going to let him die, are you?" another cried out.

"All right," Houdini motioned to Bess, taking his time about everything. "He says his son saved me. I guess the least I can do is reciprocate and save that kid's old man."

Houdini threw off his boxer's robe and made a brief statement to the press, while the seconds ticked furiously by.

"Harry, goddammit!" Bess shouted impatiently.

"I can't watch him kill himself. What would old King George think of us New Yorkers?" He chuckled caustically.

"Harry, for God's sakes," Bess shrieked.

"All right, all right!" Houdini knew what he was doing.

And with that, he hit the water, like Elmo Lincoln. A gymnast's front dive, hands and toes pointed, ankles mated, shoulders flat.

Houdini breast stroked downward along the stray cable

that held the cage. The water was warm, by Houdini's standards, murky, fast. Sixty feet of cable had gone down. Doyle was a good twenty feet below the surface. The poor fellow's ears had probably burst.

For half a minute up above, there was silence on the pier. Nobody knew what was happening under the water, what fate was in store for poor Sir Arthur Conan Doyle. Stories had already been filed that morning, to appear in the afternoon edition, describing Doyle's pathetic desperation: how he had lost to Houdini and the scientists, and was now trying futilely to make his mark in Houdini's territory. He was bound to fail. Doyle could deliver a rousing speech at Carnegie Hall. But he should stay out of New York Harbor. His spiritualism was nothing more than hypochondriac vapors and monastic fairy tales, one reporter had written.

Houdini continued down, moving fast. He'd jiggle the key lock on the cage, upsetting the delicate balance of tumblers, break inside, hit the hidden lever, thus opening every single lock on the crate, burst the steel bands with his own sideways strength (a matter of pectoral practice), grab Doyle, burst his handcuffs, push off the top of the cage and, using the cable as a lead line, make it back to the surface in less than twenty seconds. Even if Doyle had already lost it, swallowed water, gone unconscious, Houdini would have him topside long before the onset of any serious injury, or brain damage. He hoped.

As these strategies strutted about in Houdini's head, he caught sight of white dissolving salts, then bubbles, a broad, fuzzy barrage of air pockets racing toward the sky.

And suddenly, inconceivably, there was Doyle himself, swimming single-mindedly upward, chest expanded, eyes half-lidded, in an ascension-lined gesture of complete equanimity, like a caryatid afloat, a sleeping Pallas Athene, done in soft marble, dreaming of Heaven and floating there unhurriedly.

Houdini was blinded by a light that egressed with Doyle, a halo between white and cobalt, usurping the normal bile-black sheen of bilge tanks, sewer boats and fuel barges that crisscrossed these waters. Maybe it was the light from the sun piercing through the clouds above, maybe not. Whatever it was, it was a light that transfigured and dazed. Houdini's own lungs caved in. He lost his air and reversed his direction, utterly rampaged, turned around.

They both reached the surface at the same second. A cheer rose up that detained immigrants could hear a mile away.

They were ten feet from the rusted metal ladder that dangled off the pier, just touching the low tide mark. Houdini reached for it, then deferred to Doyle.

"After you," Doyle insisted.

The two of them treaded water, waves bobbing them up and down, out of earshot from the hovering multitudes above.

"How did you do it?" Houdini demanded to know, shaken inside.

"Ask my son," said Doyle brazenly.

"You're serious?" Houdini gasped.

"Kingsley may stutter, but his meaning is clear." Doyle paused, empathizing with the unbeliever in the water beside him. "I know it's hard for you, Harry."

"You're right, Arthur. It's very hard for me. I'm . . . I'm . . ." The words dropped away from him. He felt slack, silent, out of wind . . . *A miracle, astounding! No, it had to be a trick—he tricked me!* He blathered on introspectively, at a loss, swimming toward the ladder, imperiled by ambiguities.

But as he neared the rungs that dangled from the pier, he started to consider the possibility that Doyle might inadvertently have touched off the latch releases. If Doyle had truly studied Houdini's methods—as he'd alleged—the Sherlock in him might well have figured out the cage. Houdini's doubts doubled over with ferocity. *That's got to be the explanation!* he reasoned.

But he also was well aware that the cage had been reinforced with new engineering tricks. How could Doyle have known?

For all of his raging suspicions, Houdini felt glad for Sir Arthur. Glad that the man could hold onto his faith, whatever the real explanation, glad that their last moments together had been spent with a certain amount of dignity. And glad that they had achieved a mutual coming to terms. Houdini preferred things to be clean, satisfactory, resolved. He was no longer in the mood to create any pain. He was tired of hurting inside.

The two men clung to the metal ladder, and awkwardly embraced. There might have been tears on their cheeks, though nobody—not even Bess—would be able to tell, not coming out of an ocean.

Total fanfare had broken out above. Lady Doyle wept, got out of the car and approached the edge. Amy Beckwell intuited that a small miracle had occurred and embraced her.

"He did it!" Amy uttered triumphantly.

"Did you ever have any doubt?" Lady Doyle added.

Frank stood warmly next to Amy. "How you doin'?" he said noncommittally.

"Doing okay," bleated Amy.

Frank brushed something out of her hair. His hand lingered there, long enough for both of them to acknowledge exchanged tenderness and to really look at each other and realize that life must go on.

The press ribbed Doyle mercilessly as he labored up the ladder to the deck, then dried himself off. There were hoots and "told you so's" from all quarters. A large flock of bread-scouting sea birds circled the mob.

Police now held back the two stars. "Give 'em some room, boys!" they shouted.

Houdini withheld his thunderstruck secret knowledge. He was a study in perplexity, not eager just then to ponder the possibilities.

But he quietly admitted to Doyle, "There's no need to take any abuse from these creeps, Arthur. My fault for inviting them. I apologize. A miracle's a miracle. Go ahead. Tell them the truth. I certainly didn't save you."

Doyle paused, grinning, then looked up from his towel, with which his wife was drying his hair. "Maybe I just got lucky, Harry."

"What do you mean?" Houdini threw out, on the defensive now, unsure, torn between stupefaction and release.

"I'm not saying," Doyle spoke slowly, weighing his words. "There's no need for other fools to try such things and be killed. Let this remain our secret. How about it?"

Bess looked at her husband with a sparkle in her eyes. She knew. In her own heart, she had hoped for Sir Arthur's legitimacy, if not all along, then certainly on this day.

Houdini nodded. "I like you," he said. "I've decided that I *really* like you."

"That's decidedly mutual," replied Sir Arthur.

The two men shook hands and eventually, amicably, parted ways.

18

Freedom

Crowborough, Sussex, England, seven years after the events that took place in New York Harbor. The date is July 6, 1930. The home of Sir Arthur and Lady Doyle.

When Charles Lindbergh soloed to Paris, Doyle was one of nearly four million fans who wrote him a congratulatory letter. The momentous day that young Gertrude Ederle of New York started across the English Channel, stroke by stroke, Doyle, who had followed the event closely, put on his own tank suit, got into the water and emanated psychic assistance. And when Richard E. Byrd flew to the South Pole, Doyle sat out in a snowstorm in front of his house, mystically communing with the far-off commander. The *New York Times* rated Byrd's expedition as the most noteworthy event of 1929, even more impressive than the stock market crash. Doyle concurred.

And when William Jennings Bryant lashed out at Clarence Darrow, saying "You believe in the age of rocks. I believe in the rock of ages," Doyle laughed hysterically. He knew that both men—representing God and Great Ape—were saying the same damned thing, and neither realized it. That was the story of mankind.

Amidst Doyle's industrious efforts to carry on his own spiritual crusades, to travel, to write more books and to remain ever au courant, he managed to have a rather inconvenient heart attack. Two days after surgery, he'd stated jovially, "The bruised heart begets the spiritual soul." Doyle was living by his beliefs.

He soon ignored his doctor's warnings, ate as he pleased, got little sleep. He toured Africa and Scandinavia and wrote another half-dozen books, including a two-volume history of spiritualism, and the last work of Sherlock Holmes.

More recently, Doyle had been immersed in the enervating legal advocacy of a London medium ludicrously charged with violating the antiquated Witchcraft and Vagrancy Acts, first instituted during the Reign of George II. The process was exhausting him.

One beautiful July day in 1930, his doctor and old friend, Lionel Vercombe, dropped by for a chat about the latest cancer drugs, or cricket, or the inflation of German marks. Doyle wasn't listening. Standing several feet away, he stared at a blank page in a rare book that he held in his hands.

The book started to tremble. An inner voice clamored for vowels, and then issued its susurrant, air-sucking observation: *It's you!!!*

Houdini! There! In his mind's eye . . .

The noble countenance, the force of his presence, pressed in upon Doyle's ribs, so that there was no mistaking the direction to which he had been coming all along. Doyle gasped. His eyes were crimped beneath the half-formed image, and the heat of tears started to well. Tears from both sides. Tears of both times. He shook his head. His legs went limp.

"Arthur?" Lionel inquired, starting to get up from the Aubusson-covered sofa. "Are you all right?" The good doctor extended his hand.

Far away, in the murky haze of a distance, Doyle saw Harry Houdini crumpled on the floor, writhing, surrounded by the hordes of Detroit. Engulfed in thunderous applause. Hats falling back down. And on the stage, mired, frantically working himself along some ghostly path toward freedom, between the multiple layers of crushing constraint, in hideous pain, his old friend.

Doyle's hand clutched at his heart. The book—a first edition, in German, of Kant's *Dreams of a Spirit-Seer*—fell onto the floor.

A voice cried out. "The door, Betcham, get the door!" Lady Doyle had observed her guests arriving for dinner.

Lionel braced Sir Arthur. "I'm all right," Doyle replied. "False alarm."

But Doyle knew all the signs, which had been markedly escalating. He was on the verge. Excitement usurped fear. There was nothing to be done. Only to give in, willingly, freely.

Over dinner, Lady Glenco's local gossip, Sidney's troubles in London—his new young flame had dumped him for a painter—and Sir Henry's latest philanthropic coups swept past Sir Arthur without the slightest effect . . .

The glue keeping him to table talk was dissolving, and like a helium balloon of consciousness, he could feel a force pulling him upwards, away . . .

And then, it struck again. Doyle could see him.

"Oohhh!" Sir Arthur cried, falling backward from the array of old friends, pulling an embroidered rose-patterned white linen tablecloth with him, and wine glasses, and a bouquet in its ceramic vase. Explosions. *Oh my god!*

"Arthur!" Lady Doyle screamed.

His head hit the stone floor, and at that instant, his eyes, dulled with a shivering inwardness, saw the final shackle being broken free of the angry wrist. The portion of bone had snapped with a loud crackle, caving in to allow the steel enough room to slip off.

"Ahhhh!" came the groan.

Doyle's inward gaze was locked onto Houdini, years before, somehow, in some purgatory of cross-channeling, radio waves, psychic penumbras, tandem throes; he saw him thrust his hands through the curtain, jutting his head out.

Doyle observes Bess off on the sidelines.

"Harry!" Bess weeps internally.

Doyle sees Houdini try to stand, but his knees are cemented into the position of a tea master from having kneeled on them for so long without benefit of the blood's circulation.

The crowd—over five thousand paying customers—is mindlessly genuflecting with ovation, like a savage tribe on the warpath. For nearly four hours they have sat and waited expectantly throughout Houdini's torture. Bess's torture. Her husband would not give in, despite her highly emotional protests.

Now Doyle sees Joe and Royale run onto the stage and hold Houdini's arm, assisting him to his feet.

Bess rushes forward onto the center stage as well. Her husband has changed colors. He has utterly mutilated himself. She thinks to spit in the face of Hodgekiss, the sadistic challenger who'd done this to her husband. But there's no time.

It is just before midnight, October 24, 1926. An ambulance is waiting outside the back stage door. Bess hurriedly turns things over to the impresario and proceeds with Joe and Royale to get her husband the hell out of there.

It is freezing outside. The streets are iced over. Houdini keeps murmuring about the "heat."

They rush him directly into surgery at Grace Hospital. Bess is beside him. Orderlies and nurses and masked surgeons move in with trays, oxygen machines, scalpels.

Hand me those scissors . . .

Nurse, scalpel . . .

The glint of shining steel surrounds him. An injection. *Get the needle, that one, get it in*, a voice orders on the edge of frenzy.

Doyle sees all this, as he feels his own body being picked up, carried away—*up the stairs*, a voice decrees.

He lies back, visiting psyche upon psyche, with the one man who meant anything to him these last years, side by side, their final moments. Together.

Houdini's head is softly spinning as he lies drugged on the cold metallic emergency-room table. Spinning into yet another time, another dimension, which Doyle can see as well.

The sleigh is softly moving, gliding through the fresh bitter snow. His hook is dangling beside the lock on the outside.

Get it! Get in! Houdini cries. But the movement of the horses has made the task impossibly difficult.

The steel has burned the skin on his knees, palms, buttocks, forehead, the tip of his nose. He's only managed to keep his fingertips free, and they are hopelessly numb, frostbitten.

Please! he begs the fates.

Nothing gives. He can't fight anymore. His head rests against the steel. His ear and cheek begin to burn against the raw, cold dry-ice metal of the vault.

There is darkness. The sleighman has stopped at an inn for the night. The horses are silent, cloaked in winter stillness.

Houdini has no sense of time. No strength. No feeling. His breathing has covered him with the frost of final reckoning. He sits hunched and naked against the unrelenting steel shanks of the *carette* in which Chief Lebedin and his soldiers placed him, fifteen hours before.

It's now or never, he realizes.

His arm is a dumb, mute, frozen thing. The fingers must act independently. Nervous impulses are diverted around the unwilling arm, directly from the brain, which still functions.

Quivers in Russia. Quivers in Detroit. Quivers in Sussex. All of a single quiver.

He has little time. It was only the movement of the troika,

the warmed exhalations of the horses, the inherent friction of
the wheels, that just slightly increased the temperature to
keep him alive. But now, the vast, motionless, frozen, fifty-
below-zero Russian night has settled in.

Suddenly, there is a click. A holy clicking click. And another. His hook has caught the tumblers.

Like that, the steel door to the vault swings open. Houdini
can't move. His position has been frozen for too many hours.

To die this way, after having secured his release! His tears
freeze down his cheek. The aroma of cooking, the warmth of
a wood-burning stove, the sight of lights and rising chimney
smoke—all within reach.

But you did it! Doyle's inner logic confides. *You see! No
one else but you could have survived!*

Houdini exerts every ounce of mind control to crawl out
of the sadistic steel vault. But he cannot. His knees are broken, the cartilage frozen solid. Houdini is too cold to cry.

After a while the horses whinny. A drunken *muzhik* has
stepped out into the night and is burping and peeing circles
in the snow.

"Hey! Mister! *Gospodin!*" Houdini rustles a few pathetic
sounds, frantically trying to recover what little Russian he'd
studied.

"*Uh? Kto tam?*" the drunk mutters. *Who's there?*

"*Pomegaete menye, pozhaliste!*" Houdini pleads, his
voice gnarled and rasping with the acute onset of double
pneumonia, at the very least. *Help me, please!*

The drunk is wearing knee-high mukluks. He's disoriented, looking around. There is gaiety from inside the well-
lit inn. Stars twinkle across the deep forested snows of the
arriere-pays back country.

The muzhik steps up to the troika.

"*Shto vwee dyelaete?*" he says in some confusion. *What
are you doing?*

He laughs uproariously at the naked idiot before him,
reaches in and pulls Houdini out of the damned vault. Some
of his skin is stripped off by the steel plates as Houdini falls

on his face into the snow. His body is the color of a sky-blue heaven, of gangrene, or the faded halo that figured so prominently in six hundred years of icons.

The drunkard lifts Houdini, staggers, falls, rights himself and carries Houdini into the inn, where Houdini is wrapped in wool by the fire, and several stiff shots of vodka are forced down his throat.

Houdini isn't a drinker. He passes out.

You see, destiny called to you; as it calls to you now reverberates in Doyle's head.

The spinning escalates. The drug is wearing off. The surgeons have cut him open, only to sew him right back up again. A gangrenous appendix, advanced peritonitis. Temperature of 104. The *Streptococcus virulens* will take twelve hours to conquer him, the doctors say with morose but unflexing finality.

His frozen cheek is warmed by a kiss. Bess is there, looking over him.

"Where am I?" Houdini blurts.

Doyle's eyes burrow into the past, monitoring his blood pressure, expanding thoughts, hovering aura of light, Houdini's breath. All these vital signs are Doyle's own signs, these final thoughts Doyle's thoughts, these grappling hands and well-wishing circle of friends, and churning gut. This confederacy of last tidings—the same. Undifferentiated finitude of passing hopes and final rites.

Days transpire. Bess is camping out beside him. Lady Doyle sits beside her sleeping husband. The doctors have thrown up their hands. Maybe he'll escape again, the chief surgeon speculates. He's outlived every scientific prediction.

Of course he'll escape! Doyle seconds with a rakish grin.

"What?? Arthur? Can you hear me?" Lionel presses, seeing that he has suddenly come to. Lionel's sleeves are rolled up, and there are a lavender ceramic commode, a bowl of hot water and plenty of towels on a little side table.

"Is he smiling?" Lady Glenco asks, confused.

"Please," says Lady Doyle, thanking Lady Glenco, Sidney and Sir Henry. She wants them to go home, now. There's nothing more they can do here.

Doyle's right hand lies across his chest and holds onto the bicep of his left arm.

Lying still, Doyle makes out a procession of masked figures. They are wandering down a corridor. There is whispering . . . *Shhh, shhhh*! . . . And then they enter the room they've been looking for.

"Trick or treat!" they all shout with a repressed volume, obedient to the circumstances of their visit.

Houdini exerts himself, looking up from his bed. The sheets are soiled.

"It's Halloween, Harry. Some of your local fans have come to say hello," Bess says in a weakening voice, fighting back tears.

Houdini tries to thank the children for coming. A gaunt smile graces his sunken face.

Hours later, Doyle—who lies somewhere between sleep and the laboring of lungs for air—sees Houdini stir, and follows his every move. The master magician is setting the groundwork for the most brilliant escape of his entire career.

Houdini props himself up against the pillows with great effort and starts to speak.

Bess's heart is pounding. She sees that his every word is excruciating. But he must speak. And she must hear.

Doyle, whose supine oblivion itself counts as a difficulty, whose every breath and thought requires exertion now, the holding back of a pain that conspires to avalanche throughout his veins, nevertheless gathers the strength to watch Bess and Harry. It's all that Sir Arthur can do to keep focused. He has willingly given up the sight of Lionel and his wife. Because he knows that something grand is happening, and that both he and Houdini are locked together in its embrace.

"I will come back to you," the once defiant magician whispers. "You must believe that . . ." Houdini's words strain with an uncanny freshness, weak but hallowed, faint but pellucid.

"Harry . . . Oh God . . . Harry!" Bess sobs, her voice forever broken now.

"Listen to me, Bess. Please."

She raises her head and clings to his hands. She can't believe this is really happening.

"And the word I shall utter to you . . . the word, is . . . *believe*."

To the side of Doyle's bed, Lionel goes to relight the one candle that has suddenly expired. But Lady Doyle shakes her head. There's no need now. The sun is already rising over the fields and hills of Sussex.

Lionel takes Sir Arthur's pulse, then leaves the room to bring up the children, who are solemn and terrorized by the prospect.

Lady Doyle sits beside her husband, admiring his mortal form for the last time, expressing all that love and tenderness which is in her power.

When a hard jolt, like an incoming Atlantic breaker, wracks Sir Arthur's whole body, he lurches upward, full of adamant will and hope; he opens his eyes, stares into that sunrise, which now seems to engulf him, and, with a look of surprise and noncomprehension, something beyond his capability to control, his mouth forms the word "*believe*!" so that it is audible and clear, before washing back out to some distant sea, leaving his body still and tranquil.

The word hangs there, a final summons. Lady Doyle knows. Even if it is not yet her time to divine from whence the word has really come.

Epilogue

A few days after Houdini's tragic death in October of 1926, Bess found a letter waiting for her, stashed amid her perfumes.

"Sweetheart, when you read this I shall be dead. Dear Heart, do not grieve. I shall be at rest by the side of my beloved parents, and wait for you always—remember! Yours in Life, Death and Ever After."

She realized that he must have written it two months before. Why? How? For what purpose? Her perplexity soon adopted a vow of veritable silence.

At the funeral at Cypress Hills, the rabbi indicated that

there were some secrets that Houdini could never share, and that would never be shared.

Houdini's head was pillowed atop the hundreds of letters from his mother.

The Elks were there in force, as well as the St. Cecile Lodge of Masons, and the Society of American Magicians. They all sung "Beautiful Isle of Somewhere." A white lambskin was laid upon the bier, and evergreen—a symbol for the immortality of the soul—was placed upon the casket, as thousands filed by, paying their last respects.

Frank Lattimer subsequently wrote a letter to Doyle, who lived on another four years. He and Amy Beckwell had taken up together, and were considering marriage. But first, Frank was on his way to Bavaria. Holstein had vanished, and was rumored to be consorting with the German Fascista, and with Hitler.

Sir Arthur had been convinced that the story about Houdini's ruptured appendix was "apocryphal." Despite the depositions of five leading surgeons, the signed affidavits by the Canadian students and the confirmation by the insurance company that had paid out a claim on the basis of accidental death, Sir Arthur suspected foul play by some medium.

Frank had a gut instinct about it, as well. And then he came to be convinced: the young Japanese exchange student who'd punched Houdini in the stomach was apprehended in connection with a bank robbery by Canadian authorities. They turned him over to Dr. Seyberts, at the Barbie Pecker Middlestein Sanitarium. Seyberts subjected him to a host of experiments, as well as injecting him with the same truth serum that had been used on Baker Massy. The Japanese student, in and out of consciousness, eventually mentioned being employed by a fat man, named Holstein.

Frank came to understand that the "Princess" was actually a transvestite named Ernest Holstein, who had supposedly paid the "student"—a hired killer from Japan—to do away with Houdini. There was an interesting motive, Frank stated in his letter to Doyle. It appeared that Dr. Weiss, Houdini's scholarly and retiring father, had long ago been forced to flee for America with his family following a duel in which he'd killed a man in Budapest. The man had slandered the Jewish religion and bullied the unwilling Weiss into a fight. That man was Ernest Holstein's own father.

Frank had the confession of the Japanese, but it was no proof of anything, certainly not in a court of law, the confession having been drug-induced.

But Frank was a Pinkerton. In his letter to Sir Arthur, he made it clear that he would not sleep until Holstein was put away, once and for all.